UNIQUELY AFRICAN?

African Christian Identity from Cultural and Historical Perspectives

EDITED BY:

James L. Cox and Gerrie ter Haar

RELIGION IN CONTEMPORARY AFRICA SERIES

Africa World Press, Inc.

P.O. Box 1892
Trenton, NJ 08607

P.O. Box 48
Asmara, ERITREA

Cover design: Roger Dormann
Book design: Raphael Freeman

Library of Congress Cataloging-in-Publication Data

Uniquely African? : African Christian identity from cultural and
historical perspectives / edited by James L. Cox and Gerrie ter Haar.
    p. cm. -- (Religion in contemporary Africa series)
Includes bibliographical references and index.
 ISBN 1-59221-113-5 -- ISBN 1-59221-114-3 (pbk.)
 1. Christianity--Africa, Sub-Saharan. I. Cox, James L. (James Leland)
II. Haar, Gerrie ter. III. Series.
 BR1430.U55 2003
 276--dc22

2003015459

Religion in Contemporary Africa Series
*Series Editors: James L. Cox and
Gerrie ter Haar*

This book is dedicated to the late Dr Gustav Deveneaux
Former Head of the Department of History
Fourah Bay College, University of Sierra Leone

Contents

Acknowledgements

This is the final book to be published under the auspices of the African Christianity Project, which was funded from 1992 through 1998 by The Pew Charitable Trusts in Philadelphia, Pennsylvania and which was administered from the University of Edinburgh, Scotland. The Project also received invaluable assistance from the University Twinning Programme (UNITWIN) of Utrecht University in The Netherlands. The participating African institutions in the African Christianity Project deserve particular mention: The Department of Theology and Religious Studies in Fourah Bay College, University of Sierra Leone: The Akrofi-Christaller Centre for Mission Studies and Applied Theology in Akropong-Akuapem, Ghana; The Department for the Study of Religions in the University of Ghana, Legon; The Department of Religious Studies, Classics, and Philosophy in the University of Zimbabwe; The Department of Theology and Religious Studies in the University of Botswana; The Department of Theology and Religious Studies in the University of Malawi, Blantyre; The Centre of African Studies, Eduardo Mondlane University, Maputo, Mozambique; and the Department of Religion in the University of Namibia.

Special gratitude is expressed to the local organisers of the West African conferences from which a number of the articles for this book are derived: Professor Kwame Bediako for the Ghana Conference of September 1994 and Dr Leslie Shyllon for the Sierra Leone Conference of April 1997.

The commitment shown to the study of Christianity in its various forms throughout Africa by the late Dr John Bennett, who served as principal advisor to the African Christianity Project, and by Professor Andrew

Walls, who originally conceived the idea for the Project, are gratefully acknowledged.

Finally, thanks to Valerie Smith for help with preparation of the text.

Dr James L Cox, *University of Edinburgh*
Professor Gerrie ter Haar, *Institute of Social Studies, The Hague*

Preface

Setting the Context: The African Christianity Project and the Emergence of a Self-Reflexive Institutional Identity

James L. Cox

THIS BOOK REPRESENTS the last publication to result from the African Christianity Project, which between 1992 and 1998 through major funding from The Pew Charitable Trusts in Philadelphia, Pennsylvania, enabled the Centre for the Study of Christianity in the Non-Western World in the University of Edinburgh to support research into a wide range of subjects relevant to African Christianity. Through the Project, African scholars received funds to conduct research, publish articles and books, present papers at conferences and develop a network of professional contacts across Africa and Europe. The present volume contains a selection of edited papers relevant to or presented at two conferences organised by the African Christianity Project, one conducted in September 1994 in Accra, Ghana under the theme, 'Christianity and Nation-Building in West Africa' and the other in April 1997 on 'Christian Engagement with African Cultural Dynamics', held in Freetown, Sierra Leone. Although these conferences were located in West Africa, the Project made it possible for academic staff from linked universities in eastern and southern Africa to participate. In order to understand the context for a volume such as this, therefore, before commenting briefly on the scope of the present volume, I will outline the major aims, notable achievements and institutional significance of the African Christianity Project from my perspective as co-ordinator from 1993 through 1998.

Edinburgh and the African Christianity Project: Background

In 1982, Professor Andrew Walls founded the Centre for the Study of Christianity in the Non-Western World (CSCNWW) in the Department of Religious Studies in the University of Aberdeen. Five years later, due to severe financial restrictions in Aberdeen culminating eventually in the closing of the Department, Walls transferred the CSCNWW to the Faculty of Divinity in the University of Edinburgh, where he gradually re-built a programme based on postgraduate teaching, research and the accumulation of extensive bibliographic resources (a major portion of which Walls had carried with him from Aberdeen to Edinburgh from his own substantial personal collection of materials on Christianity in the Non-Western World).

Soon after arriving in Edinburgh, Walls began exploring ways to expand the research potential and funding base of the CSCNWW at its new institutional home. This eventually resulted in an application for funding to The Pew Charitable Trusts, which in the early 1990s had launched a major programme within its religion section emphasising research on global Christianity. Rarely do circumstances conspire so favourably for obtaining funding, and, in 1992 the Centre for the Study of Christianity in the Non-Western World was successful in receiving a grant in the amount of $500,000 for three years to conduct a research project studying Christianity in Africa under the name 'The African Christianity Project (ACP)'. In 1995 a second grant was approved by Pew for a further $425,000 aimed at carrying the research project to its completion in December 1998.

From its inception, the African Christianity Project addressed specifically the need for thorough and competent academic studies into Christian life and communities in sub-Saharan Africa and their subsequent impact on world Christianity. Over its seven year life, ACP cultivated a growing consortium of departments and institutions of theology and religious studies in Africa and Europe. When I was appointed co-ordinator in 1993, informal links had already been forged between Edinburgh and the Universities of Malawi, Zimbabwe and Botswana in southern Africa, and with the

University of Sierra Leone and the Akrofi-Christaller Centre for Mission Research and Applied Theology in Ghana. In 1994, the Religion Programme of the University Twinning Project (UNITWIN) in Utrecht University in the Netherlands became a participating institution and brought with it the Department of Religion and Theology in the University of Namibia and the Centre of African Studies in Eduardo Mondlane University in Mozambique. Shortly after major funding for a further three years was approved by The Pew Charitable Trusts in late 1995, the Department for the Study of Religions in the University of Ghana, Legon, joined the consortium as a partner institution with the Akrofi-Christaller Centre.

One of the conditions of the second round of funding was that an additional $100,000 should be raised from sources other than Pew. This was accomplished with major institutional support from the University of Edinburgh, the University of Utrecht and Westminster College, Oxford. In addition, during its second phase, the Project, although maintaining a co-ordinator in Edinburgh, gradually re-defined its programme as centred in and developed by African institutions. Significantly in this regard, an International Committee was formed in early 1996 consisting of representatives from each participating institution to monitor and oversee the overall Project and to become the body with which the co-ordinator worked closely and to whom he was ultimately responsible.

The Project's Aims and Achievements

Between 1992 and 1998, the African Christianity Project developed seven major programmes: 1) regional conferences in Africa and in Edinburgh; 2) seminars in Edinburgh and the link institutions on African Christianity; 3) research fellowships in Edinburgh for academics working in any African university or theological institution; 4) research fellowships in African universities undertaken by members of staff in the linked institutions in Africa; 5) an African theology lectureship in Edinburgh; 6) a major cumulative bibliography and resource sharing programme; 7) publications.

Conference themes during the life of the Project included: Peace and development in southern Africa (Malawi 1993); Rites of passage in contemporary Africa (Zimbabwe 1994); Christianity and nation-building in West Africa (Ghana 1994); Assessing research on African Christianity (Edinburgh 1995); Christian engagement with African cultural dynamics (Sierra Leone 1997); and Christianity and gender issues in African traditions (Harare

1998). Publications of three books directly attributable to the Project's conferences have resulted (Cox, 1998a; Cox, 1998b; Phiri, Ross and Cox, 1994), with this volume comprising the fourth such publication.[1] In addition, scholarly monographs, journal articles and teaching resources have resulted from academics participating in the Project's activities. Beyond promoting research on Christianity in Africa, the Project strengthened regional links among African universities, established a network for collaborative research in Africa and Europe and encouraged young African scholars to conduct postdoctoral research.

One of the most tangible accomplishments of the project resulted from the bibliographic programme, under the direction of Elizabeth Leitch, whose post was upgraded to that of ACP librarian for the second phase of the Project. By 1998, Mrs Leitch had completed the systematic cataloguing of published, unpublished and archival materials relevant to Christianity in Africa at the Centre for the Study of Christianity in the Non-Western World and at its linked institutions. By the conclusion of the Project, she had entered these onto a file available as a CD-ROM. In addition to listing available resources, between 1996 and 1998, Mrs Leitch, visited libraries in Sierra Leone, Ghana, Mozambique, Zimbabwe and Namibia where she scanned 2,448 files (each file representing one page of a document). During 1998, these files were checked for quality. Where the quality was good enough, the file was converted from a picture file into a Word for Windows text file. As a result, 160 documents were stored as Word files on computer. In addition, 564 pages (58 documents) were kept as picture files. All of these documents subsequently were transferred to CD-ROM and are now available for researchers to consult. It should be noted that funds were provided by ACP for the employment of librarians at the Akrofi-Christaller Centre in Ghana and in the Department of Theology and Religious Studies in the University of Malawi. Mrs Leitch worked with the African librarians on her visits and trained them in the use of the scanner. Currently, both institutions have scanners and are developing resources based on local archival, unpublished and dissertation materials.

The Lasting Contribution of ACP at Edinburgh: Institutional Self-Reflexivity

The scholarly significance of the African Christianity Project for the study of Christianity in Africa still awaits evaluation. One factor, however, needs to be emphasised: the Project's devolving power relationships between the central organisation in Edinburgh and the linked institutions in Africa. From an idea that had been born of a vision for research in the Centre for the Study of Christianity in the Non-Western World at its new base in Edinburgh, the Project developed deliberately into a shared programme dominated by African institutions. The themes for its conferences originated in Africa, the fellowships undertaken between African institutions were determined by African colleagues and many of the benefits were aimed directly at African departments of theology and religious studies. Although the great bulk of the funds originated in North America and accounting from the co-ordinator was to North America, and although the Project was administered from Europe, the eventual aim was to devolve power towards Africa.

In my view, this objective, which became formalised in 1996 with the creation of the International Committee, exemplifies what I am now calling a self-reflexive institutional approach. During a major consultation to evaluate the Project held in Edinburgh in 1995 and attended by representatives of each link institution, that funding agencies almost always dictate specific programmatic objectives and retain final control over any pivotal decisions was underscored as an ethical and administrative issue requiring urgent attention during the next phase of the Project. This call for European self-awareness was translated by the central co-ordinating body in Edinburgh into a calculated strategy, requiring sensitivity towards all of the interested parties (including the funding agencies and institutions in North America and Europe), aimed at systematically deflecting power away from the centre towards the regions. The emphasis of the African Christianity Project, therefore, gradually shifted from an Edinburgh-based programme to one aimed at empowering participating African departments of theology and religious studies with resources for research and the means to establish lasting links with colleagues across the continent.

The African Christianity Project and the Significance of this Volume

The problem of the hegemony of Western scholarship, which the African Christianity Project sought to address by devolving power to the African institutions, is examined in this book through contributions that explore 'uniquely' African identities from cultural, educational and national perspectives, including the encounter of Christianity with traditional societies. By analysing constructs either created in the West, such as the concept of culture, or those imposed from the West, particularly educational systems and national boundaries, the authors of this book reflect on the problem of African identities in a world dominated by Western ideological and religious systems. They do this by raising a series of questions: 1) Can specifically African identities be defined and clarified? 2) If so, what forms would such identities take in the light of Western cultural, educational and national constructs, especially in their Christian composition? 3) How could African identities be translated into Western modes of communication to promote an understanding of the 'African' outside of the African continent? 4) What effects would African identities produce on concepts of culture, educational systems and the idea of nationhood? 5) How could innovative African self-understandings interact with traditional Western methodologies? 6) What would uniquely African identities suggest for the interpretation of Christianity, Islam and Traditional Religions in Africa?

Each contributor to this volume deals directly or indirectly with some aspect of these questions. The first section of the book, including my own article and the contribution of Henk van Rinsum on 'knowing' the African, outlines the theoretical nature of issues relevant to describing African identities, particularly Western and Christian projections of the 'other'. This is followed by specific studies focusing on diverse problems created by the Christian encounter with cultural, educational and national identities as experienced in various regions throughout western and southern Africa. Finally, a concluding section examines identity in the 'new' African churches, one by Afe Adogame on an African Initiated (Independent) Church in Nigeria, another on the new African Pentecostal Churches by Ogbu Kalu and a third by Gerrie ter Haar that explores African Christian identities in Europe. These concluding articles seek to make explicit for the reader how this volume sheds light on the central question of this book: 'What, if anything, can be described as uniquely African?'

It is in this connection that this volume represents a fitting conclusion fully consistent with the aims of the African Christianity Project. By examining African Christian identities from various perspectives, the authors of this book continue the shift begun in the second phase of the Project towards self-reflexivity in institutional settings. From diverse historical, social and theological perspectives, each contributor poses an incisive challenge for Western academic, political, economic and ecclesiastical structures. In the end, by examining uniquely African identities, the authors raise fundamental ethical questions, the answers to which may shed light on the lasting legacy of the African Christianity Project itself.

Notes

1.   James L. Cox (ed.), *Rites of passage in contemporary Africa*, Cardiff: Cardiff Academic Press, 1998: James L. Cox, *Rational ancestors: Scientific rationality and African Indigenous Religions*, Cardiff Academic Press, 1998; I. Phiri, K.R. Ross and J. Cox (eds.), *The role of Christianity in development, peace and reconstruction: Southern African perspectives*, Nairobi: All Africa Conference of Churches, 1994.

Introduction

What Role do Institutions of Theology and Religious Studies Play in the Engagement With African Cultural Dynamics?

Leslie E.T. Shyllon

(This paper by Dr Leslie Shyllon, Head of the Department of Theology and Religious Studies at the University of Sierra Leone, constituted the keynote address at the West African Regional Conference of the African Christianity Project, held at Fourah Bay College, Freetown, Sierra Leone from 3rd to 6th April 1997.)

An Overview: The Condition of Africa

This Conference is concerned with the complex dynamics created by the interactions between African culture, Christianity and institutions of higher education in Africa, which largely have replicated European or American models. Before addressing these relations specifically by tracing the history and current problems in theological and religious studies in West Africa, I want to present a preliminary overview of some of the most pressing issues facing Africans today.

A pre-emptory glance of the map of the world will show that Africa covers a large land mass geographically. It is made up of several countries and races. These countries are separated from each other by valleys and large bodies of water as well as by deserts. In terms of population, Africa has some of the most populous countries in the world, for example, Egypt and Nigeria. Despite the rape of Africa by the slave trade, colonisation and its accompanying exploitation, the continent is still vibrant. It is not an exaggeration to assert that Europe and the Americas have become what they are today through the bodies and sweat of Africans. Africa was demoralised, deflowered and abused and is still being exploited and its people oppressed and discriminated against today, sadly at times by the Africans themselves.

Africa is known for its many races and ethnic groups and customs, each with its own group interests. Many conflicts in Africa, whether political, social or religious, emanate from such ethnic interests. In many African countries, the masses are excluded from decision making processes and any meaningful participation in issues affecting them, as well as in the political structures of their nation. Africa has had more coups since independence than any other continent in the world. Hence militarisation continues to be entrenched as a mode of political rule and a way of life or culture. The increasing pre-dominance of military or paramilitary or pseudo military or ex-military in positions of political power is a common phenomenon in Africa.

Economically, Africa consists of countries that have achieved a variety of economic growth and development; nevertheless, most countries, despite their independent status, are among the poorest in the world. This is a poverty of human and material resources, and justifies the nomenclature 'Third World'. African countries top the list of world debtors. These debts oppress and enslave Africans, and are likely to continue to do so for genera-tions to come, since the conditions imposed by the world multinational finance agencies have made it impossible to pay the debts. This means that Africans will remain 'third world' countries.

The economic situation of the greater part of Africa is characterised by the masses living in abject poverty while a few enjoy a comfortable and affluent existence. The grinding poverty of the masses, despite claims to economic progress and social mobilisation, attests to the basic socio-economic fact that the gap is widening between the rich and the poor. Coupled with this is the continuous control of the economy of African countries by imperialistic powers principally through the World Bank, the International Monetary Fund and Multi-National Corporations. African economies thus are under the perpetual control of external forces on which they are totally dependent. Moreover, unemployment is very high in most

African countries resulting in the migration of many of the educated and professionals to Europe and the Americas. Many Africans studying abroad refuse to return home at the end of their study simply because the conditions at home are subhuman.

The socio-economic and political realities of Africa have aggravated and provided additional causes to the traditional sources of social conflict: suppression of minorities, rivalries between ethnic loyalties and religious tensions within the countries of Africa. Ideological conflict and foreign intervention persist but some movements of social and political transformation are apparent in different countries, and these have constituted a major force for socio-economic and political changes in Africa. Through and by these movements the disadvantaged are demanding their right to full participation in decision making bodies in life and in the transformation of the religio-socio-economic and political realities of Africa.

Religion and Culture in Africa

Religion and culture interact in Africa, the complexity of which has resulted in a cultural-religious symbiosis. Outside influences and indigenous traditions have been in a process of confrontation for many centuries which is presently unresolved. Africa is undergoing a crisis of culture caused by forces of assimilation from the indigenous practices towards Westernisation and Islamisation. Modern Africans now are the inheritors of two heritages.[1] One is traditional and the other foreign. For example, when Europeans and Arabs arrived in Africa as missionaries, the Christian missionaries added the image of the triune God to African traditional deities, while the Muslims added the image of a fierce and exclusive monotheism. To Africa's customary and tribal taboos, the colonialists added civil and international law; the churches the Ten Commandments, and the Muslims the *Sharia*. To Africa's welter of tribal languages and dialects, the Europeans introduced supposedly unifying languages such as English, French, Spanish, Italian and Portuguese. With these languages, Africans are considered linked to one another and the wider world.[2]

Tensions are created when the old traditions come into contact with modernisation. Cultural gaps develop when some Africans embrace the new knowledge whereas others resist the new ways. Traditional African customs in this situation appear to drag Africans backwards away from progress and thus separate traditionalists from those living in the new culture, most of whom have embraced either Christianity or Islam. Nevertheless, the traditions of Africa are resilient despite the impact of outside cultural, social and economic forces.

A complicating religious factor results from the growth and development of new African religious movements, which pose great challenges to all three religions of Africa: Islam, Christianity and Traditional Religions. Such movements experiment by crossing the divide between traditional religion on the one hand and the new technological modern Christian and Muslim complex on the other hand. These herald necessary changes in the society and in the African mind. Nowhere is this more evident than in the efforts to produce a genuine African Christian theology.

Culture: A Formative Factor of Theology

Culture as a formative factor of theology deals with theology's character as an intellectual discipline, and with its intention to find expression in the clearest and most coherent language available. It is equally clear that to produce an intelligible theology, one has to use the language of the culture within which particular theologies are created. Consciously or unconsciously, every theologian is influenced by the categories of thought and intellectual climate of the culture out of which he or she has come. Recognition of the cultural factor is equivalent to acknowledging that there is no final theology, normative for all ages. The task of theology needs to be done again and again because its formulations are culturally conditioned; it needs reinterpretation as cultural forms change.

This explains why we in West Africa are saddened by the fact that after nearly two hundred years of Christianity in West Africa, no serious attempts have been made, before now, to produce West African theologies. The reasons for this situation are clear: first, missionaries from the West believed that West Africans had no culture; they had to be provided with Western culture. This situation has been rightly described as cultural imperialism. Second, West Africans were taken from their traditional backgrounds and environments and placed in Western orientated mission compounds; this gave the impression that to become a Christian, one has to cease to be a West African, and become English, American, German or French. Third, the people who trained for the ministry were subjected to excessive brain-washing: their theological diet consisted of pre-packaged theologies, ethical systems, pastoral methods, homiletical practices, all imported from

Europe and America. Even the examples used to illustrate parish visitations were taken from Britain or France. Furthermore, it was clearly stated that to create cultural theologies was to betray the faith once committed to the saints and so cut oneself off from the mainstream of Christianity. All these factors led to the failure of African Christians to produce an African Christian theology.

With the modern recognition of culture as one of the major sources of theology, however, African Christian theology is being worked out by African scholars. It is now recognised that many expressions in the New Testament were readily understood in the first century but are meaningless in the modern context. For example, the term 'Person' from Latin *'Persona'*, though meaningful to those who formulated the creeds in the patristic era, had quite a different meaning from that which it carries today.

In stressing the cultural factor in theology, there is the danger that African theologians may endeavour to be relevant to the times, simply for the sake of preserving African values by merging the content of revelation into cultural forms so that it becomes subject to African cultural ideals. This gives a glamorous sanctity to the ideals and institutions of one's own culture. This is what Karl Barth criticised, when he wrote: 'From belief itself capable of taking the place of content, man has brought it under his management'.[3] On the other hand, Paul Tillich defends this and claims: 'I am not unaware of the danger that in this way the substance of the Christian message may be lost. Nevertheless, this danger must be risked, and once one has realized this, one must proceed in this direction. Dangers are not a reason for avoiding a serious demand.'[4] Thus a creative tension must be maintained between the demand for relevance and intelligibility and the need for maintaining the primordial revelation. It should not prove impossible to find a way between these two extremes and this can best be done if theologians accept and teach openly the cultural factor in theology, and endeavour to handle it in full awareness of its potentialities. As McQuarrie has said, 'Let me try to exclude this factor, then it will work unconsciously for it is inescapable'.[5]

Culture, Theology and Educational Institutions in West Africa

It is against the background of the confrontation between African traditions and Western Christianity and in the light of my comments on the cultural formation of theology that I wish to outline how the modern theological institutions in West Africa were born. Writing in 1950, Bishop Stephen Neill commented on the training of the ministry in West Africa in the following way:

> The Training of the Ministry in West Africa is not an academic question of Geological syllabuses and technical details, but a burning question of the adequacy of the church to fulfil its God-given task at a turning point of history.[6]

This comment coming in 1950 interestingly enough sets out the basic principles of the role of theological education in West Africa since 1827. In that year, the Christian Institution was established in the foothills of Leicester Peak near Freetown (later moved in 1819 to Regent Village and then to Freetown under the new name Fourah Bay College) 'to train [men] to become teachers in the schools which had been established by the Church Missionary Society (CMS) and to serve as lay-workers, preaching at church services and teaching at sunday schools'.

Able students like Ajayi Crowther[7] came back for a second spell and studied Hellenistic Greek and Doctrine. But even at that early stage, its curriculum was 'A sound English Course', Arabic, Local Language, Grammar, Dictionaries and Bible translations, Music (for pleasure), all grounded 'on the impregnable rock of Holy Scripture'.[8] Arabic had been added in 1852.[9] as was Mathematics,[10] an achievement which according to Max Warren 'put it a long way ahead of any but the dissenting academics in contemporary England'.[11]

Fourah Bay College was affiliated to the University of Durham in 1876, and after the first set of students graduated in 1879, there was a flow of students from Nigeria preparing for the sacred ministry of the church. By 1900, at least 55 out of a total of 112 'Native Clergy' working under the Church Missionary Society in West Africa had been trained at Fourah Bay College.

After 1879, undergraduates not intending to be ordained were also admitted to Fourah Bay College. They also studied Theology, many of whom became catechists and lay workers in the church. The graduates were taught Islam with Arabic, and the catechists in particular learnt the Temne (local) language. This programme continued until 1912, when a

Post-Graduate Diploma in Theology was introduced. It consisted of two parts: part I substituted for the final year BA subjects; part II added a year of additional theological study beyond the BA.

Alternatively, a student could complete an ordinary BA and undertake both parts I and II in a Post-Graduate year. In the 1930s, a BA (in Divinity) was introduced by the University for students training specifically for the ministry, but who did not wish to spend four years as university under-graduates. Meanwhile, a three year ministerial course was established for non-matriculating students to suit the changing conditions of the times, with special consideration for older men. In 1955 a Faculty of Theology was established, but it was later merged with the Faculty of Arts.

In 1952, the Department of Theology introduced two projects to increase the relevance to the courses studied to the local situation. First, seminars were held to which both staff and students and clergy and lay-persons were invited. Some of the materials presented in these seminars later were published in the *Sierra Leone Bulletin of Religion*, launched in 1959, under the editorship of Andrew Walls. Second, an Easter Vacation Course for Clergy was begun so that those already in the ministry could take a fresh look at theological questions. The highlight of these vacation courses was an examination of Evangelism which was later published in 1960 in a series called the *Aureol Pamphlets*. Various other *Aureol Pamphlets* were published including *Christian Theology in Independent Africa*, edited by Harry Sawyerr, which appeared in 1961.

In 1960, by permission of the University of Durham, an Honours BA Degree in Theology was introduced, which included a study of West African Religious Thought Forms as an optional subject. In 1966, new curricula were introduced as part of the larger plans to establish an independent University of Sierra Leone. As a part of these changes, the Department of Theology decided that every student at each level of study should take a course in African Traditional Religion. Students in the Honours course were to study African Traditional Religion for two years. Islam was also provided for, if and when staff were available. Meanwhile, other theological institutions had been established in other parts of West Africa such as the Methodist Theological School in Lagos (1893) and Richmond College for West Africa (Methodist) in Freetown 1901 as a Central Methodist Theological College for West Africa.[12] With the creation

15

of other universities in West Africa in the post-1948 years, each with a Department of Theology or Religious Studies, instruction in Theology or Religious Studies was (and is still) provided at degree and post-graduate levels in the new institutions.

One further development must be noted. By 1950, church established theological institutions had been founded in two other West African countries:

(a) Nigeria: Wesley College, Ibadan (Methodist); and Melville Hall, Ibadan (Anglican); Southern Baptist College at Ogbomosho; the United School at Awka, later Trinity College, Umuahia.
(b) The Gold Coast (Now Ghana) St Augustine (Kumasi-Anglican), Trinity College (Kumasi-Methodist and Presbyterian).

In 1950, the International Missionary Council set up three surveys of the training of the ministry in Africa The first of which was conducted by Bishop Stephen Neill in British East and West Africa.[13] Since the Universities which had been established along West Africa each had a Department of Theology or Religious Studies, the Bishop made the following recommendations:

(a) 'One United Theological School (should be established) for the whole of Northern Nigeria',[14] its work conducted in English.
(b) The whole of Theological training for ordinards in Ghana should be concentrated around the then University College of Ghana (New Ghana University), or a new College should be started at Kumasi where St Augustine's College (Anglican) and Trinity College (Methodist and Presbyterian) can co-operate.[15]
(c) A special hostel for candidates for the ministry should be provided at Fourah Bay College in connection with the new University College.[16]

Such was the beginning of the situation which ultimately led to the establishment of Immanuel College in Ibadan, and Trinity College in Legon, both within walking distance of the Universities of Ibadan and Ghana respectively; and in Sierra Leone, the Theological Hall (College) and Church Training Centre; although this is much more distant from the Fourah Bay College campus than was intended originally.

The Development of New Curricula:
Theology *and* Religious Studies

One of my major interests in this keynote address is the role played by Theological and Religious Studies Institutions in the Christian engagement with African Cultural Dynamics. In this regard, we should note with interest that prior to the affiliation with Durham, the Greek New Testament was read through 'from cover to cover parsing every verb during a three year course'.[17] After the affiliation with Durham, the course in Theology included topics required for preparation for the ministry of the Church of England using books like Pearson *On The Creed*, Gibson *On The Creed*, and the *Thirty-Nine Articles of the Church of England*. Church history was covered from the earliest times to the (then) present day. When Fourah Bay College became affiliated to the University of Durham in 1876, its already progressive curriculum was extended to include 'Latin, Greek, Hebrew, Arabic, History and Geography, Comparative Philosophy, some branches of natural science, and extras, French and German'.[18]

In other words, most of Anglophone Africa inherited the British tradition that Theology was the queen of the sciences and, therefore, was on the agenda of University education. Some called it Theology, others called it Divinity. And as I have already suggested, as it developed in Africa, it was a carbon copy of what obtained in Europe and was thus a Department of Christian Theology, which did not reflect the totality of African realities which were religiously pluralistic. By the end of the second half of the twentieth century, however, a change began to take place with the creation of Departments of Religious Studies in the new Universities, all of which introduced courses more relevant to the West Africa situation, like the Sociology of Religion, African Studies, the study of African Traditional Religion, West African Church History, with more emphasis on the students learning to use their minds and depending less on accurate reproduction of the books they read or the lectures they heard.

These new Departments of Theology and/or Religious Studies today start with the conviction that while religion is a construct of the academic imagination, in reality there are several religious traditions in West Africa which define the raw material for the scientific study of religion. These departments now are taking seriously the religious pluralism of the society and are attempting forge peaceful co-existence despite the divergent truths which all these religions offer. As Professor C. Baeta puts it, in these departments 'it is not religions at all that are being placed side by side under one roof – but people, men of different faiths'.[19]

This means that the metamorphosis from Theology to Religious Studies is more than a semantic question; it is saying that the study of religions is not mere science, but also how human beings construct their hopes and fears in relation to ultimate reality. In the new situation, the study of religions holds dialogue not only with philosophy, as in earlier days, but also with the social sciences.

Cultural Realities and the Church

In the new Theological and Religious Studies Departments in the institutions of West Africa, there is an understanding that neither the church nor the institutions are an island unto themselves, but that they are inextricably bound up with the society and the world. They therefore engage in contemporary issues of society in their theological education. In their study of practical theology and Christian ethics, for example, issues such as the context of poverty with its diverse indices leading to a sense of hopelessness in people are examined.

In situations of political instability, as has been the case for many years in Sierra Leone, departments of theology and religious studies call attention to marked injustice and abuse of human dignity. In theological courses, students are equipped to reflect on social, political and economic problems in their own contexts. Graduates, both ordained and lay, are thereby taught to employ social science methods to better face the cultural realities of the contexts in which they will work. For example, although the study of African Traditional Religions fosters respect for African culture, the academic study of African culture also encourages a critical and analytical attitude among students. Commitment to any ideology is rejected as a substitute for competence; rather academic excellence and technical proficiency are made necessary components of theological education in West African institutions of today. This is why West African departments of theology and religious studies offer a curriculum which provides insights into the struggle for justice, creativity and freedom in particular African contexts.

Practical Issues: The Role of Women in Higher Education and, Training for the Ministry

An increasing number of women pursue a study of the Bible, doctrine and other theological subjects within the ambit of a BA Degree in general studies in Fourah Bay College, and no doubt in other similar institutions in West Africa. Theological education over the years has been dominated by men, a fact reflecting the traditionally inferior place of women in African society, as well as in the church due to patriarchal models.

Despite the fact that many women are now reading theology at university level, until lately, they have been hardly in evidence in top positions in church or in academic institutions. Very few university departments of theology and religious studies in Africa had women in faculty posts before the 1960s, although in commerce, civil service and teaching, women were attaining leadership positions.[20] Although more women are attaining postgraduate degrees in theology and religious studies and being appointed to academic posts in Africa today, it is clear that more needs to be done in this area.

Theological education, particularly in the eye of the church, moreover, needs to be seen as a legitimate form of ministry. Buildings and curriculum alone do not make theological education. Good teachers provide the basis on which a solid theological education must be built. That is why the church has always impressed that theological education and ministerial training are central to its life and witness. I therefore venture to assert that churches must be intentional in training people for the *Teaching* Ministry as a 'Career', and accept that this teaching ministry is a respectable engagement in its own right.

The churches must therefore support African departments of theology, and religious studies and not always want to send their students to do postgraduate studies in Europe and America. The churches must close their ranks in theological education as their limited resources are not enough for multiple denominational or sectarian institutions. What is required in the circumstance is long term planning and perhaps an endowment fund.

The single truth is that all our plans can only be realised if there are adequate financial resources. At present the funding of our non-University Theological Institutions, such as seminaries, Bible Schools and theological halls is done in a rather haphazard way which portrays a dependency syndrome. There is no doubt that most of our African churches are poor, reflecting the general poverty of African societies, partly as a result of wrong priorities and also as a result of their need to learn from the independent African churches how to generate the spirit of giving on a large scale.

The subjects of ministry and training the clergy are therefore areas where it could be seen most clearly how the gospel and culture are inextricably bound. If theological education, particularly at tertiary level, is to have its perspective right and continue to play a role in the Christian engagement with African cultural dynamics, it needs to have clarity on the nature and shape of the ministry on the African continent. Why not learn the lesson offered by the ministry in African Christian Independent Churches, which have taken seriously the African context and the traditional concepts of ministry?

African Cultural Priorities

A minister in the traditions associated with African Independent Churches is not just a ritual specialist, but a person of power. Such power is most evident in cases of healing and exorcism. Besides, in African Independent Churches the minister is a kind of lineage head, to whom people come for counselling, advice and solution of their problems, both material and spiritual. That is what makes the minister most influential and makes his or her ministry attractive, respected and relevant. It becomes therefore a challenge to mainline theological education to equip people for such ministries that are particularly relevant to African cultural and spiritual expectations.

Over the years, and to be specific during the missionary era, the historic churches have lost sight of the healing tradition, which remains at the centre of African culture. This has occurred despite the accounts in the New Testament that testify to the healing ministry of Jesus, which resonates closely with the traditional African experience in which healing is a function, if not the primary function, of religion. As such, African Christians are dissatisfied with the differentiation between so-called physical and spiritual healing, which seems to have become accepted in mainline, missionary founded churches. If the mainline church does not begin to take seriously the African emphasis on healing, as Aylward Shorter notes, 'there is a real danger of heterodoxy or even schism.'[21]

Finally, let me again emphasise in summary that the stresses and strains that go on in the study of theology and religious studies remind us that there can be no final perspective in which we can rest and be content. Every theology is culturally and historically conditioned. What Christian theology can hope to do, therefore, is to express the content of the Christian faith without undue exaggeration, omission or distortion, in the clearest and most coherent language available for its own age and communities. If this conference can achieve insight into how African cultures themselves define our age and communities, a clearer role for departments of theology and religious studies in the Christian engagement with African cultural dynamics may emerge from our deliberations.

Notes

1. H. Sawyerr, 'Tradition in Transit', in J.S. Pobee (ed.), *Religion in a pluralistic society*, Leiden: Brill, 1976: 85–96.
2. Luke N. Mbayo, *The reshaping of African tradition*, Eungu SNAAP, 1988: 76–77.
3. Karl Barth, *The Word of God and the word of man*, New York: Harper, 1957: 70.
4. Paul Tillich, *Systematic theology volume 3. Life and spirit: History and the Kingdom of God*, London: SCM: 4.
5. John MacQuarrie, *An existentialist theology: A comparison of Heidegger and Bultmann*, New York: Harper and Row: 13.
6. Stephen Neill, *Survey of the training of the ministry in Africa, Part 1*, London: International Missionary Council, 1950: 40.
7. S. Johnson, *The history of the Yorubas from the earliest times to the beginning of the British Protectorate*, London: Routledge, 1921.
8. James Denton, 'History of Fourah Bay College' In *Jubilee Volume of the Sierra Leone Church*, London, 1917: 251. See also, T.J. Thompson, *The jubilee and centenary volume of Fourah Bay College, Freetown: Sierra Leone*, Freetown: Elsiemary Printing Works, 1930.
9. Denton: 258.
10. Denton: 232.
11. Max A Warren, *Social history and Christian mission*, London: SCM, 1967: 112.
12. D.L. Summer, *Education in Sierra Leone*, Freetown,: Government of Sierra Leone, 1963: 125f.
13. See, Neill, 1950.
14. Neill: 42.
15. Neill: 52.
16. Neill: 57.
17. Denton: 262.
18. Summer: 98.
19. C.G. Baeta, *The relationships of Christians with men of other living faiths*, Accra: Ghana University Press, 1971: 8.
20. A. de Rocchietti, 'Women and the people of God', in, E. Tamez (ed.), *Through her eyes: Women's theology from Latin America*, Maryknoll: New York: Orbis Books, 1989: 96–117.
21. Aylward Shorter, *Jesus and the witchdoctor*, London: Geoffrey Chapman, 1985: 18.

Part One

THEORETICAL PERSPECTIVES

Chapter One

African Identities as the Projection of Western Alterity[1]

James L. Cox

THE ACADEMIC STUDY of African cultures, religions and societies originated in the late nineteenth and early twentieth centuries from disciplines as diverse as linguistic and textual studies, anthropology, history, sociology, archaeology, and what became known as the science of religion (*Religionswissenschaft*). The primary aim of such scholarship until the 1960s was to provide an objective description, largely for the Western academic community, of various aspects of African life. For example, historical studies sought to determine the development of African religions, often with a view to exposing the 'primitive' nature of their rites and beliefs.[2] Anthropologists identified a wide range of subjects from clan structures and lineage systems to processes operating within rituals, particularly life cycle rituals.[3] Scholars within the phenomenological approach emphasised 'understanding' African religions, but often from within Western categories such as belief in a Supreme Being, concepts of evil and how salvation is effected.[4]

Post-modern analyses, which have dominated methodological discussions for the past two decades, have introduced significant changes in the way African societies are being studied. These include acknowledging that no 'objective' or reified knowledge of African communities is attainable. 'Understanding' an African experience reflects not so much an African perspective as it does the perceptions of the researcher. This viewpoint destroys all-encompassing explanations of African cultures, limits knowledge to specific interchanges between particular researchers and researched communities, and challenges assumptions that descriptions from any of the major fields studying African societies can be regarded as 'true'.

Post-modern research methodologies thus can be classified as 'deconstructionist', but ones which result from Western self-reflection where the questions posed and problems identified are relevant exclusively to Western scholarship. For example, in his discussion of Postmodernism and Buddhism, Stephen Batchelor suggests that post-modern thinkers take for granted 'the plurality and ambiguity of perception, the fragmented and contingent nature of reality, the elusive, indeterminate nature of self'. Such a radical dispersion of knowledge has resulted from the deconstruction by Western philosophers of unitary explanations of reality, the so-called metanarratives of Batchelor's 'European Enlightenment Project'.[5] This same point has been made by Phillip Mellor and Chris Shilling who suggest 'that what is mistaken for postmodernity is in reality a series of circumstances and experiences which are the direct product of certain features of modernity'.[6] Mellor and Shilling prefer the term 'reflexive modernity' to postmodernism, because it shows clearly that the contemporary 'deconstruction of thought' remains fully consistent with the principles of the European Enlightenment. This domination of intellectual discourse by Westerners perpetually restricts Africans to the role of foreigners in the academic language game until they learn to play according to rules of scholarship dictated by disciplines operating in Western universities.

A similar analysis has been suggested by Terence Ranger who, in his discussion of 'postcolonial' methods, refers to 'hybridity' not only as 'the cultural condition of Third World intellectuals' but as 'the condition of all contemporary society'. Ranger argues that the traditional methods of Western social anthropology, for example, in such an intellectual climate are inadequate for understanding contemporary African realities. 'The old colonial relations of dominance and authority need to be replaced by social science as dialogue, as participation'.[7]

Colonial dominance and authority persist on a practical level today through African universities, which as mirror images of Western institutions, are facing increasing problems, some of which are financial and others political, but at their core may be ideological. Many African universities, such as those in Nigeria, Sierra Leone and Zimbabwe, have been closed periodically by government authorities. Nevertheless, African students continue to be trained in African universities in Western methods and African students still travel at great personal cost to Europe and America to obtain higher degrees. Methods for discovering African identities could clarify if part of the crisis in African higher education can be traced to the imposition of Western methodologies in preference to viable African alternatives.

Western educational models for studying African cultures and religions, moreover, have spread throughout Africa carrying with them the methodological assumptions implicit in an all-encompassing explanatory scheme supported by scientific rationality, even when these have been posited in a Christian guise. Although, as I have noted, post-modern analyses have challenged these assumptions, they have operated more like an intra-familial squabble rather than offering radically new perspectives; post-modernism makes little sense outside of the modernist context. I propose in the remainder of this chapter, therefore, to outline a method which suggests ways not only to surpass the modernist agenda, which prescribed how concepts such as culture, religion, education and nationhood were introduced from the West to Africa in the first place, but how to transcend the post-modern critique itself. In order to provide a context for this analysis, I want to outline the current debate, which I regard as highly divisive among scholars of religions, between those who stress either 'insider' or 'outsider' methodologies.

Polarities in Methodologies in the Study of Religions

In their introduction to *Religion in Africa*, Walter van Beek and Thomas Blakely define religion in a way which demonstrates that Western academic approaches to the study of religions tend to fall into two rather polarised camps, one which may be called broadly empirical and the other theological.[8] Van Beek and Blakely's definition of religion as 'human interaction with a culturally postulated nonfalsifiable reality' underscores the opposition between what sociologists (borrowing from a linguistic distinction) call the *etic* (outsider's) and the *emic* (insider's) approach. The outsider is one who conducts research on religious communities of which he or she is not a member. The insider is one who portrays what it is to be a member of a religion as one who actually is (or at least knows what it feels like to be) an adherent and a participant in the religion under study.

In the van Beek-Blakely definition, the outsider's view is shown by their emphasis on religion as a culturally specific human response to what must always remain from a scientific perspective a merely postulated, but entirely nonfalsifiable reality. Van Beek and Blakely suggest that this definition safeguards the study of religions from theology. Just like other disciplines in the human sciences, such as anthropology, psychology or sociology, scientific approaches within the study of religions seek to understand and interpret aspects of human religious behaviour, without passing judgements on their truth or value.

Van Beek and Blakely call their approach an example of 'methodological agnosticism', a phrase used widely in religious studies by scholars as diverse as Ninian Smart and J.G. Platvoet, who also refers to this method as the 'non-cognivist position'.[9] The term methodological agnosticism indicates that the postulated beliefs of any community are nonfalsifiable utilising any scientifically accepted instruments for testing. The approach is methodological in the sense that it employs techniques of description and observation to arrive at an understanding of the phenomena under study. Since what is nonfalsifiable cannot be observed, the academic study of religion limits itself to describing how believers relate to and understand what they postulate to be real. Van Beek and Blakely explain:

> Most people do not claim that they can – at will – directly observe God, an ancestor, or a witch at work. However, this does in no way detract from the reality of widely held beliefs; in fact, the fundamental impossibility to falsify religious content is one major foothold of religion and a source of the bewildering variation and multiplicity of forms.[10]

Those who maintain the van Beek and Blakely position frequently refer to scholars such as Mircea Eliade or W.C. Smith, who seem to affirm the reality of the believer's object of faith, as religionists, defined by Platvoet as those who study 'religions not only for academic reasons, i.e. for the sake of the religions themselves ... but also for a religious reason, for the sake of their own religious view of life'. By contrast, religionists refer to those like van Beek and Blakely who deny the verifiability (and hence, falsifiablity) of the transcendental source of religion as 'reductionists', defined again by Platvoet as those who study 'not the religions themselves, but the ways in which religions function in societies and in the human psyche and the ways in which religions are determined by non-religious factors'.[11]

That these opposing positions remain polarised today can be demonstrated by a quick review of some recent writers who have commented on methodological issues in the study of religions. One scholar who highlights the polarity is John Hick, who in his book entitled *An Interpretation of Religion* maintains a religionist position or what he calls 'a religious interpretation of religion' in opposition to 'reductionist accounts advocated by such thinkers as Feuerbach, Freud, Durkheim and their successors'.[12] Although he acknowledges the value of reductionist critiques of religion, particularly in the light of religious diversity with its implications for cultural relativity, Hick contends that 'this vast and multifarious field of human faith is nevertheless not wholly projection and illusion, ... but constitutes our variously transparent and opaque interface with a mysterious transcendent reality'.[13]

Hick's position is strongly opposed by advocates of reductionism, such as Ivan Strenski, who in his book *Religion in Relation* argues that competing theories of explanation form part of any scientific methodology. Accepted explanatory theories are challenged and superseded using specific or 'reductionistic' disciplinary tools, derived from varying fields such as sociology, psychology, economics or politics. Reductionism in this sense does not represent a closed system of analysis which explains everything in terms of its own presuppositions, but what Strenski calls an empirical 'openness to theoretical change'.[14] In Strenski's view, religionists actually limit the field of enquiry in the study of religion because they depend on a 'theological programme' which contends that if a transcendent reality does not exist, 'the history of religions ... would be impossible'.[15]

Opposition to methodological agnosticism emanates not only from theologians such as Hick and Smith and from Eliade (whom Strenski calls a crypto-theologian), but also from social anthropologists such as Michael Bourdillon of the University of Zimbabwe. In an article discussing anthropological approaches to African religions, Bourdillon argues that academic neutrality on religious matters is based on the flawed premise that the scholar of religion can or should exclude personal judgements from academic discourse. Bourdillon contends that 'our personal judgements are relevant to academic debate, and academic debate can affect our personal judgements'. By accepting this, scholars acknowledge that they view reality from limited perspectives. 'If we are aware of our limitations, we can enter into academic debate in an undogmatic way, ready to listen and to learn'. The best way to do this, rather than denying that we hold personal judgements, is to 'make explicit the value judgements behind our academic work'.[16]

At this point, Bourdillon appears to be calling for honesty on the part of the researcher by disclosing personal perspectives both to the community being researched and within the academic arena. What he means by a personal judgement, however, seems to go beyond intellectual honesty. He notes that in today's world, each person has a number of religions to choose from and 'our choices arise from judgements about what different religions offer and how true are their perspectives'. In this multi-cultural and pluralistic situation, it seems to Bourdillon that responsible academic work aims at assisting individuals within changing cultural settings 'to decide on positive values they wish to adopt'. Bourdillon admits that his position could be regarded as theological since it often is asserted in the study of religions that 'theology requires some kind of commitment while the study of religions is essentially neutral'. Against this view, he says, it is difficult, if not illegitimate, to distinguish between personal and academic judgements. Although the task is difficult, therefore, academics in the study of religions need to define 'cross-cultural criteria for judgements'.[17]

Methodological Conversion as a Starting Point

In the debate over methodologies in the study of religions, the polarities I have just outlined, created by advocates of what may variously be called the insider-outsider, non-reductionist-reductionist, religionist-empiricist positions, suggest a need for innovative thinking in methodologies. In my most recent book, *Rational Ancestors*,[18] I develop a theory, based on Raimundo Panikkar's 'diatopical hermeneutics'[19] and David Krieger's 'methodological conversion',[20] in which I affirm my own faith in scientific rationality while seeking to understand and interpret the indigenous religious expressions in Zimbabwe. I have sought to apply the method in a concrete situation to demonstrate an innovation in religious methodologies going beyond the traditional phenomenological categories of *epoché* and empathy and also attempting to overcome the problems Bourdillon notes in so-called academic neutrality or the position of methodological agnosticism.

Although I am not going to repeat here what I have written elsewhere,

I do want to press forward with the basic concept that to understand an 'other' requires me in some sense to adopt the identity of the other. This forms the basis for Panikkar's method, which he says comes naturally to him, since his identity is comprised of two religious 'others', the Hindu and the Christian.[21] Following Panikkar, Krieger suggests that we must internalise the 'other' into our own identities, so that we can, like Panikkar, be both-and, rather than either-or, in Panikkar's case both Hindu and Christian, or as I suggest in my book, both a scientific rationalist and an indigenous African believer.[22] This process is strictly methodological and intended to promote understanding of both the subject and the object of research.

As this is outlined by Krieger in the context of interreligous dialogue and adapted by me for the purposes of scholarly research, seven stages emerge:

1) The researcher begins by employing what Krieger calls 'all reliable methods', including the empirical, historical-critical, philosophical and phenomenological to critically analyse his or her own tradition.
2) The same critical tools are then applied to the tradition the researcher wishes to understand.
3) Understanding of the tradition changes to conviction, just as the scholar is committed to his or her own tradition.
4) This enables an internal intra-religious dialogue to occur within the researcher which is characterised by the search for a 'common language' capable of 'expressing the truth of both religions'.
5) The internal dialogue becomes external when the scholar's interpretation is presented to representatives of the other tradition.
6) The same stages are presupposed for those the scholar is seeking to understand.
7) New interpretations are tested in the dialogue between the traditions. Where they are found inadequate, the researcher returns to the level of intra-religious dialogue and starts afresh.[23]

The Krieger-Panikkar approach, as I have adapted it, assumes that the researcher is committed to, and by using the proper critical tools, can speak for his or her own tradition. It also assumes that the scholar can learn to experience what it is like to adhere to the tradition under study and thus apply the same critical analysis to it as was done with the original tradition. In this way, the scholar interprets both one's own as well as the other's 'faith' through an intra-personal dialogue (just as Panikkar did as a Hindu-Christian) before actually testing the interpretations reached through the methodology in actual field studies. Although this approach eventually involves the researched community in the process of research, I believe recent studies of the 'other' can deepen the method by making it less dependent on a model of inter-religious dialogue and hence more valuable for empirical research.

The 'Other' Within

In recent years, the study of Otherness, or what is called 'alterity' has become a central theme across many academic disciplines. This has been documented in a book that appeared in the Amsterdam Studies on Cultural Identity series, edited by R. Corbey and J.Th. Leerssen entitled *Alterity, Identity, Image*.[24] In their introduction to the book, Corbey and Leerssen note: 'The Other has been placed on the agenda by pursuits as diverse as women's studies, literary image studies, psychology, philosophy, and, most importantly perhaps, in the social sciences'.[25] Although Corby and Leerssen fail to include the academic study of religions in their list (unless they subsume it under the social sciences), the movement to study alterity and identity is precisely what Panikkar and Krieger have sought to do, and what I have tried to apply in an African context.

In the Corby and Leerssen volume, a particularly helpful paper for the discussions of this book exploring uniquely African identities, is presented by Ernst van Alphen, lecturer in literary theory in the University of Nijmegen. In his article, entitled 'The Other Within', van Alphen does not address religion directly, but he is concerned with the same issues implied by the insider-outsider discussions I described above. By examining the categories of hermeneutics, epistemology and psychoanalysis, van Alphen sheds light on how 'outsiders' gain knowledge of and understand cultures and societies of which they are not a part.[26]

Van Alphen suggests that, from a hermeneutical perspective, we have tended either to idealise or to denigrate the 'other'. He calls the former tendency 'exoticism' and the latter 'nationalism'. From an exotic perspective, the culture of the other is regarded as superior to one's own thereby implying a negative regard for one's own identity. A hermeneutic of nationalism, on the other hand, regards one's own identity as superior to the identity of the other thereby creating images of other cultures as dangerous, weird, inferior or evil.[27]

In either an exotic or nationalistic depiction of the other, the interpretation provided results entirely from the image which the subject holds of itself. The alleged superiority or inferiority of the other is not based in objective reality, but on an imputed value based on self-identity. Van Alphen concludes: 'This implies that the concept of alterity does not have the same status as that of identity. While "alterity" is a screen for the imagination, "identity" is the content of that imagination'. This leads van Alphen to conclude that alterity '*is* nothing, has no meaning' (emphasis his). It operates simply as a 'device' for meaning-production induced by self identities.[28]

An epistemology delineating how we project identity and alterity as objects of knowledge thus becomes critical. Van Alphen, following the philosopher J.L. Austin's distinctions between locutionary, illocutionary and perlocutionary speech acts, argues that identity and alterity are defined not by what is said about them, but by the effects they produce in those who speak about them and in those who hear what is spoken about them. Austin defined locutionary speech as the simple act of saying something. A locutionary act that also performs an action, such as asking or answering a question, giving some information or issuing a warning is an illocutionary speech act. A locutionary act, which produces certain consequential effects on the feelings, thoughts or actions of the one hearing the speech or in the one making the utterance, is perlocutionary. In other words, in perlocutionary speech, what is spoken about is known in the act of speaking it. For example, if I instruct someone to 'Close the door', I am performing an act by giving the order. The action is contained in the statement and thus is perlocutionary, or performative.[29]

Austin added that language to be perlocutionary does not require an explicit statement of the act to be performed, but could employ 'in place of the explicit formula ... a whole lot of more primitive devices such as intonation, for instance, or gesture'. Simply saying 'Dog!' with the proper intonation and gesture could warn a would-be victim of an imminent attack. 'Our explicit performative formula ("I promise ...", "I order you ..." etc.) serves to make explicit and at the same time more precise, what act it is that the speaker purports to perform in issuing his utterance.'[30]

That identity and alterity are best understood as performative and thus similar to perlocutionary speech acts is evidenced through the psychological dimensions of experience.[31] Van Alphen argues that Freud's psychoanalytic theory demonstrated that the self and the other are not distinct but one and the same. 'The other is part of the self. We are our own others. The other is always the other within'. Thus, when we speak of identity and alterity, we refer to that which directly affects the self. Freud's concern was not with the 'integration of the other' but with the 'disintegration of the self'.[32] In his description of the technique of psychoanalysis, for example, Freud described the neurotic ego as one that 'is no longer able to fulfil the task set to it by the external world (including human society)'. It is so disturbed that 'its organization is impaired, it is internally split apart, it is no longer capable of any proper synthesis, it is torn by discordant impulses, unappeased conflicts and unsolved doubts'.[33] By focusing on how psychoanalysis raises 'the mental processes' in the ego 'to a normal level' and thus returns to the patient 'once more ... the possession of his ego', Freud showed how ego states affect the perception of the other and thus function to interpret the other for the self. This leads van Alphen to conclude: 'Identity and alterity are not "givens", they are not presences behind the self or the other, but changeable products of the ongoing process of constituting a self-image'.[34]

Implications of Identity and Alterity for Innovations in Religious Methods

What does van Alphen's analysis of identity and alterity imply for innovations in religious methodologies generally and for identifying African identities specifically? Van Alphen himself suggests the answer: 'The only way to know the other is by letting the other speak about me, by giving the other the position of "I". The reason for this is that when I speak about the 'other', I am immediately involved in demarcating my own self image. By extension, when the 'other' speaks about me, the other also is engaged in a process of self-definition.[35]

For methodologies aimed at examining cultures and identities, this implies that research proceeds legitimately only when contracts of understanding are formed between the researcher and the so-called researched communities. The contract entails dialogue in the fullest sense of the term, where the researcher outlines the purpose and the process of the research and speaks performatively (with effect) to what traditionally would be regarded as the objects of the research. This reveals to members of the researched community nothing about themselves, but a great deal about the researcher. Particularly when researchers speak of the objects of research (alterity), they transport the other into themselves and thereby make their own identities transparent. The counterpart to this occurs when a researcher invites (not compels) members of the researched community to speak about their perceptions of the researcher and the research project. Based on the premise that the other is always the self within, and that the self within can be known only through affect and effect, this methodology provides the only sure way to attain understanding of the other.

This method, moreover, confirms what anthropologists, ethnologists and empirical scholars of religion have argued persistently, that reliable studies of the other emerge only after a researcher has experienced a long exposure of living within and among the people under study. What is innovative in this approach is not the time and commitment involved in the research, but the epistemological process of discovering the other in the self, of knowing alterity through identity.

In the end, the distinction between researcher and researched becomes blurred, if not destroyed altogether, by this methodology. This is why 'the other within' position can be depicted as incorporating both Panikkar's diatopical hermeneutics, which steps outside of boundary discourse and power relations, and Krieger's fourth stage in methodological conversion, which turns the identity of the inner self into that of the other. The knowledge which results from these innovative methods thus cannot convey knowledge of the 'other' in some objectified and reified understanding of knowing. The findings of this kind of research depend on the specific interactions between identities and others, what van Alphen calls the 'interlocutionary situation'.[36]

In my view, this approach to the study of religions overcomes the polarities created by the classic insider and outsider distinctions in research, and thereby defuses the controversy between religionist and reductionist methodologies. It also advances the Panikkar-Krieger methodology beyond its close alliance with models of inter-religious dialogue and their clearly articulated theological aims. The 'insider within' method assumes that the researcher remains always the insider because what is outside is always projected from the inside. The researched also always remains an insider with respect to the one conducting research. The two meet only when they incorporate the respective others within.

Any uniquely African identity in this context will emerge as a form of alterity to Western research initiatives. What the African says about the West, its history of colonialism and its intellectual domination will reveal far more about the African's sense of self than it will about the Western imperialist agenda. I am suggesting, therefore, that the best way to read the articles of this book is to understand them as projections of the self-perceptions of the authors, as reflections of identity through discussions of alterity.

Notes

1. This article is a revised version of Occasional Paper 18 of the British Association for the Study of Religions (1999), which was printed under the title: 'Alterity as identity: Innovation in the academic study of religion'. It is used here with permission.
2. E.E. Evans-Pritchard, *Theories of primitive religion*. Oxford: Oxford University Press, 1965; J. Thrower, *Religion: The classical theories*, Edinburgh: Edinburgh University Press, 1999.
3. J.L. Cox (ed.), *Rites of passage in contemporary Africa*, Cardiff: Cardiff Academic Press, 1998: x–xii.
4. J.L. Cox, 'Ancestors, the sacred and God: Reflections on the meaning of the sacred in Zimbabwean death rituals', *Religion* 25 (4) 1995: 339–355.
5. S. Batchelor, 'The other enlightenment project: Buddhism, agnosticism and postmodernity,' in U. King (ed.), *Faith and praxis in a postmodern age*: 122–123.
6. P.A. Mellor and C. Schilling, 'Reflexive modernity and the religious body', *Religion* 24 (1) 1994: 27.
7. T. Ranger, 'Postscript: Colonial and postcolonial identities', in R.P. Werbner and T.O. Ranger (eds.), *Postcolonial identities in Africa*, London: Zed Books, 1996: 271–272.
8. W.E.A. van Beek and T.D. Blakely, 'Introduction', in T.D. Blakely, W.E.A. van Beek and D.L. Thomson (eds.), *Religion in Africa*. London: James Currey, 1994: 3–20.
9. N. Smart, *The science of religion and the sociology of knowledge*, Princeton: Princeton University Press, 1973; J.G. Platvoet, *African Traditional Religion: A reader*, Harare: University of Zimbabwe, Department of Religious Studies, Classics and Philosophy, 1990.
10. Van Beek and Blakely: 1.
11. Platvoet: 21.
12.. J. Hick, *An interpretation of religion. Human responses to the transcendent*, London: Macmillan, 1989: 1.
13. Hick: 9.
14. I. Strenski, *Religion in relation: Method, application and moral location*, London: Macmillan, 1993: 5.
15. Strenski: 2.

16. M.F.C. Bourdillon, 'Anthropological approaches to the study of African religion', in J. Platvoet, J. Cox, and J. Olupona (eds.), *The study of religions in Africa: Past, present and prospects*, Cambridge: Roots and Branches, 1996: 151.

17. Bourdillon: 149–150.

18. J.L. Cox, *Rational ancestors: Scientific rationality and African Indigenous Religions*, Cardiff: Cardiff Academic Press, 1998: 99–115.

19. R. Panikkar, *Myth, faith and hermeneutics*, New York: Paulist Press, 1979: 9–10.

20. D. Krieger, *The new universalism. Foundations for a global theology*. Maryknoll: Orbis, 1991: 53.

21. Krieger: 45.

22. Krieger: 50–61; Cox, *Rational ancestor*: 117–136.

23. Krieger: 75–76; Cox, *Rational ancestor*: 167.

24. R. Corbey and J.Th. Leerssen (eds.), *Alterity, identity, image: Selves and others in society and scholarship*, Amsterdam: Rodopi B.V., 1991.

25. R. Corbey and J.Th. Leerssen, 'Studying alterity: Backgrounds and perspectives' in Corbey and Leerssen (eds.): viii.

26. E. van Alphen, 'The other within' in Corbey and Leerssen (eds.): 1–16.

27. Van Alphen: 2–3.

28. Van Alphen: 3.

29. Cox, *Rational ancestors*: 71.

30. J.L. Austin, 'Performative-constative', in C.E. Caton (ed.), *Philosophy and ordinary language*, Urbana, Chicago, London: University of Illinois Press, 1963: 25–26.

31. Van Alphen: 5.

32. Van Alphen: 11.

33. S. Freud, *An outline of psycho-analysis* (translated by James Strachey), London: The Hogarth Press, 1949: 46–47.

34. Van Alphen: 15.

35. Van Alphen: 15.

36. Van Alphen: 5.

Chapter Two

'Knowing the African': Edwin W. Smith and the Invention of African Traditional Religion

Henk J. van Rinsum

They say that they are merely *doar*, simple people, and how can simple people know about such matters? What happens in the world is determined by Spirit and Spirit can be influenced by prayer and sacrifice. This much they know, but no more; and they say, very sensibly, that *since the European is so clever perhaps he can tell them the answer to the question he asks* [emphasis mine].

E.E. Evans-Pritchard[1]

Introduction

Nowadays, books with 'three-dimensional' picture cards are available in every bookshop. These cards display at first sight only a regularly repeated configuration of lines and colours which express no picture, meaning or message. However, a hidden picture with a remarkable depth emerges from such a page when one holds it close to one's eyes and focuses them onto it in a particular manner. It may be assumed that hidden depths of texts may likewise be made to reveal themselves by examining them and their contexts closely. In this article, texts on the construct 'African Traditional Religion' are scrutinised in order to uncover layers of meaning which were concealed in the process of textualisation.[2]

The subject of the October 1990 issue of the journal *Religion* was 'African Religion'. The contributions in it by Rosalind Hackett and Rosalind Shaw focused on the concept of African Traditional Religion as a cultural construction.[3] They located its origin in the use of Judaeo-Christian terminology and theology by missionaries when they 'translated' elements of the belief-systems of the people they were trying to convert.

Both Hackett and Shaw emphasised the important role which Geoffrey Parrinder and his 'decontextualised 'catalogue' style' played in the development of the concept 'African Traditional Religion'.[4] It was, moreover, Parrinder who was the first to use it in his *African Traditional Religion*.[5] Its adoption and propagation by leading African theologians like E. Bolaji Idowu and John S. Mbiti in the period of cultural and religious decolonisation and Africanisation made African Traditional Religion into the dominant paradigm in the study of the indigenous religions in Africa. Westerlund has shown how this concept of African Traditional Religion was institutionalised in many Departments of Religious Studies at African universities.[6] As Shaw said:

> African Traditional Religion was constructed as the single, pan-African belief system comparable to Christianity, a mega-homology in comparison to the much more limited delineation of equivalence (and presumed African inferiority) in missionary cultural translations and in the work of scholars such as Westermann.[7]

The aim of this article is to study constituents of the genesis of the construct African Traditional Religion. By going beyond Parrinder, I wish to identify scholars who may be regarded as the pioneers of this concept. I intend to reconstruct how, and under what circumstances, African religious systems began to be translated into Christian terminology and theology. I will concentrate on the influence of Edwin W. Smith (1876–1957), editor of the publication *African Ideas of God*, in laying the foundation of the concept of African Traditional Religion. I want to show that Smith was one of the pioneers in defining the contours of this concept to which others later on referred. This is not to downplay the importance of individuals in the history of missionary work in Africa, like Bishop Colenso in South Africa, who deviated from a general pattern of derogatory thinking as far as African religion is concerned. But these individuals cannot be grouped together in a 'strategic location' to a coherent body of texts on African Traditional Religion. They served as what may be called 'proto-pioneers'.

I will make use of the concept of 'Orientalism' developed by Edward Said, in order to localise the position and influence of Edwin W. Smith. It is also the concept of 'Orientalism' that tried to unmask the intricate relationship between knowledge and power. If one 'knows' a person or a group, one is in a position to 'master' this person or group intellectually. But such domination also affects the knowledge which is acquired about them and the ways in which it is translated into our codes. In my opinion, Western missionaries played a critical role in 'knowing' and thereby domesticating the religious 'other' through a Western epistemological order.

The Contribution of Edwin W. Smith: Biographical material[8]

Edwin W. Smith was born on 7 September 1876 in Aliwal North (Cape Province, South Africa) which was the main centre of the Primitive Methodist Mission in Southern Africa. His father, John Smith, was an influential minister in the Primitive Methodist Church. That church had separated from the Wesleyan Methodists in Britain in the early nineteenth century not so much because of differences in theological doctrines but because it practised open-air-camp meetings in which they tried to reach the poor classes in the Midland industrial areas. This approach was condemned by the Wesleyan Methodist authorities as 'extreme revivalism'.[9]

The mission activities of the Primitive Methodists, as they were called, were initially limited to their home country. In 1860, the church decided to start missionary work in Africa. The mission in Aliwal North was opened in 1870. John Smith was posted there in 1874. He strongly advocated that mission work of the Primitive Methodists in Africa be expanded. After a tour to the French missionaries in Basutoland in 1884, he reported:

> I saw exactly what I wanted to see – a real missionary agency in full operation, and a heathen people in the process of being transformed into a Christian nation. This has made me more

41

dissatisfied than ever with our position at Aliwal. It has become to me simply unbearable. If we mean to do lasting missionary work we must go out into the clear open field of untouched heathenism.[10]

In 1888 the Smith family returned to England. John Smith served as Missionary Secretary of the Primitive Missionary Committee. He was the driving force behind the missionary expansion of the Primitive Methodists who decided in 1888 to open a mission in the land of the Mashukulumbwe, as the Ila people were called at that time, in what is now Zambia. It was not until 1893 that the first pioneer missionaries of the Primitive Methodists reached the area of the Mashukulumbwe. No doubt, John Smith had a lasting influence on young Edwin. Not only his missionary zeal but also his progressive thinking with an open mind for other religions must have had an imprint on Edwin who decided to follow the tracks of his father.

Edwin Smith was sent to Elmfield College, the Primitive Methodist boarding school in York. Edwin Smith did not receive a formal theological education, but in 1897 he entered the ministry of the Primitive Methodist Church and left Great Britain for his missionary work in Africa among the Ila in 1898. First he worked in Basutoland with French missionaries who had been visited by his father. He received a training in the local African languages there. Due to the Anglo-Boer war he had to wait until 1902 before he and his wife could travel to Northern Rhodesia. In July 1902 he arrived in Nanzela, his first mission post. During his stay there he wrote his Handbook of the Ila language that was published in 1907 by Oxford University Press. In 1907 the Smith family returned to England on furlough. In 1909 they went back to Africa and established a new station in Kasenga. In this period Smith was preparing, together with Andrew Murray Dale (resident magistrate in Namwala), the ethnography *The Ila-speaking peoples of Northern Rhodesia*. In 1915 he returned to England. Being a diabetic, it proved impossible for him to return for longer periods to Africa.

After his return to Europe, he served as a chaplain with the British troops in Belgium. Then he found a job with the British and Foreign Bible Society, first as a secretary for Italy and afterwards for Western Europe. He became literary superintendent in 1922 and editorial superintendent in 1932. In this capacity he had the ultimate responsibility for the translation activities of the society. He left the society in 1939.

Smith became one of the founding fathers of the International Institute of African Languages and Cultures in 1926. He served as a member of the executive Council with, among others, Sir F.D. Lugard, Professor Lucien Levy-Bruhl, Dr J.H. Oldham, Rev. Professor Wilhelm Schmidt svd and Professor C.S. Seligman. He had joined the Royal Anthropological Institute as an ordinary fellow in 1909 and served the Institute as its President in 1933–1935.[11]

Smith served as visiting professor at Hartford Seminary, Connecticut between 1939 and 1943, and at Fisk University (Tennessee) from 1943–1944. In 1937 he received an honorary D.D. from Wesley College, Winnipeg. He was the editor of *Africa* from 1945 to 1948. Smith was married to Julia Fitch who died in 1952. They had two children: a son, who had died during their mission period in Africa, and a daughter. Smith died on 23 December 1957.

Edwin W. Smith and African Traditional Religion

As editor of *African Ideas of God*, Smith wrote a thirty-five-page comprehensive introduction which I take as the synopsis of his thinking on African religion. He started with a reference to a meeting he once had with Emil Ludwig in Khartoum.

> One of my fellow-guests was the eminent biographer, Emil Ludwig. Having learnt that I had been a missionary in Central Africa, he drew me aside after the meal and questioned me at great length – indeed, he monopolized me for the rest of the evening. 'What does Christianity do for the African?' he asked. 'Does it increase his personal happiness, and if so, how?' I spoke of the release from fears. 'What fears, and how release?' I pictured the fears and told how we try to induce a personal trust in a living, present, loving God who is stronger than any evil power. Mr Ludwig was puzzled. 'How can the untutored African conceive God?' It surprised him when I said there was no need to persuade pagan Africans of the existence of God: they are sure of it, but not sure of Him as a living power in their individual experience. He was frankly incredulous. 'How can this be?' he said. 'Deity is a philosophical concept which savages are incapable of framing.' I doubt whether I convinced him. (Smith 1950: 1).[12]

It is not without reason that this short story frequently featured in later apologetic contributions on African Religion.[13] Those contributions all had but one objective which is shared with the contributors to *African Ideas of God*: to show that Africans were indeed capable of framing deity as a philosophical concept. The aim of the publication was therefore clearly defined by Smith: 'Among Africans who have not come under the influence of Islam, Judaism or Christianity, is there any awareness of God? If so, what idea of Him have they formed?'[14]

According to Smith symbols played a dominant role in the religious thinking of Africans. Africans used symbols to express their religious feelings. Smith related his analysis of the role of symbols in African religions to a discussion of the origin of religion:

> Obeying the universal impulse to exteriorize the emotionally apprehended supersensible world, Africans take, for the most part, celestial phenomena as symbols of the Supreme Being. [....] Such symbols not only spring from emotion; they generate emotions of awe and gratitude which are directed towards the Deity they symbolize.[15]

Smith is following here the tradition of scholars like R.R. Marett and Rudolf Otto for whom the concept of awe was crucial in their theory of the early development of religion. Religion was held to have developed in stages or phases. Smith referred to Marett's sketch of its development to the stage in which a transcendent Personality, a Creator emerges. As the title *African Ideas of God* already implies, the dominant theme here is theism; it is about ideas Africans have about God. Therefore Smith set out 'to relate the African's theism (such as it is) to other phases of his religion'. These phases are spiritism and dynamism. Following Marett, Smith concluded that these stages, phases or categories 'may certainly be found existing contemporaneously among any one people'.[16]

The lowest of the three stages, dynamism, was discussed first by Smith. He defined it as

> the belief in, and the practices associated with the belief in impersonal, pervasive power or energy, something akin to the Polynesian *mana*, which is likened to an electrical fluid that

44

could charge persons and things, and be diverted from one to another.[17]

The whole concept of dynamism became the object of an academic debate which was strongly influenced by the work of Placide Tempels who wrote a little, but very influential book on Bantu philosophy. Early concepts of dynamism, drawing on the Polynesian idea of a cosmic Mana as defined by Codrington, were focusing on a mystic energy which occupies African practice and thought. This energy was interpreted as one continuum, all-pervasive, in things and human beings. The concept of Tempels was focusing on a *'force vitale'* in terms of individual forces in which one should differentiate in kind and classes according to the potency of this energy.

The major question for Smith was how to relate the phase of dynamism to theology; what is the connection between this essential energy and the belief in God? Put in other terms: is the Supreme Power thought of as 'It' or 'He'? He defined a number of criteria to distinguish the High God from the cosmic Mana. The High God has personality, a personal name; he has a life and consciousness; he is anthropomorphic; he is a Being who is not human; he is Creator or Constructor; he is ultimate power and authority; he is worshipped and he is regarded as judge.[18]

> These criteria, as readers may apply them to the deities described
> in the following chapters, lead me to the judgement that we
> have to do with a High God and not with an abstract Power or
> natural potency, 'Cosmic Mana'.[19]

According to Smith 'so many Africans are aware of Something, other than themselves and other than the Supreme Being, that makes for righteousness'. This missing link between dynamism and theism is the phase of spiritism defined by Smith as 'the belief in, and the practices associated with the belief in, beings who are either (*a*) free nature spirits who never were human, or (*b*) discarnate human spirits'.[20]

The emphasis with the Bantu is on 'human beings who continue to live in the unseen world'.[21] These are called the *mizimu*. Spiritism is important because it gave Smith a clue to the understanding of a fundamental characteristic of African religion: 'It is an essential element in

African belief that "living" and "dead" exist in symbiosis, interdependent, capable of communicating one with the other'.[22] Especially the *mizimu* determine the well-being of people. They are the 'guardians of traditional morality'.[23] Taking the unseen world as a starting point, Smith went on to define religion:

> If the essence of religion is a sense of dependence upon supersensible powers who are able and willing to help, then we are in the presence of religion when Africans commune with their kinsmen in the unseen world, who have enhanced powers associated with their new status and particularly as mediators between man and God.[24]

Mediators are necessary because in Smith's perception of African religion God is 'the complete Other, the absolute sovereign, external to his own creation, so far remote in his solitary glory as to be unapproachable save through intermediaries'. At the same time, this God is thought to be immanent in man. 'But God is not all unlike man'.[25] Smith was now finally entering the third phase of religion, theism. He observed Africans seeking power to satisfy their physical and psychical needs. 'He wants to feel safe in this uncertain and hostile world'.[26] Many of these needs are satisfied by his dynamism and spiritism.

> But alike in the experience of individuals and of society, Africans sooner or later reach the frontier line beyond which neither dynamism nor spiritism can satisfy their needs: they do not meet all the facts, nor adequately solve the problems of life. That is where God comes in. He is the ultimate Controller of natural forces and of human destiny.[27]

In short, God is the last resort when all other helpers fail (Smith 1950: 30).[28]

Having said this, Smith needed to answer only one more important question: 'How came Africans, like other peoples of simple nature, to conceive the idea of God?.[29] Smith raised a possibility which brought him back within the parameters of his own conception of religion:

46

This intellectual argument [i.e. the natural curiosity] is accompanied by, or induced by, an emotional apprehension. [...] the inquiry ends in the wonder of awe, before that which, the more it is understood, by so much the more transcends our understanding. [....] Africans share in that wonder, inarticulate as they may be ....[30]

This last sentence is the clue to the further understanding of Smith's thinking on African religion. All human beings share the wonder of awe simply because 'the self-revelation of God is present and continuous'.[31] Here we are clearly entering the area of theology, a theology of fulfilment. Smith was taking a stance against the theology of Karl Barth, the theologian who can be regarded as the proponent of the exclusive revelation through Jesus Christ. Smith here approvingly quoted the theologian Emil Brunner who said:

Apart from real revelation the phenomenon of religion cannot be understood. Even the most primitive polytheistic or pre-polytheistic idolatrous religion is unintelligible without the presupposition of the universal revelation of God which has been given to all men through Creation.[32]

Edwin W. Smith's Writings

Edwin W. Smith was a prolific writer.[33] The development of his thinking about African religion can be traced in the following publications.[34] I already referred to the ethnography that he wrote, together with Andrew Murray Dale, *The Ila-speaking Peoples of Northern Rhodesia*. This ethnography was published in 1920 but the text was already available in 1915.[35] The parts dealing with the belief-system of the Ila were written by Smith. They already carried the marks of an evolutionary scheme from dynamism to theism. It seems justified to argue that his stay among the Ila was decisive for his thinking on African religion in general. This material is therefore interesting because the ethnography was one of the first books of Smith in which he wrote about African religion and also because some of the epistemological problems we have touched upon can be elaborated through this material. Since I turned to the text of the ethnography dealing with the belief-system of the Ila in another article,[36] I will here briefly highlight some of the other publications of Smith, written and published between the publication of the ethnography in 1920 and *African Ideas of God* in 1950.

In 1923 a small booklet was published with the allusive title *The Religion of Lower Races, as Illustrated by the African Bantu*, which indicates his evolutionary thinking.[37] But I must add that Smith apologised for this title, which the publishers forced upon him. Twenty years after its publication, he refused to sign a copy of it in the New York Library[38] and he omitted the title of this booklet from the lists of his publications. The content of this little book rehearsed the scheme developed in the Ila ethnography: it started with dynamism and ended with the Supreme Being, though the latter part was not developed as well as it is in his other works.

The Secret of the African, published in 1929, contained the lectures which Smith delivered at the invitation of the Church Missionary Society in 1927 and 1928. In nine chapters Smith unfolded his ideas on African religion for an apparently missionary audience. Referring to Rudolf Otto's *Das Heilige*,[39] 'which has exercised so great an influence over our thinking in recent years', he followed Otto closely and defined the basis of African Religion as 'a feeling of the uncanny, a thrill of awe and reverence, a sense of inferiority and dependence'.[40] In his chapter on the relationship between religion and magic, Frazer's theory on magic was rejected by Smith who grouped magic with dynamistic religion. Marett was praised for having labelled the pre-animistic stage of religion as dynamism.

African Beliefs and Christian Faith, published in 1936, was written to serve as teaching material in Africa to African students, evangelists and pastors. It was written in basic English to facilitate its translation into African languages. Smith admitted that it is certainly not meant to be a complete manual of Christian theology:

> I have limited myself to the Doctrine of God. This is, in my opinion, the most fundamental of Christian doctrines, and the most vital in teaching Africans. It provides the best approach to Africans through their own beliefs.[41]

The book is divided into three parts. First, Smith dealt with 'Belief in God among the Africans'; it is followed by 'Belief in God among the Jews'; and the book is concluded by 'The Revelation of God in Jesus Christ'. The comparison of African theism with that of the Jews was important for Smith, because the Jews 'like Africans, went far on the road but did not get into the full light' of the revelation of God in Jesus Christ.[42] In this booklet, Smith concentrated for obvious reasons on belief in God. But it is of interest to note that, although his evolutionary scheme is present in his discussion of the relationship between force and God, he did not mention dynamism as a developmental phase explicitly. Smith seemed to anticipate the growth of African theism and in tune with it de-emphasised his evolutionism. His emphasis on African theism can partly be explained by the fact that he was writing for an audience of African Christians.

Four years before the publication of *African Ideas of God* a little book called *Knowing the African* was published. This book was a compilation of lectures mainly given by Smith at the Canadian School of Missions at Toronto while serving as visiting Professor at the Kennedy School of Missions at Hartford. His audience consisted mainly of candidates and missionaries on furlough. Chapter Six, 'Some Aspects of African Religion', resembled closely the matter and structure of the introductory survey in *African Ideas of God*. Religion's three phases of development, dynamism, spiritism and theism, featured prominently, but it is remarkable that Smith started with spiritism first in this chapter. He posited as the key element of African religion the 'constant coming and going between the two worlds; the seen world and the unseen world'.[43] And this division between the so called living and the so called dead with its accompanying 'reciprocal obligations', brought him to his definition of religion:

> I believe myself that, among the many who have attempted to define religion, Schleiermacher comes nearest the truth: "The essence of the religious emotion," he said, "consists in the feeling of an absolute dependence".[44]

For yet another reason spiritism was an important developmental stage because it opened access to the phase of theism. There seemed to be 'certain powerful chiefs who remain in the unseen world to protect their community and to act as intermediaries between them and the Supreme Being'.[45] He referred in this case to the spirit of Shimunenga, a local divinity in Kasenga which was one of Smith's mission posts. From spiritism Smith now turned to dynamism. He referred first to Frazer's unsatisfactory division between religion and magic. He observed: 'Africans believe that something is at work – some mystic force is released and works'.

> I had, I remember, reached this point in my research when Dr Marett's book *The Threshold of Religion* came into my hands. It was an illumination. He held out for the widest possible definition of religion. Since he wrote, the notion of pre-animistic religion has found a place in our thinking. Much of what used to be labelled Magic is now seen rather to be religious because it relates to the specific emotion of awe which men experience in the presence of the supernatural.[46]

Smith here used the word dynamism, which he admitted borrowing from Marett.[47] In this phase of dynamism, people 'become aware of power or powers which excite wonder and awe.'[48] It is the 'awesome holy'.[49]

Smith then moved to theism as religion's crowning phase. He began by admitting that missionaries are in for problems if they presume to present data about theism among Africans. The following quote presents in a nutshell the problematic on which this article focuses:

> A missionary who speaks or writes on this subject expects to have his testimony questioned. We are supposed to be incapable of weighing and criticizing the evidence, and to read much more than is warrantable into what Africans tell us, because we want to prove a thesis. We have been accused of manufacturing names for God; and some people have said that what we report as African belief is nothing more than a reflection of our own teaching. I do not admit the criticism as applicable to myself. I have no theory to maintain. I only want to get at the facts.[50]

Smith rejected the theory of Father Schmidt about a primeval monotheism. Smith preferred the 'Marettian scheme, viz. that Africans, and others, have risen to a recognition of a Supreme Being by personalizing the all-pervading potency of which I have spoken'.[51] The main question is whether the Power is '*He*' or '*it*'? Based upon his experiences among the Ila, Smith's conclusion is clear. There was certainly the idea of a Supreme Being. Ancestors were the intermediaries between him and men. And this theistic belief was, of course, a starting point for missionaries.

> I still believe that in presenting Christianity to the African one should begin where the African has left off; and that it is for us to develop all the rich promise that lies in their awareness, however vague it may be, of a Supreme Being. We have to make God real to the Africans and lead them to concentrate upon Him all the devotion they now give to ancestral spirits and charms.[52]

Indeed, theism is shown here as the ultimate phase in the development of religion.

The 'Definer' Defined

Smith's definition of religion may be reconstructed from several passages in the books discussed so far.[53] Key elements in it are human experience of the supernatural as real, the sense of awe and feeling of absolute dependence before it. We may locate Smith in a tradition of defining religion as 'the manifestation of the holy'.[54] Platvoet mentioned in a footnote that this tradition occurred mostly in combination with the definer of 'religion as communication' which is also the case with Smith's definition of religion.[55]

This tradition stemmed from the liberal theology as it developed in the second half of the nineteenth century. Under the strong influence of Schleiermacher, it stressed the religious experience and intuition in reaction to rationalist positivism. Major elements of liberal theology are the reality of a supernatural world and humanity's dependence on it; the *sui generis* nature of religion; and its irreducibility to a human fallacy. In addition, religion is an essential part of all human cultures. The differences in religion are the products of the relative degree to which they are affected by the phases of development.

This liberal theology had a formative influence on Smith. One document to support this thesis is the photograph of Smith's study at Nanzela station in 1904 mentioned by Young. It showed newspapers and many books, and among the latter Fairbairn's *The Philosophy of the Christian Religion*.[56] Fairbairn was a leader in liberal Christian thought at the close of the nineteenth century; a favourite author of John Smith, Edwin's father, and closely associated with Dr A.S. Peake, Tutor at the Hartley Primitive Methodist College whose writings must also have been known to Smith.[57] Smith must also have been influenced by the 'nature myth' school taking his deep interest in the development of languages and in protological myths.

This reconstruction of Smith's definition of religion is important. It shows that Schleiermacher's feeling of dependence, Marett's definition of Mana, and Otto's concept of Awe have moulded the minds of pioneer liberal missionaries like Smith and Junod.[58] Platvoet correctly contended that (operational) definitions of religion used by scholars, 'are derived not solely from the object of study, but from the interaction between the data of the religion(s) to be studied and the scientific interests and views of the scholar'.[59] The fact that Smith apparently had internalised this concept of religion as the manifestation of the Holy is a major element in a recontextualisation of his writings. It must have had a decisive influence on the way he observed and textualised his experiences during his stay among the Ila. Smith perceived the deep felt, 'innate' indigenous religious awareness of the Africans among whom he worked.

I locate Smith not as an individual on his own but as an important representative of a group of pioneers who initiated the development of the notion of African Traditional Religion. How can we assess this fundamental shift in conceptual thinking? It is precisely the use of a specific definition of religion which brought Smith the tool to 'define' and through that, to 'invent' African Religion. Note, for example, his opinion on magic. In the Frazerian tradition there was a sharp dividing line between magic and religion. Smith disagreed and brought magic within the realm of religion by means of his definition. Magic is then transformed to the phase of dynamism, the phase of the belief in the all-pervasive force, Mana in the words of Codrington. This is very important because it ascertained the Africans as people having a religion. Moreover, the religious experiences which they have, they share with other people. Like them, they feel dependent on the 'Other' World. And religious experiences imply that they communicate with the supernatural world. This implied almost by necessity the phase of spiritism. And through the 'Marettian scheme' of personalising the all-pervasive force, one enters the phase of theism.

One may argue that Smith is here merely following the lines of evolutionary thinking which was common in this period of time. Undoubtedly,

Smith is strongly influenced by evolutionary thinking.[60] Often he characterised the Ila as being in a state of infancy from where they will grow to maturity.[61] But for Smith, the differentiation of African religion in phases was not necessarily thought to be a linear development. And it should also not be interpreted as a linear development in the process of conceptualising religion by Smith for already in 1907 he observed the existence of African theism.[62] This pyramidal categorisation was manifest in all the writings of Smith. And throughout his writings this line of thinking was disseminated not only in missionary but also in academic circles of that time. Later scholars like Parrinder, but especially Mbiti and Idowu, started from this phase of theism where Smith ended up in his evolutionary thinking.

How then can we interpret Smith's position in the development of a Western discourse on African Traditional Religion? In the introduction to this article I suggested the answer when I referred to the concept of *Orientalism* as developed by Edward Said.

Orientalism and Discourse

In 1978, the Palestinian scholar of literature, Edward Said, who teaches at universities in the United States, published a book *Orientalism*, in which he developed the notion 'orientalism'. Building on ideas of Foucault he analysed Western academic discourse about the 'Orient', the East. It is, he said, a 'style of thought based upon an ontological and epistemological distinction made between "the Orient" and (most of the time) "the Occident"'.[63] Said considered 'Orientalism' to be a 'Western style for dominating, restructuring, and having authority over the Orient'.[64]

A discourse like 'Orientalism' acts within, and strengthens the existing power-relations through which We, the West, dominate the Other, the East (and which we try to maintain). This domination is intimately linked with knowledge. The West is in a position to know the Orient, to master the Orient intellectually. In such a discourse images of the Other are being constructed. I define discourse as a configuration of speaking, writing and imaging in a certain period of time based on a regulating and controlling principle. Whether images of the other are 'true' or not is ultimately not relevant for it is proper to such a discourse to cause people to believe these images; it prevents them from questioning their truth. All that matters is the practice resulting from the images. In this way, these images not only determine our own practice but also the practice in respect of the Other.

Although discourse can be regarded as overlapping with ideology, it is more comprehensive. If one takes a broad definition of ideology, for example. that of Therborn, one is still referring to human subjectivity: it (ideology) includes 'both the "consciousness" of social actors and the institutionalized thought-systems and discourses in a given society. [...] not as bodies of thought or structures of discourses *per se*, but as manifestations of a particular being-in-the-world of conscious actors, of human subjects'.[65] In the Foucault-inspired notion of discourse this human subject is absent although, as we will see, Said was deviating from Foucault in this respect. I also want to differentiate between discourse and 'invented traditions' as defined by Hobsbawm and Ranger. In their terminology tradition is taken to mean a 'set of practices'.[66] I am here interested in the formation of texts from which tradition resulted.

Said has shown how the intellectual authority of the concept of 'Orientalism' may be analysed. He distinguished between the strategic location of an author, i.e. the position of an author within his texts with regard to the material he is writing about, and the strategic formation, that is the relationship between text and the way clusters of texts, textual genres, in the end preserve the discourse within which they function. Authority is directly linked to 'exteriority'. This concept of exteriority is crucial: ' ....the orientalist is outside the Orient, both as an existential and as a moral fact. The principal product of this exteriority is of course representation'.[67]

This exteriority is also connected with a vague idea of altruism. Since the Orient is not able to represent itself, 'we' are willing to do this on its behalf. This notion has especially been strongly developed by missionaries in the past. They displayed a highly developed sense of altruism. This is well illustrated by a quote from Placide Tempels' *Bantu Philosophy*:

> We do not claim, of course that the Bantu are capable of formu-
> lating a philosophical treatise, complete with an adequate vo-
> cabulary. It is our job to proceed to such systematic development.
> It is we who will be able to tell them, in precise terms, what their
> innermost concept of being is. They will recognize themselves
> in our words and will acquiesce saying, You understand us: you
> know us completely: you "know" in the way we "know".[68]

There is virtually no better way for expressing the superiority inherent in dominance through knowledge than through the altruism that Tempels displayed.

Through representation the 'Other' is made 'visible': 'And these representations rely upon institutions, traditions, conventions, agreed-upon codes of understanding for their effects, not upon a distant and amorphous Orient'.[69] Said has shown that the process by which the Other is represented develops along its own consistent pattern:

> My analyses consequently try to show the field's shape and internal organization, its pioneers, patriarchal authorities, canonical texts, doxological ideas, exemplary figures, its followers, elaborators, and new authorities.[70]

It is important to note that Said, unlike Foucault, assigned an important role to individual authors in the development of a discourse.

> Yet unlike Michel Foucault, to whose work I am greatly indebted, I do believe in the determining imprint of individual writers upon the otherwise anonymous collective body of texts constituting a discursive formation like Orientalism. The unity of the large ensemble of texts I analyze is due in part to the fact that they frequently refer to each other: Orientalism is after all a system for citing works and authors.[71]

Said was interested in revealing 'the dialectic between individual text or writer and the complex collective formation to which his work is a contribution'.[72] Said clearly diverged here in a fundamental way from Foucault for whom the subjectivity of an individual writer did not matter at all. Clifford criticised Said for this 'hybrid' approach. In his view, it resulted on the one hand in a mix of tradition and ideas, and on the other in a notion of 'discourse' inspired by Foucault, in which individuals play no role.[73] Though Clifford had a point here, the approach of Said still seems appropriate when the aim is to understand what elements play a crucial role in the genesis of a discourse. A discourse is not a static entity but a dynamic formation. Though it must be admitted that there is no direct causal link between a subject, an author and a discourse, I follow Said in emphasising the role of authors and their texts in the formative processes of the discourse, not as subjects who sustain a discourse but as writers whose textual products are located in a certain relation to a body of texts.

An analysis in the vein of 'Orientalism' demands that attention be paid to the role which authors and texts played in the context of the power relations prevailing at the time when their texts were written and read. According to Said, an intimate relationship exists between knowledge and power. Knowledge of the 'Other' implies that one can take a position towards the 'Other'. The 'Other' is object of scrutiny, of academic research and, in the case of Africa, of missionary zeal. Through knowledge of the Other we are in a position to 'create' the origin and the future of the civilisation of the Other. The Other is becoming a fact, a thing.

> To have such knowledge of such a thing is to dominate it, to
> have authority over it. And authority here means for "us" to deny
> autonomy to "it" – the Oriental country – since we know it and
> it exists, in a sense, *as* we know it..[74]

Knowledge thus acquired from a position of power will reinforce the power-relations. This knowledge will be regarded as authoritative. Said stressed the constitutive element of unequal power-relations. Any writer who is representing another cultural tradition, another cultural experience, will never escape the constitutive effect of existing power-relations.

Since its publication, *Orientalism* has provoked fierce criticism because Said postulated an intimate interrelationship between knowledge and power. He has been criticised as 'totalitarian' for leaving no room for alternative ways of representations in the West nor for independent voices from the 'Other' side. Marcus and Fischer therefore argued that *Orientalism* had been effective as a polemic only and mainly had an impact among academics (Marcus and Fischer, 1986). Despite the fundamental criticisms which have been levelled against *Orientalism*, the perspectives developed by Said offer a valuable heuristic instrument which may be usefully employed when analysing the ensemble of early texts on 'African Traditional Religion'.

African Traditional Religion as a Discourse

What I did in this article is to replace the concept of 'Orientalism' by the construct 'African Traditional Religion'. It emerged, after all, as an attempt to represent the religious experience of the African 'Other'. I see African

Traditional Religion as part of a comprehensive Christian missionary discourse characterised by Mudimbe as the 'authority of truth'.

> Missionary orthodox speech, even when imaginative or fanciful, evolved within the framework of what, from now on, I shall call the authority of the truth. This is God's desire for the conversion of the world in terms of cultural and socio-political regeneration, economic progress and spiritual salvation. This means, at least, that the missionary does not enter into dialogue with pagans and "savages" but must impose the law of God that he incarnates. All of the non-Christian cultures have to undergo a process of reduction to, or – in missionary language – of regeneration in, the norms that the missionary represents.[75]

All elements of the religious belief-systems of those groups, which were subject to the mission activities, were reduced in the end to the dominating system of belief of those missionaries. The cultural construct African Traditional Religion was therefore a constitutive part of a wider colonial discourse. The nucleus of the construct is a pyramidal categorisation of the religious belief systems of the African peoples which ranges from an all-pervasive power at the base to a Supreme Being at the top.

If we want to analyse the shape and organisation of the construct African Traditional Religion as a body of texts as Said did for Orientalism, we have to identify pioneers, patriarchal authorities, canonical texts, followers, elaborators and new authorities. In this way we can build up a library of knowledge on African Traditional Religion and position Smith in this discourse.

Pioneers

I consider western missionaries like H.A. Junod, T. Cullen Young, J. Roscoe, D. Westermann, and especially Edwin W. Smith to be the pioneers of a systematic, coherent development of the concept of African religion. Influenced by liberal theology, they all worked at the beginning of this century in Africa and showed a similar positive appreciation of the belief systems of the peoples among whom they lived. Their works were a turning point in the history of Western representation of African indigenous religions. Their appreciation of certain elements of the indigenous religions compelled this new brand of liberal missionaries to textualise their views and experiences in ethnographic texts. These textualisations, either missiological literature or anthropological material, were intended to represent the 'Other' in his/her religious experience. It resulted in a wealth of ethnographic material about different peoples in Africa. Their ethnographies were regarded as classics for many years.[76] These missionaries played a prominent role in the development of the academic discipline of anthropology from its paradigm of the 'armchair anthropologist in the metropolis' to the paradigm of the 'experienced fieldworker'.[77]

Patriarch

> When, some fifty years ago, Geoffrey Parrinder first went to work in West Africa as a young man, there was really very little at all he could have read on the subject of African Christianity. He could turn to some books on the subject of African religion and society by Edwin Smith and others.[78]

It seems appropriate to attribute to Geoffrey Parrinder the title of patriarchal authority. In his writings he firmly established the notion of African Traditional Religion (in singular!) as a pan African belief-system notwithstanding local and regional differences. There were quite a few connections between Parrinder and Edwin W. Smith. They both started their career as missionaries sent by the Methodist church to Africa. When Parrinder wrote his PhD thesis on West-African religion, Smith was one of his examiners (together with E.O. James). Smith wrote a foreword to Parrinder's *West African Religion* which was published in 1949 by Epworth Press.[79]

Andrew Walls has suggested that *West African Religion* was one of the first publications in which 'the fourfold categorization of the divine hierarchy, based on collections of names in African languages: Supreme God, Divinities, Ancestral Spirits and power located in specific objects' was introduced.[80] In this respect I disagree and refer to the writings of Edwin W. Smith who, as I have shown, laid the basis for this way of defining the religious Other. This was also confirmed by Parrinder himself when in 1970 he wrote that 'Edwin Smith also gave a model for African religious thought, regarding it as a pyramid'.[81]

In 1954, Parrinder published *African Traditional Religion*. He was the first author to define the body of beliefs of Sub-Saharan Africa and give it a place among the 'world religions'. But, as Walls rightly said, 'What Parrinder has done [in his 1954 publication] was to draw out the implications of the Smith symposium'.[82] Walls referred to a publication edited by Edwin W. Smith to which also Parrinder contributed. This brings us to one of the canonical texts.

Canonical Text

There is certainly not just one canonical text in the development of the discourse of African Traditional Religion. But I assume that the publication *African Ideas of God* will rank highly in any list of canonical texts.[83] Edwin W. Smith was without any doubt its initiator and *auctor intellectualis*. African theologians and African scholars of religion like Idowu and Mbiti frequently referred to *African Ideas of God*; a symposium published in 1950. It looks as if, in the terminology of Edward Said, this publication acted as a canonical text, a pivot in the development of the discourse.[84] *African Ideas of God* was a publication which consisted mainly of contributions by missionaries who focused on the alleged perception of God by African peoples. Westerlund characterised the publication as a 'break-through of a theology of continuity among the Western theologically-trained scholars who were concerned with African religion'.[85] The concept of God acted as the interface between Christianity as a dominating religious system imported by Western missionaries to Africa and African Religion as defined by later African scholars of religion. Westerlund said:

> In the theology of continuity it is, above all, God who represents the continuity. African scholars therefore tend to accentuate His role, while the importance of other aspects of African Religion, some of which are not easily compatible with Christian theology, is played down.[86]

Followers and Elaborators

A line of succession may be discerned starting with Smith and Junod as pioneer missionaries of the new type. It proceeded from them to the authors of canonical texts such as *African Ideas of God*, to Parrinder as patriarch, and on to other scholars who may be termed 'the followers and elaborators' in Said's terminology. Especially Mbiti[87] and Idowu qualify as such. On the one hand they seemed to have followed the path of Smith and Parrinder. It was Parrinder who supervised the thesis of Idowu for his degree of Doctor of Philosophy on which he based his later publication *Olódùmarè, God in Yoruba Belief*[88] In 1973 Idowu published *African Traditional Religion: a Definition* in which he elaborated on different aspects of African Traditional Religion, 'studied from the inside and in true perspective'.[89] On the other hand they also specified the concept, since they wrote their texts in a new era of decolonisation from an African perspective. They tried to 'Africanise' the missionary legacy. At this point it is relevant to refer again to Mudimbe when he argued that 'Western interpreters as well as African analysts have been using categories and conceptual systems which depend on a Western epistemological order'.[90] This dependency on a Western paradigm is precisely the crucial issue in respect of these 'followers and elaborators'.[91] Is it at all possible for African scholars like Idowu, Mbiti and successive African scholars of religion, to escape the dominant epistemological order which was imported and imposed by Western missionaries?

New Authorities

Apart from pioneers, patriarchs, followers and elaborators, Said discerned also 'new'authorities'. In recent years such 'new authorities' have also emerged in the field of the study of the religions of Africa. Among them are African scholars as J. Olupona, F. Mbon and U.H.D. Danfulani. They reject the homogeneous conception of African Traditional Religion because they practise a multi-disciplinary, and multi-dimensional approach which is strongly influenced by the methodologies of the social sciences and the historical study of African societies and religions. As a result, they emphasise the contesting elements in the indigenous religions of particular groups which do not well harmonise with the Judaeo-Christian interpretation of them as much as those which do.

Taking this programmatic design, I concentrated in this article on one of the missionary pioneers, Edwin W. Smith. What he did in his writings was to *re*-present the religious Other. As an element of a discourse, this knowledge of the 'Other', which is based on representation, will in turn function as what I call prescriptive knowledge for the Other. Because a discourse functions within existing power-relationships, the Other eventually 'recognises' himself in the representation constructed of him. From this angle, conversion is not an active achievement of a person who decides to adhere to another religion for whatever reason but a subtle process of recognition of an imposed image of one-'self'.[92]

In this respect the use of the definition of religion as manifestation of the Holy had another significant rationale. It is important to note that the tradition of defining religion as manifestation of the Holy stemmed from a group of scholars like Rudolf Otto who worked and lived within the boundaries of a distinctive Protestant tradition. In his massive and provocative thesis, Balagangadhara defended his point of view that it is Christianity itself that does not allow something 'other' to religion. Referring to especially Schleiermacher and Otto, he argued that the definition of religion as the individual religious expression of the Holy, the wholly other, presupposed as a framework of 'religion', the Christian religion.[93]

From this perspective, the group of missionary pioneers played a crucial role in the development of the discourse on African traditional religion. On the one hand, they ascertained that pagans in Africa did have another religion, an African religion. On the other hand, however, they defined it as one which foreshadows the Christian religion, thereby not only dominating it and relegating it to the distinctly inferior position of a nascent Christian religion, but also effacing its otherness as historically distinct, plural and independent objects of research. As Balagangadhara said:

> In simple terms, the basic mechanism in the spread of religion is its *effacing of the otherness of the other*. The other is transformed into an 'image' of the self. Otherness becomes another variant of the self. There is no 'other' to religion – but merely another religion. Effacing the otherness is possible if and only if there exists a framework which does not allow an otherness. [....] This is how the heathen and the pagan – peoples without religions – end up being incorporated into theology: members of the pagan religions.[94]

Representing the religious 'Other' in a context of domination produces a specific definition of the religious 'Other'. But at the same time the reverse is also valid. Using a certain definition of religion produces a specific representation of the religious 'Other'. Edwin W. Smith was very influential, both in missionary and in academic circles, in propagating a specific concept of religion of the 'Other' by defining and representing African religion as 'another religion', but one waiting for fulfilment.

Notes

1. E.E. Evans-Pritchard, *Nuer religion*, New York and Oxford: Oxford University Press, 1956: 316.
2. I regard 'textualisation' as an intricate process of observing, interpreting, conceptualising and finally writing. This process produces a text which is subject to re-interpretation by its readers.
3. R.J. Hackett, 'African religions: Images and I-glasses', *Religion*, 20, 1990: 303–309; R. Shaw, 'The invention of "African Traditional Religion"', *Religion* 20, 1990: 339–353. Shaw did not define the concept 'cultural construction' but referred to V.Y. Mudimbe, *The invention of Africa: Gnosis, philosophy, and the order of knowledge*, London: James Currey, 1988. Mudimbe spoke about European constructs of Africa as elements of a discourse. Hackett used the term 'construction of cultural categories and the ideological foundations of academic discourse'. See Hackett: 303.
4. Shaw, 'The invention of "African Traditional Religion"': 343.
5. E.G. Parrinder, *African Traditional Religion*, London: Hutchinson, 1954. Also, Personal communication from Geoffrey Parrinder.
6. D. Westerlund, *African religion in African scholarship: A preliminary study of the religious and political background*, Stockholm: Almquist and Wiksell, 1985. See also, J.G. Platvoet, 'The institutional environment of the study of religions in Africa south of the Sahara', in M. Pye (ed.), *Marburg revisited: Institutions and strategies in the study of religion*, Marburg: Diagonal Verlag, 1989: 107–126.
7. Shaw, 'The invention of "African Traditional Religion"': 345.
8. For a short biography of Edwin W. Smith, see, M.J. McVeigh, *God in Africa: Conceptions of God in African Traditional Religion and Christianity*, Cape Cod, Massachusetts: Claude Stark, 1974. The Rev. John Young has recently completed a biography of Edwin W. Smith: W.J. Young, *The quiet wise spirit: Edwin W Smith (1867–1957) and Africa*, Petersborough: Epworth Press, 2002.
9. P. Bolink, *Towards church union in Zambia: A study of missionary cooperation and church union efforts in central Africa*, Franeker: Wever, 1967: 65–79.
10. Bolink: 68.
11. His second Presidential Address was titled: *Africa: What do we know of it?* In the conclusion Smith gave the following answer: 'Very little as yet'. See, Edwin W Smith, 'Africa: What do we know of it?' *Journal of the Royal Anthropological Institute* 65, 1935: 1–81.
12. 'The whole subject in perspective: An introductory survey, in, Edwin W. Smith, *African ideas of God: A symposium*, London: Edinburgh House Press: 1.
13. See, J.O. Awolalu, 'African Traditional Religion as an academic discipline', in E.M. Uka (ed.). *Readings in African Traditional Religion: Structure, meaning, relevance, future*,

Bern: Peter Lang, 1991: 125; E.B. Idowu, *Olodumare: God in Yoruba belief*, London: Longmans, 1962: 30; G.O.M. Tasie, 'Africans and the religious dimension. An appraisal', *Africana Marburgensia* 9 (1), 1976: 57.

14. Smith, *African ideas of God*: 1.
15. Smith, *African ideas of God*: 13.
16. Smith, *African ideas of God*: 13–15.
17. Smith, *African ideas of God*: 16.
18. Smith, *African ideas of God*: 21–22.
19. Smith, *African ideas of God*: 22.
20. Smith, *African ideas of God*: 23.
21. Smith, *African ideas of God*: 23.
22. Smith, *African ideas of God*: 24.
23. Smith, *African ideas of God*: 25.
24. Smith, *African ideas of God*: 26.
25. Smith, *African ideas of God*: 27.
26. Smith, *African ideas of God*: 28.
27. Smith, *African Ideas of God*: 29.
28. Smith, *African ideas of God*: 30.
29. Smith, *African ideas of God*: 30.
30. Smith, *African ideas of God*: 30–31.
31. Smith, *African ideas of God*: 32.
32. Smith, *African ideas of God*: 32.
33. Cf. Hastings: 'Its [Africa's] chosen author was the scholarly Edwin Smith who had been born on a South African mission station in 1876, had become a master of Bantu languages as well as a Methodist missionary in central Africa, the writer of a prodigious number of books about African and missionary subjects and, in 1950, had only just given up the editorship of the International African Institute's quarterly *Africa*.' A. Hastings, *A history of African Christianity, 1950–1975*, Cambridge: Cambridge University Press, 1979: 41.
34. I confine myself here to the books that Smith wrote on African Religion. For an exhaustive bibliography of Smith, see McVeigh.
35. Edwin W. Smith and Andrew M. Dale, *The Ila-speaking peoples of Northern Rhodesia*. 2 vols. London: Macmillan and Co, 1920.
36. Henk J. van Rinsum, 'Edwin W. Smith and his "raw material". Texts of a missionary and ethnographer in context', *Anthropos* 94, 1999: 351–367. 1999.
37. Edwin W. Smith, *The religion of the lower races, as illustrated by the African Bantu*, New York: The Macmillan Company, 1923.
38. I owe this information to Rev. John Young.
39. R. Otto, *Das Heilige. Über das Irrationale in der Idee des Göttlichen und sein Verhältnis zum Rationalen*, Breslau: Trewendt and Granier, 1917. The text was translated into English and published in 1923 as *The idea of the holy: an inquiry into the non-rational factor in the idea of the divine and its relation to the rational*, New York and London: Oxford University Press.

40. Edwin W. Smith, *The secret of the African*, London: Student Christian Movement, 1929: 21–22.

41. Edwin W. Smith, *African beliefs and Christian faith*, London: Lutterworth Press, 1936: 13.

42. Smith, *African beliefs and Christian faith*: 80.

43. Edwin W. Smith, *Knowing the African*, London: Lutterworth Press, 1946: 103.

44. Smith, *Knowing the African*: 105.

45. Smith, *Knowing the African*: 106.

46. Smith, *Knowing the African*: 110–111.

47. He traced the (use of the) concept of dynamism back to A. van Gennep. See, Edwin W. Smith, 'African symbolism', *Journal of the Royal Anthropological Institute of Great Britain and Ireland* 82 (January–June), 1952: 34.

48. Smith, *Knowing the African*: 111.

49. Smith, *Knowing the African*: 113.

50. Smith, *Knowing the African*: 115.

51. Smith, *Knowing the African*, 117.

52. Smith, *Knowing the African*: 120.

53. See especially, *The secret of the African*: 22; *Knowing the African*: 105, 111; *African ideas of God*: 26, 27, 30–32.

54. J.G. Platvoet, 'The definers defined: Traditions in the definition of religion', *Method and Theory in the Study of Religion* 2 (2), 1990: 180–212.

55. Already in 1907 Smith referred to Tylor and his 'minimum definition of religion'. See, Edwin W. Smith, 'The religion of the Bantu', *Primitive Methodist Quarterly Review*, January, 1907: 18.

56. A.M. Fairbairn, *The philosophy of the Christian religion*, London: Hodder and Stoughton, 5th ed., 1907.

57. J.W. Young, 'Edwin Smith: Pioneer explorer in African Christian theology', *Epworth Review*, May, 1993: 80–88. Eric Sharpe placed Fairbairn in the tradition of the scholars of religion who 'view the religious quest of mankind as divinely inspired, and as finding its fulfilment in Christianity'. See, Eric Sharpe, *Comparative religion: A history*, London: Duckworth, 1986 (2nd ed.): 149. *The Philosophy of the Christian Religion* was published in the series of the Gifford-Lectures as was *Varieties of Religious Experience* by Prof. W. James (1902), a book which Smith also mentioned in his ethnography.

58. Junod in his *The Life of a South African Tribe* defines religion as 'the feeling of man's dependence on higher, supranormal powers to which he has recourse to help him in his distress' See, H.A. Junod. *The life of a South African tribe. Vol. 2: Mental life*. London: Macmillan, 1927: 595.

59. See, Platvoet, 'The definers defined': 182. Platvoet added that these interests and views, and the operational definitions of religions are 'constantly corrected and reformed' by the data. He has scholars of religion in mind who explicitly reflect on operational definitions of religions and their very limited heuristic and analytical functions. Outside this group and this use, definitions will often not be reformed by, but be imposed upon the data. Those definitions must be subjected to the methodological prescrip-

tion of reform by the data. I hold that the writings of Smith and most certainly his ethnography, which was meant to be a scientific endeavour, can be analysed along the lines of the processes of interaction as outlined by Platvoet in his article.

60. John Young mentioned that Smith had a copy of Darwin's *On the Origin of Species* among his books in 1904.

61. In his *The Religion of the Lower Races* Smith said that we should remember 'that we are all pupils in God's great school and that if, by His grace, we are in the higher class, it is not for us to despise those who are in the kindergarten'. (Smith 1923:8).

62. Smith, 'The relgion of the Bantu': 19.

63. E. Said, *Orientalism*, New York: Pantheon, 1978: 2.

64. Said, *Orientalism*: 3.

65. G. Therborn, *The ideology of power and the power of ideology*, London: Verso, 1980: 2.

66. E. Hobsbawm, 'Introduction' in E. Hobsbawm and T. Ranger (eds.), *The invention of tradition*, Cambridge: Cambridge University Press, 1983.

67. Said, *Orientalism*: 21.

68. P. Tempels, *Bantu philosophy*, Paris: Présence Africaine, 1959: 25.

69. Said, *Orientalism*: 22.

70. Said, *Orientalism*: 22.

71. Said, *Orientalism*: 23.

72. Said, *Orientalism*: 24.

73. J. Clifford, *The predicament of culture, twentieth-century ethnography, literature, and art*, Cambridge: Harvard University Press, 1988: 268–271.

74. Said, *Orientalism*: 32.

75. Mudimbe: 47–48. See, especially chapter 3, where the power of speech is shown to be important in this respect. A dominant theme for Mudimbe is the relationship between knowledge of the 'Other' and power.

76. Smith wrote the major part of the ethnography *The Ila-speaking peoples of Northern Rhodesia*. He wrote this ethnography together with Andrew M. Dale, a government official in Northern Rhodesia. H.A. Junod wrote *The life of a South African tribe* in two volumes dealing with the social and mental life of the Thonga-people.

77. In Van Rinsum: 351–367, I analyse the ethnographic works of some of these missionaries against the background of the discussion on the 'ethnographic authority' as initiated by James Clifford, among others.

78. Hastings, *History of African Christianity*: 201.

79. E.G. Parrinder, *West African religion: A study of the beliefs and practices of the Yoruba, Ewe, Akan, and kindred peoples*, London: The Epworth Press, 1949.

80. A.F. Walls, 'A bag of needments for the road: Geoffrey Parrinder and the study of religion in Britain', *Religion* 10 (2), 1980: 144–145.

81. E.G. Parrinder, 'Monotheism and pantheism in Africa', *Journal of Religion in Africa* 3, 1970: 85.

82. Walls: 147.

83. *African Ideas of God* was first published in 1950. In 1961 a second revised edition was published, edited by Geoffrey Parrinder and in 1966 a third edition was published.

84. Etherington refers to Edwin W. Smith's landmark anthology. See, N. Etherington, 'Recent trends in the historiography of Christianity in southern Africa' *Journal of Southern African Studies* 22 (2), 1996: 213.
85. See, Westerlund: 51. In this respect I also refer to: J.G. Platvoet, 'Review of Westerlund, D., *African Religion in African Scholarship: A Preliminary Study of the Religious and Political Background*', *Journal of Religion in Africa* 15 (3), 1985: 244–248.
86. Westerlund: 46.
87. In his influential *African Religions and Philosophy* (1969) Mbiti did not yet follow Parrinder's unitary model. He spoke deliberately 'of African traditional religions in the plural because there are about one thousand African peoples (tribes), and each has its own religious system'. In his *An Introduction to African Religion* he shifted from the plural to the singular, yet maintained an independent stance from the Parrinder-Idowu paradigm by never writing 'African traditional religion', but consistently terming it 'African religion'. See, J.S. Mbiti, *African religions and philosophy*, London: Heinemann, 1969: 1; J.S. Mbiti, *An introduction to African religion*, London, Heinemann: 1975.
88. E.B. Idowu, *Olodumare: God in Yoruba belief*, London: Longman, 1962: viii.
89. E.B. Idowu, *African traditional religion: A definition*, London: SCM Press, 1973: xi.
90. Mudimbe: x.
91. I refer to Platvoet, 1996, who made a distinction between 'Africa as object' and 'Africa as subject' in the history of the study of religions of Africa. In using the discourse-perspective the polarity of 'object' versus 'subject' as 'insider' versus 'outsider' loses some of its relevance. In a footnote Platvoet himself characterised these categories as 'problematic'. See, J.G. Platvoet, 'From object to subject: A history of the study of the religions of Africa', in Jan Platvoet, James Cox and Jacob Olupona (eds.), *The study of religions in Africa: Past, present and prospects*, Cambridge: Roots and Branches, 1996: 105.
92. See also Mudimbe: 48, who characterised 'African conversion' as 'the sole position the African could take in order to survive as a human being'.
93. S.N. Balagangadhara, *'The heathen in his his blindness.': Asia, the west and the dynamic of religion*, Leiden: E.J. Brill, 1994.
94. Balagangadhara: 368.

Part Two

CULTURE AND IDENTITY

Chapter Three

Educational Institutions and Christian Engagement With Societal Challenges

U.D. Anyanwu

Perspectives and Background

This paper examines educational institutions and Christian engagement with societal challenges, largely based on data from Igboland, Eastern Nigeria – an area considered typical of the southern Nigerian situation on a number of grounds. The area has one of the highest densities of Christian communities or populations in the region. Also, like the rest of many areas in West Africa, Igboland has had unbroken and expanding Christian presence since the last quarter of the nineteenth century. It thus exemplifies the success of Christian missions in West Africa, particularly in terms of the speed and spread of converts as well as the acceptance and utilisation of Christian religious, educational and health programmes and institutions. For some Christian groups (the Catholics, for example) Igboland houses the largest number of clergy, seminaries, religious organisations and educational institutions inspired and nurtured by the forces or agents of Christianity.[1] Furthermore, until the incursion of Islam into some parts of Igboland since the 1970s, Christianity remained the only historic religion with structures and adherents in the area, challenged only by traditional religion which progressively lost ground to Christianity.

Thus, to a considerable extent, Igbo society is an ideal instance of the collapse of traditional religion in West Africa because of Christian pressures, making Christianity the dominant religion of the people. In fact, in the context of Nigeria, with some justification, Igboland, or Eastern Nigeria for that matter, is perceived as the vanguard for the defence and perpetuation of Christianity; a perception that often made the people the first target of most anti-Christian uprisings or attacks. Igboland is also a distinct model of the fruitful use made of education (or educational institutions) in the fostering of evangelisation.[2] It thus offers an excellent case for the analyses of issues, trends and results of the symbiotic relations between educational institutions and Christian engagement with societal problems in West Africa.

Igboland, moreover, illustrates the fact that an authentic and autonomous church or Christian history is still valid, possible, relevant and desirable in contemporary non-western (erstwhile colonial) societies, where, because of nationalistic, patriotic and ideological considerations, some scholars erroneously propose that such history can only be evaluated when contextualised within the broader history of imperialism and colonialism.[3] Of course, while it is true that Christianity in some ways facilitated colonial attainments, it is equally true that in both the short and long term, the mission of colonialism was not synonymous with that of Christianity or indeed the Christian missions.[4] One subject in the social, economic and political evolution of Igboland which highlights this truth unambiguously is the use made of educational institutions in the Christian effort to overcome societal problems.

The Aims of Christian Educational Missions in Igboland

The basic concern of missions in the building and development of educational institutions (first primary schools and later secondary schools) was the planting and nurturing of Christianity. Though there were initial differences among the missions on this subject, by the 1920s, it had become a generally accepted position that 'the school is a major facilitator of Christian religion in Igboland and the rest of West Africa'. As a result, the first set of primary and post primary institutions were solely mission schools. The missions were in charge of the schools and the management programmes were designed to satisfy the denominational aspirations of the respective missions. The Church Missionary Society, Roman Catholics, Methodists, and Presbyterians were among the first denominations to establish and operate schools and churches in Igboland. As the works[5] of Ekechi (1971), Isichei (1976), Igwe (1987) and Anagbogu (1995) confirm, the respective denominations engaged in competition and rivalry in their efforts to establish schools and churches, leading to the existence of many unviable or sub-standard schools as well as hostile relations among the constituent populations in the Igbo communities where the denominations operated. Joseph Shanahan's appreciation of the significance of the school in the work of evangelisation is indeed typical and shows why it was easily a source of rivalry and competition.

> The school is becoming more and more a providential instrument of incalculable good in our hands. If we go from town to town talking only about God, we know from experience that much of our effort brings no result. But no one is opposed to the school.[6]

The Dike Committee of the 1960s noted that

> everywhere the opening of a missionary outpost was accompanied by the erection of a school. During the first fifty years of their existence and over, the voluntary agencies (as the educational missionaries came to be called) depended almost entirely on funds from overseas for their pioneering work in education: as has been indicated elsewhere systematic and sustained government support by way of grants-in-aid emerged a decade ago. Throughout the century of their existence the voluntary Agencies have dominated the educational scene in this Region: and, as a result, all Eastern Nigerian leaders in Church and State, in business and education, owe their training in whole, or in part to missionary enterprise. The committee found everywhere evidence of the widespread and wholesome influence which the missionaries have exerted throughout the Region. Everywhere their unrivalled contribution to the moral, educational and material progress of the East is acknowledged.[7]

This tribute is well deserved. However, we must not gloss over related issues or matters which also contributed to trends on the development of education and educational institutions. Government policy was among them. Initially, government was opposed to the building of schools by the missions. But by the 1920s, government policy shifted in favour of partnership involving the maintenance of standards, regulation of management and the giving of grants-in-aid to deserving institutions. Government's change of policy was determined mainly by two main factors, namely, its inability to fund education by itself and the desire to obtain necessary clerical staff for the colonial establishment. Additionally, government also wanted to contain the negative effects missionary rivalry over spheres of influence (in terms of schools and churches) had caused in the communities. In the circumstances, the missions remained the dominant factor in the growth of educational institutions in the region.

The other issue in the evolution of educational institutions was the reaction of the communities. The people of Eastern Nigeria responded (after initial hesitation) enthusiastically to the establishment of primary and post primary schools. They easily saw the promise the school had for the social enhancement of recipients of education. As the colonial order evolved, it became obvious that the greatest beneficiaries of the social, economic and political situation were those with the *literacy* which the school provided. In other words, while the missions sponsored educational institutions primarily to promote evangelisation, the people accepted the educational institutions largely for utilitarian materialist reasons. It is true that many who passed through the educational institutions became converted to Christianity or at least became less faithful to the practices associated with traditional religion, yet it would be misleading to conclude that the school system was seen by the people as a total substitute for indigenous cultural views on the social, economic and political development of the people. Indeed, a major paradox of the school system was that while it laboured hard to install Christian structures and approaches in the society, its products (like the teachers, clerical officials, professionals) tended to offer alternatives that were often opposed to the desire of the Christian authorities to increase their hold on the government and society. The school system was partly bedevilled by inter-denominational rivalries and so there was no consensus among the various Christian denominations on the place of government or the state in the control, ownership and management of educational institutions. It was in this context as well as that of the post-civil war that the government was able to take over all primary and post primary educational institutions in Eastern Nigeria in the 1970s. This was, of course, done with little or no consultation with the Christian authorities who had since the beginning of the twentieth century been the dominant providers of Western education in the Region.

What does this suggest? First and foremost, the use of educational institutions for the Christianisation of Igboland failed to receive the protection of the state. Secondly, the investment made by the Christian missions in education appeared wasted from that point of view. There is also the fact of lost hope since the expectation that educational institutions would remain key factors in the interpretation of Christianity among the people was severely constrained by the government's unilateral takeover of educational institutions – an act that made the institutions secular and which also banned religious activities in them. It is also important to stress that the total takeover was in some ways symbolic of the reality that (contrary to the original hopes of the Christian missions) Christian ideals and principles did not dominate ideas and principles derived from other sources in the social, cultural, political and economic attitudes of the people in the area of study. Expectedly, various Christian denominations have been reacting to the government control of schools and the matter has remained one of the most vexed questions in the society.[8] The Catholic authorities are more rigid on the matter than their Protestant counterparts. Nevertheless, there is growing acceptance by all denominations that schools operated by the government constrain evangelisation in Igboland.

The takeover of schools is just one instance of the societal challenges which Christianity encounters in Igboland. Other examples include the issues of social equality, cult membership and the ordering of public affairs according to Christian principles. To reduce ambiguity, there is need to elaborate on each of these issues. An appreciation of the Igbo situation regarding these issues shall, hopefully, further help us to reflect adequately on the circumstances and nature of the encounter between educational institutions and the Christian engagement with society as a whole.

Social Equality, Christianity and the Traditional *Osu* Caste System

From the very beginning Christianity has been teaching that all people and persons are equal before God. It thus abhors and condemns discrimination and all forms of repression that deny people their human rights, including political freedom, the right to own property, freedom of association and equality before the law. These principles were taught and practised by many in Igboland. However, in this connection, within Igboland there still persists a social tradition which remains a challenge to Christianity. It has to do with the *osu* caste system.

Though there is some uncertainty about the origin of the *osu* system, I agree with Onwubiko that its roots are 'in the practice of human sacrifice in Igboland.'[9] According to this explanation, the *osu* was a person sacrificed to a deity by a community or a group of people or a family to pacify 'an enraged deity to save the community, the group or the family'. Given the well celebrated equalitarian and republican setting of the Igbo socio-political structure, it is easy to understand that only a matter as overwhelming as religion could instil within Igbo culture a place for an *osu* or outcast. Even so, with Christianisation many *osu* were liberated and it was hoped that the stigma attached to them would collapse. In law and in theory this was the case. But the hard truth is that Chinua Achebe's description of the life of the *osu* remains valid for Igbo society, even as humanity enters the first years of the twenty-first century. This is so despite the fact that Igboland is rightly perceived as a model of mature and well domesticated Christianity in West Africa. According to Chinua Achebe the *osu*

> was a person dedicated to a god, a thing set apart – a taboo for ever, and his children after him. He could neither marry nor be married by the freeborn. He was in fact an outcast, living in a special area of the village, close to the Great Shrine. Wherever he went he carried with him the mark of his forbidden caste, tangled and dirty hair. A razor was a taboo to him. An Osu could not attend an assembly of the freedom, and they in turn, could not shelter under his roof. He could not take the four titles of the clan, and when he died he was buried by his kind in the evil forest.[10]

When we accept that because of the impact of education, government, urbanization and other moderating influences which compel the jettisoning of the rather crude manifestations of the *osu* system (notably, dirty hair, barring from people's assembly, visits to the residence of the *osu*, and burial in the evil forest), yet it is true that the *osu* are discriminated against in fundamental ways. Thus, they are victims of unequal and unfair treatment in Igbo society. In some sense, the condition of victims of the South African apartheid system was better than that of the *osu*. In present times, not only is it impossible for the *osu* to be the Eze or King of an Igbo region, but subtle measures are taken to ensure that he could not win or even stand as a candidate in elections at various levels of the governmental structure. Of course, inter-marriage with the freeborn is still stoutly opposed.[11] In every sense 'the *osu* system of slavery constitutes the greatest contradiction to Igbo equalitarian ideology';[12] a contradiction which has given rise to a book with the worrying title, *Can the Igboman be a Christian in View of the Osu Caste System?*[13]

Despite the religious origins of the *osu*, the persistence of the discrimination against them in Igbo society is not explicable in terms of the fear of the gods. Instead, it is due more to the social stigma which it has acquired over the long period of its existence. In some ways, therefore, the *osu* system is no longer rationally defended by both Christians and non-Christians in Igboland. As it is, it is largely in marriage and leadership affairs that the *osu* system continues to exhibit uncontrolled negative impact in Igbo society. Therefore, it remains a critical challenge to Christianity in the land.

Challenge of Cult and Cultural Practices

Membership of cults, confraternities or secret societies as well as participation in cultural practices associated with widowhood, readily indicate another variety of societal challenges to Christian engagement in Igboland. Though attitudes or interpretations may vary among the denominations on these subjects, yet the challenge they constitute has had to affect all Christians. A notable illustration of cult activities is the situation in Afikpo in Ebonyi State at the time of writing (in 1997). The Ogo Cult is practised among the Afikpo. It is open to all male adults who go through some initiation rites and perform as masquerades. In traditional times, the masquerades enjoyed uninhibited immunity as they marched through wherever they chose in Afikpo. In the process they also harassed the citizens, often beating up some and chasing the non-initiates and females into hiding. Since the 1980s, their activities and all they stood for came under severe attacks from 'born again' Christians, apparently backed by other members of the society who in principle shared in the belief of the 'born again Christians' that the entire Ogo Cult should be wiped out in Afikpo. This led over time to

75

a number of conflicts between the Christians and the adherents of Ogo Cult. The latter included Christians who did accept that the Ogo Cult had anti-Christian principles and practices. The resulting conflicts were marked by bloodshed, particularly at Amasiri (1988 and 1994), Ozizza (1984), ubam Ugwuegbu (1987), Amankwo and Akpoha in 1994. The destruction which followed these conflicts was so high (in human life and material goods) that concerned citizens were forced to form a Peace Committee while the Abia State Government, under whose jurisdiction Afikpo was at the time, investigated the conflict and issued a White Paper.[14]

Some of the provisions of the White Paper are worthy of note. They include the provision that initiation into the Ogo Cult should be voluntary or optional; oath taking or swearing should be according to one's faith; Christians should not be forced to participate in non-Christian rites and cultural practices. Moreover, subjecting mothers of twins to indignities were regarded as repugnant to natural justice, equity and good conscience and thus declared illegal. On the other hand, Christians should not advocate the total eradication of Ogo cultural practices. They should adopt inculturation of some of the practices which do not offend Christian faith and morals. Clearance should be received from the police before holding public assemblies outside church premises. Christians should restrain their new converts and teach them to respect the traditions of other people. They should also make financial contributions for the development of the community and also take active part in the administration of the funds.[15]

It can be observed that the overall tone of the White Paper was conciliatory. It reflects the government's stand on freedom of worship and of association. The government, like the committee whose recommendations formed the basis for the White Paper, showed evidence of its interest in the growth of Christianity and yet stood against fanatical measures for the realisation of such growth. In particular, government did not empower the adherents of either Christianity or the Ogo Cult to use force or violent measures to win converts to their positions.[16]

A celebrated example of challenge posed by cultural or customary demand is with reference to Nanka in the Anambra State of Nigeria at the time of writing this paper in 1997. The issue here had to do with widowhood practice. The conflict arising from this was the immediate cause of the Nanka Rising of 23 February 1993.[17] The Nanka uprising is concerned with widowhood practice among the Igbo. Custom requires that the widow should not see the late husband's corpse before burial. This is in addition to other treatments which in practice subject the widow to much punishment or torture; usually to show clearly that the widow is sorely touched by the death of the husband and yet by implication (even if fortuitously) giving the erroneous impression that the widow caused the death of her husband. Such other inhuman practices are the solitary confinement of the widow; the requirement that she should be unkempt (dirty clothing) and desolate looking. In the specific case of Nanka, a widow who allowed herself to see the dead husband's corpse was declared the perpetrator of *aru* (abomination) and the *breaker* of *nso ala* (that is, the desecrator of the land which houses the ancestors). As reported by Martins Ugonna Okafor, the proximate cause of the Nanka Uprising was that a Christian, before his death, left instructions that his wife be exempted from the widowhood taboo, that is, a wife should not see the corpse of the dead husband before burial. The affected wife with the support of many other Christians (predominantly belonging to the Catholic Charismatic Renewal) obeyed her late husband's directives. That is, she was present at all the burial rites; an action that embittered the other Christians who still had much faith in the protection of custom. Consequently, the embittered group ambushed and waylaid the funeral procession as it advanced to the compound of the deceased, demanding full implementation of the customary sanctions against the dissident widow. As would be expected, a violent clash ensued between the opposing groups, resulting in the death of two persons (a man and a woman) and injuries to several people.

The Nanka Uprising evoked much interest, leading to hard questions. A significant point is that the uprising paradoxically occurred within the Christian communities (not only Catholics). Its repercussions thus tended to shake the foundation of the entire Nigerian church and it is being seen as symbolic of the situation in the West African area generally. It thus illustrates the kind of challenge which African Traditional Religion poses to Christianity; a view held by many competent commentators including Rev. Fr. Luke Mbefo.[18] The issue here goes beyond the religious aspect. The total problem is reflected in the question: How can the African Christian be truly African and truly Christian? Both recorded and unrecorded reports indicate that the challenge exists in many parts of Christian Eastern Nigeria, including Uturu which has the distinct reputation of housing the highly regarded Marist Brothers, an organised group that manages educational

77

and health programmes which have received both national and international commendation. The present writer is aware of the long crisis (eight years old) which developed because opposing Christian groups could not agree on the date or period for the celebration of the Mbomuzo festival in Umuokeh town, in Obowo Local Government area of Imo State. As it ultimately happened, under cordial environments generated by a committed community leadership, the Mbomuzo palaver was amicably settled by the practice of inculturation by the Catholic and Anglican churches – the largest Christian denominations in the town.[19] The Umuokeh experience commends emulation in the rest of Igboland and Eastern Nigeria wherever similar circumstances exist and challenge the stability of the churches.

Governance and the Challenge of Uprising

In September 1996, disturbances occurred in Owerri, capital of Imo State, shortly after the former Military Administrator had left office. As adequately summarized by the Judicial Commission of Inquiry into the Disturbance of 24–25 September, 1996 in Owerri, the city which was reputed for its peaceful and tranquil nature (and for which it won a national award) became disturbed in the 'last two years' because the crime of kidnapping was unleashed on it. Several children were abducted; the public were excited with indignation and resentment. The kidnapping incidents were associated with the emergence of a new crop of young men of questionable antecedents who had suddenly acquired immense wealth in suspicious circumstances. They also displayed their wealth recklessly to the astonishment and resentment of the general public. The commission also reported the maladministration and unmitigated corruption of the Aneke (the immediate past Military Administrator of Imo State) administration; the recklessness with which traditional rulers conferred chieftancy titles; the collaboration by the police with the *nouveaux riche*, and the inappropriate manner in which the prison officials handled dangerous criminals in their custody. There was also the case of some religious organisations that broadcast tendentious and provocative religious programmes over the media for the consumption of the public, in some cases using human parts for illustration.[20]

This was the situation in Owerri when the police on 20 September, 1996, arrested Innocent Ekeanyanwu who was in possession of a fresh and decapitated human head, which was later identified as that of teenager – Anthony Ikechukwu Okonkwo. A few days later, Ekeanyanwu, who was under police custody, was reported dead in what were clearly mysterious and suspicious circumstances. The consternation of the public heightened, but more was yet to happen. There developed a peculiarly ominous situation whereby snakes of identical patterns swallowed up those of other species.

For the people, there was the general feeling that it was time to redress the ugly trend. The opportunity soon came. The police in public glare and press presence exhumed the headless body of Anthony Ikechukwu Okonkwo in the premises of Otokoto Hotel in the Amakohia area of Owerri. People took to the streets on the 24th and 25th of September 1996, destroying buildings and other forms of property belonging to those they associated with the ugly happenings.[21]

The commission formally identified a number of revealing factors as the remote causes of the disturbances. These are revealing because they occurred in a city and state highly reputed for the defence and practice of Christian values, structures and institutions. For purposes of brevity in this essay, I will focus on a few of them. One was the activity of the *nouveaux riche* (otherwise popularly called '419'). The '419' thronged into Owerri in large numbers between 1993 and 1994; their sources of wealth being either unexplained or unexplainable. In their recklessness they were unchecked by the authorities; they thus became wild, unruly, lawless and intimidating to the citizenry. For instance, often they drove in long convoys of flashy and expensive siren-fitted cars, accompanied by uniformed policemen. They frequently terrorised law abiding citizens by shooting indiscriminately into the air. Some of them acquired chieftaincy and other traditional titles from Traditional Rulers who were so corruptly influenced by the 419 rich men that they no longer bothered about sound character and moral rectitude as key requirements for the award of traditional titles. I have already mentioned the incident of child kidnapping. It remains to mention that the kidnapped children were used for satanic practices, ritual murder or outright human merchandising. This was technically confirmed by the discovery of the roasted body of a human being in the house of one of the *nouveaux riche*, namely, Dominic Egbukwu, whose house is known as Damaco House, because Dominic is popularly nicknamed DAMACO.

Police inaction and apparent collaboration with the 419 group was admitted even by the former commissioner of police, whose tenure was the most offending period in terms of the nefarious activities of the fraudsters and/or *nouveaux riche*. Similarly, prison officials collaborated with them; a collaboration which made it possible for two of them (the 419 suspects) in prison custody to plan and execute the abduction of a young girl, Nonye Echebiri, daughter of a prison official. One of them actually married a lady prison official while still in prison custody after celebrating the traditional wedding ceremony.

Other remote causes include the sale of Amaraku Power Station by the Aneke administration – a sale which was seen as the unjustified denial of a major community benefit from a previous administration.[22] And as if this was not enough, the commission discovered that the Military administrator and one of his commissioners did not pay up to half of the money realised from the sale into the state treasury. Closely related to this was the fact that some traditional rulers offered protection to the fraudsters and indeed facilitated their nefarious activities by utilising the immunity offered by their palaces.

Overall Image and the Concern of this Paper

There is no intention to be nihilistic by presenting only the dark aspects of developments in Igboland. There is no intention to suggest that the results of Christianity in Igboland are to be noted only for these uncompliment-ary activities. Yet, it will be untrue to suggest that these unwholesome activities do not constitute societal challenges. In every sense they do. It is true that Christianity in Igboland was for various reasons finding it almost impossible to control the adverse circumstances which bedevilled it. Increasingly, values and principles associated with the negative forces were being accepted and practised (at times naively) in the various segments of private and public affairs in Igbo society. It was the case that the champions of the negative values and principles were becoming more dominant in the ordering of political and socio-economic conditions in several Igbo communities. Indeed, a recent study of local government democracy in Nigeria confirms that such principles and values gained in strength and thus helped to ruin the efforts to achieve true or genuine democracy at that and other levels of government in Nigeria.[23] Even so, the conscience of the land and people remained dominated by cherished Christian values and principles. Indeed, what the instances of revolt or reprisals against the negative groups or tendencies confirm is that the forces of light, as nurtured by Christianity and other positive and related agencies, are still alive and resolved to execute their duties in Igboland, as in the rest of Eastern Nigeria. Furthermore, many (and the majority of the populace) still engage in various activities that testify to the glorious and noble impact of Christianity in the land. Many, both as individuals and operating corporately, espouse and live as genuine agents of the Christian message. Among them are the pastors, priests and members of the clergy and religious communities who continue to promote prayers, teaching, charity and other services that keep alive the Christian message and ideals in Igboland. They also include many lay people whose financial and other forms of contributions have proved useful for the establishment and maintenance of church buildings, mission social amenities such as hospitals, leper and maternity clinics, guest houses, youth and women's development centres, seminaries and other religious institutes. Comprehensive statistics on these are yet to be collated but it is quite obvious that some of the institutions and persons who have brought glory to Igboland and Christianity in both the past and contemporary times are deeply associated with the formative and nurturing influences of Christianity. The institutions include Trinity College of Theology, Umuahia; Bigard Memorial Seminary, Enugu; Holy Ghost College, Owerri; Methodist College, Uzuakoli; Dennis Memorial Grammar School, Nkwerre. The individuals include the several bishops and distinguished clergy in different denominations and political juggernauts like the late Dr Nnamdi Azikiwe and Chief S.O. Mbakwe.

So then, what is the overriding image? There is evidence that Christianity in Igboland has passed through a number of phases; as have the educational institutions. A great deal of the influences which have reduced the positive impact of Christianity in Igbo society (like Government and nationalist pressures) also account for the chequered nature of the role of educational institutions in promoting the cause of Christianity in Igboland and the entire Eastern Nigeria. An awareness of the main features of this chequered role is necessary for the proper appreciation of the subsequent presentation that follows in this paper. In addition, the issues already examined make it easier to understand the concerns and results of the educational institutions in the matter. Hopefully, with these and the follow up discussion it will become clearer why this author holds the opinion that an authentic and autonomous history of Christianity is valid, desirable and relevant in contemporary non-western or erstwhile colonial societies.

Pre-Civil War Situation

In the pre-Nigerian Civil War period in Eastern Nigeria, educational institutions – primary, secondary and tertiary – were directly involved with explaining Christianity to the people. This happened at two levels. Educational institutions like the teachers training colleges, which were owned by various Christian denominations, had syllabuses and schemes of work which imparted knowledge of the doctrines and teachings of Christianity to the trainees. In the case of the would-be teachers, it was compulsory for them to pass courses on religion and other aspects of the owner–denominations' teaching on the Word of God and related subjects. For instance, in the then Holy Ghost Teachers Training College, Umuahia, trainees, in addition to passing the course on Religious Knowledge organised by the Government Examination Body, sat a specific examination on Catholic Christian Doctrine. Not only was this course compulsory, but trainees who earned distinction grades in it were issued special certificates of merit, duly signed by the Bishop of the Diocese. This practice was repeated in the other Catholic Teacher Training Colleges in the then Eastern Region of Nigeria.

In addition, the religious life of denominational schools was clearly defined – with prayers and other formation programmes rigidly implemented on a daily basis. In the case of the Catholic institutions from which I draw my examples, the programmes were compulsory for all students and defaulters were subject to sanctions, usually suspension and/or outright expulsion from the schools. In all the mission schools, the staff and management usually had a specific devotion to ensuring that moral guidelines and practices as approved by the denomination were faithfully implemented by both staff and students. The structure was so thorough that the private life of staff and students was closely monitored by the agents of the denominations both within and outside the schools.

All those who were associated with the running and management of educational institutions in Eastern Nigeria in the period before the Nigerian Civil War, therefore, were *ab initio* agents of Christianity. Indeed, all teachers in the institutions were also instructors on the faith, both within and outside the schools. Many served as catechists and lay readers in their churches. It was unusual to have a teacher who was not also a formal agent of evangelisation among the students and the wider society. Teachers faithfully monitored the actions of students to ensure that they did not betray the calling of their respective denominations. In fact, at that time, the tone of each school was directly associated with the denomination which owned and managed it. And as it turned out, the few non-denominational educational institutions (particularly the Government owned ones) were not popular; being rightly or wrongly seen as lacking in the capacity for giving total or complete education. Generally, the social and political environment of the period was enabling for the educational institutions to engage fully in the evangelisation process. Admittedly, they faced a number of problems, like the clash with cultural and traditional teaching and institutions. But all in all, the pre-Nigerian Civil War period was the golden age of the involvement of educational institutions in the Christianisation of Igboland and the rest of the then Eastern Nigeria.[24] It also marked the end of the era of large scale Christian influence in the definition of education and educational development methods, means and strategies in the area. The only educational institutions exempted from this were the schools of theology, seminaries, convents and vocational educational institutions owned solely by the respective Christian denominations and/or their agencies. But these were few and very restricted since they were designed to serve only those who were in some ways being called to professional service in the different denominations.

The Post-Civil War Period

As I have already hinted, the post civil war period witnessed a declining role for the involvement of Christian missions in the running and controlling of educational institutions in Igboland and Eastern Nigeria. This was because the Government took over all educational institutions, both primary and post primary. Denominational religious activities including prayers were banned from the schools. Participation in religious activities was made optional for teachers and pupils. However, moral instructions were permitted. The government's arguments for this policy should not delay us here. Again, it is also now unnecessary to rehearse the varying responses of the Christian denominations to the takeover of schools. This is so because at the time of writing, it is safe to assert that increasing numbers of people (in Government, out of Government, and irrespective of denominations) now admit that the action was not to the positive health of the people and land. Many now realise that the negative trends in Igbo society (as indicated in the earlier sections of this paper) have some link (no matter how remotely) with the emergence of the products of the school system based on little or no emphasis on Christian principles and values which came about since the takeover of the institutions by government.

This explains why newly founded denominational schools and colleges are becoming increasingly the first choice of parents and students who desire complete and balanced education for their wards. For instance, the Marist Comprehensive Academy in Uturu, Abia State, has a student population drawn from all parts of Nigeria even though the fees charged are relatively high. The Anglicans, Presbyterians and Catholics have embarked on such educational institutions, employing the methods and guidelines which kept Christianity alive and active in the conscience of both staff and students in the pre-civil war period.

At the level of tertiary institutions, the marginalisation of Christianity is very high – that is from the point of view of the laws guiding courses and their teaching. For instance, in the Imo State University (now Abia State University), there is no Department of Religion because it was not considered a priority by the founders. Yet, it was the first truly Igbo University in the country, following the takeover of the University of Nigeria, Nsukka, by the Federal Government. Thus from its foundation in 1981 to about 1988 when the University's Centre for Igbo Studies was established, there was technically no academic unit that had (even professionally) the responsibility of teaching and carrying out other activities or programmes for interpreting Christianity to students. Of course, there was a multiplicity of denominational activities as well as pentecostal programmes which helped to keep alive the Christian interests in the University. Thus it is essentially through the Centre for Igbo Studies that Abia State University as an educational institution offers formal and statutory opportunity for scholars to participate in the Christian engagement with societal problems. But to fully understand the Centre's role in this matter we need to recall a few points. The idea to set up a Centre for Igbo Studies in the University was mooted in 1984, but actually realised in 1988. The need for such a Centre had long been felt, especially since inter-disciplinary studies started to attract increasing attention in universities all over the world. In the area of pan-national and ethnic studies, with respect to Africa, the tendency has been to set up institutes or centres for African Studies and centres for cultural studies. The university thus had two choices: either to set up a Centre for African or a Centre for Cultural Studies. The University opted for the latter because of its belief that centres for African studies (at any rate, in Nigerian Universities) have for obvious reasons (including inadequate funding) to restrict themselves to ethnic studies. Hence the cultural studies centre was designated the Centre for Igbo Studies. There is also the realisation that the Igbo, one of the largest ethnic nationalities in Nigeria, were in comparison to other ethnic nationalities of their size and history, least studied and documented for posterity.

Consequently, the Centre for Igbo Studies was set up and envisaged to be a community of scholars devoted to the study, documentation, promotion, presentation and dissemination of all aspects of Igbo life and culture from the earliest times to the present. The Centre hopes to make a significant contribution to the world of learning and to ensure the continuity of all positive aspects of the cultural attainment of the Igbo as a necessary condition of Igbo survival in Nigeria and in Africa in particular and in the world at large. To achieve its objectives, the Centre has five academic units, viz: Research; Publication; Lectures and Conferences; Documentation and Performing Arts. The Centre in its staff composition has three experts in Religion (with particular emphasis on the dialogue between culture, Christianity and modernisation) as well as three historians and two archaeologists. There are two experts in Oral Literature as well as associate staff drawn from the disciplines of English (Language), Arts, Architecture, Botany and Biology.

The Centre's study on religion has focused on the following themes:

(i)   Change and continuity in Igbo traditional religion;
(ii) World religions in Igboland, that is, Islam and Christianity;
(iii) Religion and politics in Nigeria – the Igbo dimension;
(iv) Christian missions and socio-economic development in Igboland;
(v)   Christianity and education in Igboland.

Each of these subjects has been addressed in seminars and/or academic articles by scholars in the Centre. For example, Rev Dr Agwu has produced a monograph on religious dichotomy in Nigerian politics and has written three articles on culture and Christianity in Igbo society, while the present writer has investigated extensively the role of Christian missions in the social and economic development of Igboland and presented two conference papers on the subject. Another paper which is a chapter in a forthcoming book on the subject of religion by the writer is on the changing role of indigenous religion in Igbo society. Furthermore, another colleague, Mr. E.O. Inyama has written chapters on religion in Igbo society and has been researching on the taxonomy of Igbo gods. Though the Centre does not advocate any particular denominational or even religious point of view, the work of the scholars demonstrates a general acceptance of the reality of the centrality of religion (including Christianity) in Igbo culture and civilisation. Indeed, the subject of the second annual conference of the Centre for Igbo Studies was 'Religion and Society in Igboland'. Papers were presented by seasoned scholars (including convinced Christians), notably, Professor Ikengah Metuh, Mrs Rose Adaure Njoku (who gave the keynote address) and Rev Fr Dr Nicholas I. Omenka who gave a lead paper on 'Church and Leadership in Igboland'. It is also important to note that in the first annual conference entitled 'The Igbo and the tradition of Politics' adequate focus was put on the role of religion (both traditional and Christian) in Igbo politics and leadership, particularly in the papers by Ogbu U. Kalu; N.I. Omenka, E.O. Inyama and Jude C.U. Aguwa. More recently, R.O. Aja, a Research Fellow in the Centre, has been investigating 'Christianity and Culture in Afikpo' – an interest born out of the desire to promote understanding on the matter because of the tensions and conflicts associated with the subject in the area of study. Thus, both directly and indirectly, the Centre for Igbo Studies is actively involved in scholarship to provide enlightenment on the place of Christianity in a non-Western society which is still under overwhelming influence of all sorts of pressures as it seeks to find stable bases for its social, economic and political advancement.

Even so, it is hoped that Abia State University shall soon establish a full department of religions. There are encouraging signs in this regard. The College of Education now offers the course Education/Religion and experts in Religion are being employed to teach in it. It is also envisaged that the Centre for Igbo Studies will continue to make every contribution to the promotion of enlightenment on the place of Christianity in the educational development of Igboland.

Concluding Remarks

I have tried to show in this paper that the fluctuations in the involvement of educational institutions in the promotion of Christian engagement with Igbo society were largely caused by factors extraneous to Christianity. It is also my view that the period before the Nigerian Civil War, when Christian missions had a full hand in educational institutions, was also the better period for the tone of Christians and Christianity in Igbo society. It was when the Christian mind and approach dominated group and individual strategies for solving societal problems. The post civil war period, when the Government unilaterally took over the schools, diminished the influence of Christians and Christianity and unorthodox methods became manifest in Igbo life and culture. We have shown that despite the takeover, the Igbo now show that they acknowledge the advantages of Christian involvement in the management of educational institutions. There is, therefore, much need for action to enhance the Christian presence in the educational institutions in Igboland. To do so would be a clear case of serving the justice of history.

Notes

1.   N.I. Omenka,'The impact of religion on the educational and social development of Nigeria', Paper delivered at Nguru Students Day, 1991: 8–27.

2.   See, S.N. Nwabara, *Igboland: A century of contact with Britain, 1860–1960*, London: Hodder and Stoughton, 1967.

3.   As either explicitly or implicitly, nationalists like Kwameh Nkrumah, Walter Rodney, Patrick Wilmot and Frantz Fanon.

4.   As in N.I. Omenka cited in Note 1 above.

5.   F.K. Ekechi, *Missionary enterprise and rivalry in Igboland 1857–1914*, London, Frank Cass, 1971; E. Isichei, *A history of the Igbo people*, London: Macmillan, 1976; S.O. Igwe, *Education in eastern Nigeria*, London: Evans Brothers, 1987; and Ifeanyi Anagbogu, *A History of Awka*, Awka: Chiston, 1995.

6.   J.D. Jordan, *Bishop Shanahan of southern Nigeria*, Dublin, 1949: 82. See also Ogbu U. Kalu, 'Images and lenses: The image of Igboland in early missionary writings 1841–1945', *Journal of Religion and Theology* 1 (1), 1993: 22.

7.   K.O. Dike (Chairman), *Report on the review of the educational system in eastern Nigeria No 19*, 1962: 41.

8.   Details of these are available, notably, in S.O. Igwe, *Education in eastern Nigeria 1847–1975: Development and management: Church, State and Community*, London: Evans Brothers Ltd, 1987.

9.   O.A. Onwubiko, *Facing the Osu issue in the African Synod*, Engui: Snaap Press, 1993: 25.

10. Chinua Achebe, *Things fall apart*, London: Heinemann, 1978: 143.

11. Onwubiko: 10–82.

12. V.C. Uchendu. *The Igbo of southeast Nigeria*, New York: Holt, Rinehart and Winston, 1965:89.

13. J.O.L. Ezeala, *Can the Igboman be a Christian in view of the Osu caste system?* Orlu: Nnaji and Sons Press, 1991.

14. Michael O.Njoku, 'Conflict between religious groups and Ogo adherents' *Afikpo Today* 1 (7), 1996: 32; Abia State Government White Paper, 'The Ogo/Church conflict in Afikpo, *Afikpo Today*, 1 (7), 1996: 33.

15. Cf. *Afikpo Today*, 1 (7), 1996: 32–33 and Raph O. Aja's contribution in the same journal titled 'Religion and culture in Afikpo society': 34–35.

16. Similar spirit or principles informed the Memorandum to the Ogo/Church Peace Committee, as reported in *Afikpo Today*, already cited, p31.

17. See Martins Ugonna Okafor, 'The Nanka and Owerri uprisings: The Church connection', *Wisdom Satellite* 4 (4), 1997: 17–18. Except where otherwise stated, my information on the Nanka Uprising which made news is derived from this source.

18. L. Mbefo, 'Nanka martyrs: The shadow side of inculturation', *The Leader*, Owerri, Assumpta Press, 1993: 5; and also, 'The Church Bishop Shanahann Left Behind', *The Nigerian Journal of Theology* 8 (1), 1994: 31.

19. Though there were political (especially power tussle) aspects to the crisis, the Mbomuzo Festival became a major cause because some Christians believed that particular dates were associated with idol worship while some insisted on the opposite view. Incidentally, the polarisation corresponded with the political division in the town, namely, the Oguluo ('Let there be war') and the Aririeri ('the damn them') groups. Informants include Chief James I. Okafor, Chairman of Eze's Cabinet in Okenalogho Obowo; Sir Vincent Maduforo, Chairman, Caretaker Committee, Umuokeh Obowo; Chief Sir John Kafor-Ibe, Secretary Caretaker Committee and Dr U.D. Anyanwu, President General, Umuokeh Peoples Assembly.

20. Imo State Nigeria, *Government White Paper on the Judicial Commission of Inquiry into the disturbances of 24–25 September 1996 in Owerri*, 1997: 4, hereinafter cited as White Paper on Judicial Commission of Inquiry.

21. White Paper on Judicial Commission of Inquiry: 6. Subsequent information the report is in the same source: 6–38.

22. For the people of the area in particular and the generality of the masses in Igboland, Amaraku Power Station is one of the memorable achievements of a former civilian Governor who is very much cherished for the development his administration to the people *viz*: Chief S.O. Mbakwe, Ph.D., otherwise fondly called 'Dee Sam'.

23. U.D. Anyanwu, *Local government democracy in Nigeria*, Okigwe: Whytem Publishers, 1997: 8–21.

24. Cf. S.N. Adiele, *The Niger mission: Origin, growth and impact 1857–1995*, Aba: Isaeco Press, 1996: 112–159.

Chapter Four

Christian Engagement With African Culture: Religious Challenges

Mercy Amba Oduyoye

THIS ARTICLE DRAWS on experiences of life in Ghana and Nigeria enriched by several opportunities to be in conference with Africans from across all of Africa and through a period of twenty years of intentional intensive contacts with African women in theology, in a bid to initiate a pan-African multi-religious forum for women theologians. This effort has resulted in the creation of a Circle of Concerned African Women Theologians (The Circle), one of whose concerns is a study of African Women in Religion and Culture. The on-going research of the women of The Circle furnishes the primary source for the input on African Christian women's engagement with African cultural dynamics and religious challenges, which I explore in this paper.

Christianity in the work of The Circle is varied. There are Roman Catholic sources, lay and religious, all the Western-type Protestants in Africa are represented, so are the African Independent Churches, sometimes referred to as African Initiated Churches (AICS), the prophet-healing-praying churches and the more recent Pentecostal-charismatic-prosperity churches. The whole spectrum of the expression of Christianity in Africa is present in The Circle. To approximate to anything like a profile of Christianity in Africa, it is necessary to take a wide sweep as well as sample specific brands because the engagement with African culture varies from type to type.

African culture is undergoing tremendous changes and yet in some ways the critical phases remain untouched. The rites of passage, family solidarity and expectations have only received cosmetic changes. Hastings remarks:

> It is striking how in some societies, especially in West Africa, even when the large majority of people have eventually become Christian in the course of the twentieth century, the monarchy itself has remained essentially pagan continuing to require for its very existence the regular performance of rituals forbidden to Church members.[1]

Food taboos and dress codes have experienced liberalisation and have been dissociated from family and ethnic groups. In their place are new norms and taboos linked to religious affiliation and peer groups. African musical instruments, lyrics and dances once said to be incompatible with a profession of Christianity have been dissociated from African Traditional Religion. New architecture and westernised homesteads are emphasising a style of life that increasingly diminishes diverse expressions of culture. The language is changing and young people have developed new expressions while they have to ask for the meaning of traditional African idioms and proverbs. As to symbolic language, much of it is lost on the young generation. Globalisation of electronic media has introduced elements from Euro-American and Asian culture into Africa. There is a dynamism in cultural development, all is in flux, but it is only for a few that 'things fall apart'.

Despite the pressures on traditional cultural expressions, religion continues to get high rating in Africa. 'Gospel Music' has replaced 'High Life' lyrics in Ghana and new places of worship spring up like mushrooms. Crusades and mass 'redemption' and 'deliverance' gatherings are the order of the day. Bible Study and Prayer groups abound everywhere and all night vigils and exorcisms are commonplace. Religion is the way of life of all, rich and poor, female and male. Even those who are not officially affiliated to any faith community would vouch for the importance of being religious, or fearing God. This is the ethos of 'traditional' Africa and it is very much alive today. We need to note also that Islam is strong in Africa, and that it makes no distinction between religion and other human activities. Various aspects of Arabic and Middle-Eastern and Semitic cultures akin to some African beliefs and practices have accompanied the spread of Islam. Although the religious scene in Africa is dominated by Christianity and Islam, new movements that derive from Buddhist and Hindu influences have also appeared.

The complex interaction between different types of Christianity, as reflected in the varied membership of The Circle, and the wider African religious culture defines the context for this paper. I want to address in the remainder of this article, therefore, one central question: How is the Christian engagement with a dynamic and thoroughly religious African culture best described and understood? I will address this from the following standpoints:

- The Missionary Engagement
- The African Response – AICS
- Christian Women's Engagement
- Prosperity Christianity and African Culture

I will conclude with some remarks on the interpenetration of Christianity and African Traditional Religion, which I prefer to call African Religion (AR), and how each of the factors examined is reflected in theological education.

The Missionary Engagement

The story of missionary engagement with African culture has been told and retold. It was not only the Euro-Americans, but also African collaborators, who worked to subvert African culture. Local people revealed secrets and taught Europeans the workings of African Religion and Culture. Converts, up to today, bring artefacts associated with AR to be destroyed by Christian cultic functionaries. The strategy was to show that AR was a deception and where it became necessary to acknowledge the power of the spirit world, it was always referred to as demonic. To make colonial exploitation of Africa by Europeans possible, the distortion of the African and of AR and culture was necessary. Travellers, anthropologists, missionaries aided this process by portraying Africans as 'minors' who need Europeans to help them lift themselves to the level of social, political and economic development of Europe. They discounted all the social, political, economic development of pre-colonial Africa as primitive and not worth building upon. All has to be discarded and European models introduced wholesale.

Dominating missionary accounts of their encounters with African Religion (AR) are the attempts to convince kings and priests of the superiority of Christianity. There are many accounts of kings who stood their ground. Ngqika of the Xhosa told Van der Kemp, the Dutch missionary:

> You have your manner to wash and decorate yourselves on the Lord's day and I have mine, the same in which I was born and that I shall follow ... If I adopt your law, I must entirely overturn all my own and that I shall not do.[2]

Examples could be multiplied from encounters with kings and queens of the Asante of Ghana, the Yoruba of Nigeria, the Baganda of Uganda and others. Hastings goes on to comment: 'Every side of an African monarchy and the ensuring of its power was tied to belief and practices unacceptable to missionaries.' He could have generalised to cover other leadership positions in traditional African constitutions as well as in the daily lives of individuals. When the deliberate effort to Christianise Africa hit West Africa in the 19th century, what the Euro-American Christian missionaries had to contend with was African Religion that pervaded the whole of the people's lives, but which was hidden from the missionaries' eyes because it did not have majestic ornate temples. God, the Source of Being, did not dwell in temples made with hands. There were few 'high' and 'holy' places to mark the presence of divine beings and the ancestors, but basically, the spirit world existed as an unseen dimension parallel to, but interacting with, the human dimension. The only other factor on the scene was Islam, which Christians have been discrediting and combating since the time of the crusades. Apart from Mediterranean and Nilotic Africa, however, Christian missionaries largely had been able to ignore Islam in Africa.

Missionary records abound with stories of those who succumbed to the Christian evangelisation process, only hinting at resistance to this process. Suggestions that missionaries encountered resistance, however, are found in the writings of frustrated missionaries, like Townsend, who wrote to Henry Venn in 1850: 'I do not doubt that but that the government of this country is set against the preaching of the gospel ...' The stories of resistance are yet to be adequately publicised. More recent scholarship from

African and European researchers is bringing to general knowledge that locals resisted missionary work, but we are also finding that missionaries adopted a variety of methods in their evangelistic work. Clearly, not all missionaries were negative to African culture. Some were even ready to grant the validity of aspects of African Religion.

Initially, African belief in the Supreme Being was trivialised. African cosmology was treated as an illusion. If God existed at all, the Supreme Being was described as remote and as removed from life. For some missionaries, Africa had no religion at all. Moffat called the Xhosa 'a nation of atheists'. Bentley believed people of the Congo, as he found them, were practically without religion.[3] Their conclusion was that Africans are polytheists and idol worshippers and all the missionaries needed to do was to debunk the African primal religion and spirituality and sweep away that religious structure. The African claim to a belief in one Supreme Being was challenged because it did not conform with the outward manifestations of the religions known to the Europeans. They questioned, 'Why are the divinities and ancestral spirits so prominent in African religion?'

In the wake of the missionary encounter with African Religion, researchers, both European and African, began to write on indigenous beliefs and practices. On the balance, they would always wind up saying Africans are better off as converts to Christianity in spite of the professed validity of the African system. Christianity was, after, all the culmination of the revelation of God to humanity. For such views, see, for example, E.B. Idowu's two books, *Olodumare: God in Yoruba Religion* and *African Traditional Religion: a Definition* and J.S. Mbiti's *New Testament Eschatology in an African Background*.[4] African Christian scholars have largely maintained this evaluation of AR propagated by Idowu and Mbiti. Among missionaries once in a while one comes across controversial persons like Bishop John Colenso who were bold enough to articulate the validity of the African intimations concerning God. They accepted African names for God rather than contriving others from European or biblical sources.[5] Christianity is exclusivist while AR was inclusivist. It was the inherent intolerance of Christianity that bred the confrontation with AR. While the Source Being could be assimilated as the God of Christian monotheism, the Orisha of the Yoruba, the Abosom of the Akan and the Lubaale of the Baganda had to be combated.

Specific cultural practices that have religious roots were attacked. Top

of this list was all that had to do with the veneration, so called, of the ancestors. Festivals related to nature, agriculture and the people's history always
involve the spirits of the ancestors and the divinities associated with nature.
Community with the ancestors through communal meals and prayers were
vehemently attacked. Pouring libation must have reminded missionaries of
Roman times. They were decidedly against the practice and to this day it
remains the mark of the non-Christian in Ghanaian circles. Libation called
up all the benevolent ones who dwell in the realm of the spirit beginning
with God the Supreme Being, through relevant divinities to the ancestors
including the recently departed. This 'lumping together' of God and other
spirit beings was decidedly unacceptable to the missionaries. Sacrifices associated with these festivals and with healing and reconciliation and other
rites and rituals were attacked and prohibited to Christians as unnecessary
as the final sacrifice has been made on the cross by Jesus the Christ.

Even names given to Africans during the traditional naming ceremonies could not be entered into Christian books as several reflect religious
beliefs that are said to be incompatible with Christian faith. The naming
ceremonies themselves were under attack as were other rites of passage.
Rites of passage were said to be incompatible with Christianity as were
many African religious rituals. You cannot drink the cup of Christ and
that of the divinities and ancestors. Initiation rituals into adulthood or
access to traditional royal positions as queen, king, chief or elder were
attacked vehemently. Sometimes even acting as head of an *abusua*, clan,
was forbidden as these leadership positions carried religious implications.
In some cases, missionaries crafted 'Christian coronation' rituals to install
Christian kings. Traditional practices relating to ancestors and divinities
were vigorously opposed, not always with success, but the intention was
there. Separation rites related to death were specially difficult to dislodge.

Christian worship had to be on the model of the missionary's home
church. So, as the Bible was translated, so were the hymn books, catechism
and prayer books of the home church. In most 'Western' churches in Africa
these are still in use even when they have been replaced in the European
churches. Tunes that got into European Christianity from social life were
taught to Africans while it took a great deal of struggle to get African
rhythms and instruments into the churches. These were associated with
paganism. The drum was a most feared instrument as its very crafting
involved religious ritual. Recent attempts to indigenise worship in the

Methodist Church in Nigeria, though appreciated by most, made several feel uncomfortable. Africans who oppose these developments do so for diverse reasons, chief of which is the fear of the memory of traditional worship. Protestants are known for shying away from ritual and from symbolic representations. They claim that it is alien to the Protestant heritage. One could almost hear them say with Calvin:

> It is lawful for me and all believers to reject everything the men have presumed to add to the institution of Christ ... theatrical pomps which dazzle the eyes and stupefy the minds of the simple.[6]

The Roman Catholics in Nigeria, following liturgical renewal in that church, have found it appropriate to baptise traditional liturgical forms.

By and large the ethos of missionary engagement with AR remains. African Christians are uncomfortable with what relates to African Religion. On the other hand, in rural Africa, as among traditionalists in urban Africa and abroad, elements of AR survive. It is also a fact that traditional ethical and legal systems are nowhere near being completely obliterated. The association of Western clothing with converts was perforce abandoned, although in the early days it was in the same category as polygamy and circumcision and bodily decoration, dancing, wrestling and other aspects of artistic culture.[7]

We also cannot neglect to underline the fact that there were missionaries who were roped into rain-making, although others saw them as 'the very pillars of Satan's kingdom'.[8] This shows that the world view of many missionaries was essentially the same as that of the people they sought to convert. Therefore, the belief in the existence of witches, of angels, and miracles formed a common ground with traditional African ways of thinking. Nevertheless, evangelisation and conversions went ahead because the spirits, including ancestors and those called on in traditional religion for healing, were said by many missionaries to belong to Satan's kingdom. Nevertheless, both missionaries and converts must have been convinced of the importance of the symbols of African divinities and other spirits. Otherwise why would they have gone to such great lengths to see them destroyed?[9] Throughout this complicated process, the engagement between missionaries and African Religion and Culture resulted in Africans shaping their own good news out of the Babel of idea and demands that the missionaries offered and the missionaries too were being moulded by their African context, though few would admit this.

AICS: Varieties of African Response

The African independent churches, according to Kofi Asare Opoku,

> have succeeded in stripping Christianity of its foreignness which has been a great handicap and have shown that Christianity can be expressed and meaningfully informed by the African religio-cultural reality.[10]

Writing on 'Christianity and Culture' in *International Review of Mission*, I observed that as African intellectuals continue to discuss the subject, African Christians are daily shaping a Christianity that will be at home in Africa and in which Africans will be at home.[11] In writing this I had in mind the African Instituted Churches. Approaches to Christianity that choose to depart from Western style and demands have existed for as long as there have been missionaries of European descent and their converts in Africa. Just as the Western input was varied, so has been the African response to evangelisation. The encounter with Westerners in Africa meant that Africans were forever having to work against the imposition of Western power and norms. Isichei notes that they 'grew out of white discrimination against black mission agents, disputes over resources, a general feeling, among educated Africans, of being marginalized'.[12] This move became known as Ethiopianism. Official missionary policy encouraged self-government or self-leadership, self-propagation and self-support. But on the ground it did not seem as if missionaries wanted this to happen, especially not 'self-leadership', to use the terminology of Hastings. It was inevitable that Africans would seek to participate in the Christianisation of Africa.

Many students of Christianity in Africa, including myself, have a positive view of the contribution of these Churches towards the *skenosis* of the Christ in Africa. Isichei notes that not all are of this opinion. She quotes Ogbu Kalu: 'There has been a tendency to glorify the Independent churches ... most of them are neo-pagan, engaged in non-Christian ritual'. She comments that 'all this can best be understood in terms of a wider debate, which seeks to reconcile the historically exclusivist claims of

Christianity with the desire to show equal deference to other faith traditions'.[13] The early structure of mission compounds and Christian villages were aimed at total dissociation from AR and culture, desired by both missionaries and some of their converts. Alexander Riddel of Livingstonia Mission wrote in 1880: 'The separation of the people from their tribal chief is, humanly, the only conceivable way in which they can be laid open to the reception of Christianity'.[14] True, there must have been Africans who were only too relieved to be 'liberated' from traditional obligations. Evangelisation outside this format also aimed at the same results, but there were several obstacles to its success apart from the 'paganism' associated with traditional religio-political leadership. Among Africans therefore there were both resisters and collaborators. Collaboration took many forms and was of varied intensity.

By the 1860s Africans were initiating their own churches either *de novo* or by secession from Western churches. African initiatives include anti-African Religion campaigns such as those of Wade Harris and Samson Oppong in West Africa. Here it was converts destroying the symbols of the divinities of AR, charms and amulets. In Southern Africa it was the brutality of colonialism and the arrogance of European land-grabbers coupled with what was demonstrated as a denial of common humanity to the African that fuelled the culture of resistance that came to be labelled 'Ethiopianism'. This movement was conceived more in terms of socio-political resistance that of religio-cultural assertiveness.[15] One common characteristic of Ethiopianism is the upholding of African names. This is a powerful symbol. Yoruba Christians in Yorubaland retained them *in toto* while Sierra Leoneans of Yoruba origin inserted them, but scarcely used them. Most 'Ethiopians' were soon to dissociate themselves completely from Western-led churches and to initiate independent Christian communities largely instituted by lay converts and persons who claimed to have had religious experiences.

These independents revalidated the use of African clothing for both social and religious occasions. Africans were seeking to establish their conviction that one does not have to be European to be Christian. Christianity has to be seen to be multi-cultural. This attitude of the African version of Christianity developed outside the ambit and hegemony of Western missionaries. Inside some of the early Ethiopian churches, the culture remained European and foreign to African culture. Formally robed choirs, some wearing mortar boards, participated in worship services. Pipe organs and hymns, as in the Western churches, were employed. In general, therefore, the liturgy was not indigenised when the leadership was. Neither was there any appreciable shift in theology except in refutation of the racist anthropology of the missionaries.

The prophetic churches like that of Garrik Braide's of Nigeria, the Harrists of Cote d' Ivoire, the Kimbanguists of Zaire and the Zionists of Southern Africa incorporated much that was African. They revived AR's need for seers and diviners in the form of biblical prophets. African Christians too had need for people with whom the spirit world can communicate and through whom they can receive messages. Dreams, visions and angelic visitations are all media for revelation. The spirit-possessed people of the AR found their counterparts in the AICs. They can bruise the head of Satan as surely as those of AR can detect and oust witches. The Aladura, like the Western missionaries and their converts, are vehemently opposed to AR and would not compromise with anything that has to do with the divinities and they would not accommodate any cultural practice that pander to their desires.

As in AR, the functionaries of the AICs are both women and men. Indeed, there are many women leaders and founders. In most of these churches both leaders and members are white-robed, as were some of the devotees of divinities of AR. In Southern Africa, other colours of church uniforms may be observed. Many members of AICs observe food taboos and have purity regulations, mostly for women. They take off their shoes in sacred places, which they say derives from Hebrew religion but which could as well be AR. The Aladura churches are firmly rooted in praying. In this regard Isichei observes that 'prayer sometimes become a form of technology, like traditional ritual. If the right words are pronounced at the right place and time, very specific consequences will follow'[16] Traditional prayer requests are made for prosperity, for procreation and all that brings life, victory and power. Health and healing are central to these churches, as they are to adherents of AR.

Other cultural practices like polygamy, *lobola* (often called 'bride wealth' or dowry), circumcision and especially female genital mutilation [FMG] have elicited a variety of approaches in the AICs, just as they have in the Western churches. Some Aladura would accept polygamy while others would not. As in the Western churches, many simply pretended it was not there, while others made monogamy mandatory only for the clergy. Some acknowledged witchcraft and asked people to confess and be delivered; others do not. Faith-healing is important for most, but as in AR, a more comprehensive approach is taken which sometimes involves medicines as well as psychological processes. West Africa has not had much controversy over circumcision, but where this has been an issue, the challenge has been as much for the Western churches as it for the AICs. In Kenya, while some Western churches were campaigning against it, others openly supported it or simply ignored it. One AIC went to the extent of creating a school system in which the Christian girls could claim their right to be circumcised.[17] Alice Lenshina of the Lumpa Church opposed all that she judged 'pagan': witchcraft, sorcery, beer-drinking and promoted what she found to be in conformity with the Bible.

The varied responses of AICs to traditional culture, which I have tried to outline in this section, demonstrate that Christianity in Africa is yet to find a creative way of dealing with what is traditionally authentically African and which cannot be easily criminalised or denounced on the basis of human rights. This leads me to consider the debate over the indigenous nature of a new and dynamic form of African Christianity often associated with the 'Prosperity Gospel'.

Prosperity Christianity and African Culture

A 'new religious movement' in contemporary Africa has been described by Paul Gifford as the 'prosperity gospel'.[18] This term is being used loosely to characterise a movement which very often is spearheaded by African young Christians with or without American backing. The general ethos of these movements is not unlike that of the mega-churches of the USA. They are fuelled by mass evangelisation campaigns in Africa led by European and American evangelists, who sometimes come at the invitation of the Western Churches in Africa. (I use 'Western Churches' to designate those that have direct roots in the Euro-American missionary enterprise in Africa.)

Does this movement reflect African cultural perspectives? Certainly, the theme of prosperity remains central to religion in Africa. All prayers of AR finally focus on the attainment of abundant life here and now. So poverty and suffering could mean 'wrong' religion or not enough of it. However, as we shall see, there is such a strong dissociation from tradition in the prosperity churches and an intolerance of those outside of them, that they cannot be regarded as an extension of AR. Neither do African young Christians, who are mostly products of secondary and tertiary education, find the AICs and the Western Churches adequate to the needs of contemporary Africa. It is their search for alternatives that has produced the 'Prosperity' Christianity/Churches of Africa. (for convenience we shall use Prosperity Gospel or PG for them).

The culture of poverty and crime that envelopes Africa today cannot be attributed to Christianity. On the contrary, industry, frugality and clean living have formed the core of Christian teaching in all of the churches. Both the Western Churches and the AICs preach about the evils of poverty and undertake small projects to meet the people's needs. The odds are simply too overwhelming for them, as they are for African governments, which face global economic injustice and internal political and military conflicts. In the face of this we find PG preachers all over Africa, opting to reach people with 'positive thinking' and a religion that has no room for failure. This is a form of Christianity that has no use for traditional African religion and cultural practices. Adherents are deliberately encouraged to distance themselves from all the cultural practices that the churches have dealt with ambiguously. The pouring of libation is definitely a sin. No polygamy, *lobola* or other traditional rites would be tolerated. They combat Satan, spirit possession and have power to deliver people from all these evils. The process begun by missionaries, who failed to be sensitive to other cultures, has been carried to completion by Africa's own westernised children.[19] Most visible is the replacing of the African family by the church family. Members of these churches have their lives, days and moments totally regulated by church activities and demands. They have no time for those who do not belong except to convert them to their newly found house of deliverance.

Some of the cultural shifts around elaborate marriage ceremonies might improve their economic standing or at least not burden them with debts. Some decree simplicity in dress code that may also have the same effect. Members learn to budget wisely and spend wisely, for tithing has become for them a road to salvation which includes prosperity here and now. Casting out demons and faith healing begin to replace both Western and Traditional medicine for some of the PGs.

Here we have a Christianity that is attempting to respond to the changing culture of Africa and to marginalise all that has to do with AR. For when one has nothing to do with the African divinities, which all African

Christians claim to have abandoned, and then marginalises the ancestors by refusing to go along with traditional rites of passage, other rituals and festivals, then one's separation from the religio-culture is complete. However, this does not necessarily guarantee liberation for all. A literal adherence to 'biblical culture' and injunctions leave women subjected to men in these churches and promotes exclusivist attitudes that condemn all who are 'different'. A new culture of intolerance has been added not only in the realm of culture but also Religion. The adherents of the PGs have augmented the ranks of religious fundamentalists in Africa. Their engagement with the dynamism of African culture is one of confrontation, condemnation, dissociation and the creation of a holy club of those being saved.

Christian Women's Engagement

The engagement of Christianity with African religion and culture cannot be assessed without a specific evaluation of what it has done *vis a vis* the humanity of women in Africa. African women theologians, looking at the daily realties of women, seek the root causes and struggle to find practical solutions and answers to the economic chaos and militarism that is rampant. They learn from and seek empowerment for women who have to single-handedly ensure the education and survival of their children, but who continue to socialise them to follow cultural practices that are life-denying for women. The daily reality of domination by men is all too evident in homes and in churches. Yet socialising a child against a culture is not a risk one undertakes easily. Buying into the Western Christian culture, such as the Prosperity Gospel preachers promote, the Christian culture of Africa has removed most of the traditional avenues of women's protest and resistance to domination.[20] On the other hand, they have not been able to save women from obnoxious cultural practices that demean and subjugate women.

This global challenge of the 'Church and Women' was taken up by the World Council of Churches (WCC) through its promulgation of the 'Ecumenical Decade of Churches in Solidarity with Women 1988–1998'. Mid-decade, the WCC sent teams to churches round the world to listen to their experiences of what the Solidarity with Women has meant to them. The reports from Africa make it necessary for one to state specifically the women's standpoint when dealing with the church. It becomes clear that it is only in theory that the Church is 'the whole people of God' or even those on its membership rolls. In practice the church is the leadership, the spokespersons, and in Africa most of them are men. Another clear message from the reports is the contradictory discourses on the situation of women in church and society. Most men think all is well with women and most women disagree.[21] The women live a life of appearances. Often lack of independent economic means is a key factor to women's acquiescence to oppressive culture and religion. African women will not speak out for fear that:

> Exposing the man they would deprive themselves of his maintenance.
> Exposing the problems would make the woman appear a failure.
> Exposing their suffering would mean that they were not accepting their cross, as the church has told them, and enduring the pain. (WCC)

Speaking with women one often hears them say,

> When missionaries introduced Christianity they did not really convey the message of the Lord openly and fairly. They used cultural values and scripture to keep women in the place and role they traditionally held in patriarchal societies and that the missionaries as couples also mirrored ... Tradition, culturally determined factors and hierarchical male-oriented leadership patterns promoted by missionaries play an important role in keeping women from being real participants in decision and policy-making bodies and as full leaders. Too many restrictions have and continue to be placed on women in churches (from WCC).

If in an African tradition a woman cannot perform a burial ceremony, the church does not challenge this. Instead, it becomes one more reason for not ordaining women into the sacramental ministry.

The culture of violence in Africa has a special face, since apart from the violence related to economic hardships and military conflicts which all Africans suffer, there is the violence that comes from African Religion and culture. Witchcraft accusations continue to dog the lives of women who do not conform to traditional expectations. Traditional festivals during which women are terrorised are still celebrated. Violence in the family is hardly ever admitted, or worse, is said to be the norm. Pride and self respect shut women's mouths. Where there is an engagement it is not by the church but by women seeking the revival of traditional ways of dealing with this violence or moving out of the culture of silence and acceptance imposed upon them by church and African culture. For many African churches, 'Preservation of traditional moral values seems to be a high priority as there is a feeling that Western cultural invasion ... including its moral liberalism. threatens today's (African) society' (wcc). Both church and African culture join hands with Islam to put the onus of the peoples' morality on women. The culture of victimisation and blaming the victims continue to be the order of the day under the aegis of these powers. Here too the engagement does not come from church or from Christianity but from women confronting oppressive religion and culture. Where physical life is threatened, women have begun to break away from traditional responses of acquiescence to challenge the roots of their hurts.

Women theologians have begun to speak on these issues as a group and to challenge the churches to more considered attitudes towards these issues. The stance of non-involvement has been condemned by these women as incompatible with a faith community that names itself after Jesus of Nazareth and claims to be the Body of Christ. In the first chapter of *The Will to Arise* and the whole of Part II of the book, the authors address religio-cultural practices.[22] African culture is reviewed for both its positive and negative impact on women. For most of these women, their forebears had adopted Christianity as a viable and preferred alternative to AR and Islam, but they now find that Christianity sits loosely on what affects women and often supports or finds itself powerless against AR when it is being oppressive to women. It has been easier for Christianity to support the patriarchal operation of African culture against women than to speak out against it.

There are instances where Christianity had adopted or ignored African cultural practices in order to make converts. For example, in Kenya it has ignored Female Genital Mutilation and in Nigeria it muted the protest against polygamy in order to stem the arrival of Islam. Pastors have been heard to condone domestic violence on the part of husbands, quoting the

Bible as counselling husbands to discipline their wives. In the attempt to root out polygamy early missionaries teamed up with husbands to alter the marital status of wives without consulting them. A husband became a convert and a wife simply found herself a divorcee. Women therefore experienced Christianity as a religion that undermined marriage.

What do African Christian women want to do about oppression resulting from religious teachings and cultural values? Here change is slow, even though African women are beginning to resist. A recent conference of French-speaking African Christian women looked at the subject of 'African Hospitality and Christian women's response'. They condemned the 'sexual hospitality' that some cultures expect of women. They condemned the conspicuous consumption that accompany rites of passage, especially weddings and funeral. They concluded that without their cooperation there would be no polygamy. They cited instances of sexual hospitality in the Bible as being most unhelpful. So rather than waiting for a re-interpretation of biblical expressions of 'hospitality' such as Lot's offering of his daughters to strangers, the Levi's concubine, the rape of Tamar and Dinah, and the socialization that pushed Tamar and Ruth to throw themselves on men, women will have to stop being cooperative. Their conclusion was that women have to learn to be hospitable to themselves.

The engagement of Christian women with the resilience of traditions that oppress women has moved from the culture of silence to breaking the silence. Two recent publications by members of The Circle throw the veil off the violence against women and the church's silence.[23] Women are empowering one another to nourish a spirituality of resistance. This may be summed up in Nyambura's contribution to the Pan-African conference of The Circle held in Nairobi in 1996. Reflecting on the experience of Rizpah 'concubine' of Saul [2 Samuel 21:1–14], she concludes: 'For Rizpah revenge and death were not the last words! There was an alternative. In God transformation of our attitudes, beliefs and values is possible.'[24] This, I propose, should move the churches to break their inertia and engage in a dynamic way the contemporary African culture.

Interpenetration of Christianity and African Religion

Over the past five hundred years, Christianity has affected African societies in many ways, but what we now experience as African culture has resulted from multiple agents of change. Christianity itself is culture-coded and we have seen how Victorian Christianity attempted to make Africans into Europeans. The material culture, music and liturgy were transplanted in Africa and for the most part germinated, took root and flourished. AR idiom and thought forms influenced converts, missionaries and theology. Lamin Sanneh in his theme of 'vernacularization' of Christianity[25] and E.B. Idowu in *Towards an Indigenous Church* [26] have promoted the discussion of the Africanisation of Christianity.

Reading a women's critique of culture and religion in Africa, one comes to the conclusion that to live creatively, we must dispense with ethnic superiority, relativise our own religion, admit the inevitability of paradigm shifts and accept the duty of each generation to reconstruct the received culture and religion. One unshakable principle in a women's cultural critique is the dignity of all human beings and the sacredness of all life. When Christianity supported choice of religion and promoted Western education for both boys and girls, it was going against African culture. It was destined to enable people to move out of strict role assignments in the economic and religious fields. However, in the domestic arena the impact was feeble. This has meant that a lot of women still live their lives without determining the course of it.

Theological education has played a significant role in the process of Christian engagement with African Religion. The theological institutions of pre-independent Africa were set up to educate in response to a situation in which Christianity had to establish itself as the one true religion and do so by showing how wrongheaded AR and Islam are. Christian missionary policy, as we have seen, included raising up an African elite that would promote both Christianity and westernisation. It took some decades to ordain Africans and even more to make them teachers of theology. Hastings (p. 455) describes what he calls 'the neurotic missionary anxiety about or-daining men who had not been proved by many years of theological study and controlled pastoral experience'. He cites several examples including that of the Paris Evangelical Mission, which founded the Bulozi mission in 1880 but made their first ordination only in 1950.[27]

Africans had to undergo theological education based on the needs of the mission church developed in the European context. The London University Bachelor of Divinity syllabus guided its college in Legon, Accra, until mid-1960. It offered the study of Comparative Religion, which enabled students to get some rudimentary insights into Islam and AR, but it was not intended to foster true interpenetration between the religions. It was not until I moved to the University of Ibadan, Nigeria in 1974 that I discovered the concept of the study of the interaction of religions. At that time it was in its infancy and even those of us on the faculty with our backgrounds of traditional British curricula were sceptical of this innovation. It took even longer for the idea of dialogue to surface but then and till now it is mainly conceived as between Christians and Muslims.

At the same time, all around us was the very strong influence of Yoruba culture in our inter-personal relationships, while the incessant rounds of naming ceremonies, weddings and funerals of Christians was unabashedly Yoruba and should have helped one to see the reason and the need for the offering mentioned. It was not difficult to observe the circumscription of the life of the whole people, Christian or Muslim, by the festivals and demands of traditional Yoruba religion. Why then was it so difficult to engage AR beyond the unilateral study of AR by Christian students and scholars? Even here it was the Departments of Religion in the universities and not the seminaries and colleges of the churches which undertook this study. At Ibadan we had the challenge of a couple of AICs which threatened not to sent their students to the Department of Religion if their time there would continue to be wasted with the study of AR.

It is clear to me that to move forward we must engage the many forms of Christianity in Africa and above all initiate conversations with scholars of AR, especially those of them who are practitioners and through them to the adherents of AR. That way we may learn more about how Christianity could play a positive, constructive and liberating role in Africa's dynamic religious culture.

Notes

1. A. Hastings, *The Church in Africa 1450–1950*, Cambridge: Cambridge University Press, 1979.
2. Hastings: 307–308.
3. Hastings: 325–326.
4. E.B. Idowu, *Olodumare: God in Yoruba belief*, London: Longman, 1962; E.B. Idowu, *African Traditional Religion: A definition*, London: SCM Press, 1973; J.S. Mbiti, *New Testament eschatology in an African background: A study of the encounter between New Testament theology and African traditional concepts*, London: Oxford University Press, 1971.

5. Hastings: 332–334.

6. John Calvin *The Institutes* Book IV xv 19

7. There has been no attempt to periodicise, as attitudes cut across periods. It is generally agreed however that the period of the scramble for Africa 1890–1920 bred more anti-African culture than the period before. See, Hastings, *The Church in Africa*: 398–492.

8. Hastings: 313–317.

9. Hastings: 71–77.

10. Kofi Asare Opoku, 'Issues in dialogue between African Traditional Religion and Christianity', Paper presented at WCC's Sub-Unit on Dialogue with People of Living Faiths consultation, Kitwe, Zambia, September 22–25 1986. Cited in Emmanuel Martey, *African theology: Inculturation and liberation*, Maryknoll: Orbis, 1993: 76.

11. Mercy Amba Oduyoye, 'Christianity and culture', *International Review of Mission* 84 (332/333), 1995.

12. Elizabeth Isichei, *A history of Christianity in Africa: From antiquity to the present*. Grand Rapids: William B Eerdmans, 1995: 179–182.

13. Isichei: 5.

14. Hastings: 310–311.

15. For a short exposition on the origins and nature of the term, see Hastings: 478–487.

16. Isichei: 278–291, discusses the ethos of the AICs. The approach to prayer she describes seems to me to be very close to medieval sacramental theology.

17. See unpublished Ph.D. thesis of Nyambura Njoroge. Princeton Theological Seminary.

18. See, Paul Gifford (ed). *The Christian churches and the democratisation of Africa*. Leiden: Brill, 1995.

19. Lesslie Newbigin, *Unfinished agenda: An autobiography*, Grand Rapids Michigan: William B. Eerdmans, 1985: 251.

20. See Felicia I. Ekejiuba, 'Down to fundamentals: Women-centered hearth-holds in rural West Africa', in Deborah Fahy Bryceson (ed.), *Women wielding the hoe: Lessons from rural Africa for feminist theory and development practice*, Oxford: Berghahn, 1995. She recalls the tradition in which 'women punish men who repeatedly battered their wives or who made disparaging comments about women and their reproductive anatomy'. Rape was a heinous crime and was punished; violence was grounds for divorce and return of bride-wealth. These are no 'feminist fancies' and one would have thought the Church would be behind women in this regard.

21. The reports from the visits called *Living Letters* are privileged documents so no specific identification will be made beyond what has already been indicated.

22. Mercy Amba Oduyoye and Musimbi R. Kanyoro (eds). *The will to arise: Women, tradition and church in Africa*, Maryknoll, New York: Orbis Books, 1992. This is the second publication that came out of the creation of The Circle of Concerned African Women Theologians. The research of The Circle on women, religion and culture in Africa continues.

23. See, Musimbi Kanyoro and Nyambura Njoroge (eds.), *Groaning in faith: Women in*

the household of God, Nairobi: Acton Press, 1996. Also, Grace Wamue and Mary Getui, *Violence against women: Reflections by Kenyan women theologians*, Nairobi: Acton Press, 1996.

24. The conference held in Nairobi in August 1996 had the theme 'Transforming Power; Women in the Household of God.' It was multireligious, had over a hundred women and papers covering several aspects of the theme including 'the religio-cultural roots of violence against women'.

25. Lamin Sanneh, *Translating the message: The missionary impact on culture*, Maryknoll, New York: Orbis Books, 1989.

26. E.B. Idowu, *Towards an indigenous church*, London: Oxford University Press, 1965.

27. Hastings: 455.

Chapter Five

Christianity in A Pluralistic Context: Religious Challenges in Zimbabwe

Ezra Chitando

A MARKED TRIUMPHALIST spirit characterises the study of African Christianity today. Commentators point to the amazing spectacle; the centre of Christianity has shifted from Europe to Africa in a decisive way. Whilst the numbers quoted tend to vary, there is general unanimity that Africa [South of the Sahara] is a Christian continent. Kwame Bediako subtly refers to a 'reverse mission' where the theological insights from Africa might hold special interest to the West.[1] Indeed, there are sufficient grounds for the optimism as churches continue to grow. However, there is need for caution. Is the church in Africa performing at optimum capacity? Has Christianity in its various forms adequately taken to the spirit of Africa? What are some of the challenges to be faced? This article attempts to address these questions by surveying some of the challenges facing Christianity in Zimbabwe. It is hoped that such an undertaking will bring out the complexity of issues facing the religion. In order to facilitate clarity there is need to spell out how the terms central to the discussion are being handled.

Brief Definition of Terms

'CHRISTIANITY' is a term which, like most other terms, is simple when used casually and yet complex when one tries to define it. The historian of religion W.C. Smith admitted that trying to define religion is a mammoth, even mistaken, task.[2] In the Zimbabwean context it might be helpful to stay clear of an ideological, reified and homogenising understanding of the term. Ideally it refers to followers of Christ, but on the ground people express their being Christian in strikingly different, even contradictory, ways. A study of Christianity in Zimbabwe means an examination of the 'main-line' churches, i.e., Catholic and Protestant, Independent/African Initiated Churches and the Pentecostal/Evangelical Churches. As one may already note, these categories are broad and serve to mask vast differences. It may well be that reference to Christianities in Zimbabwe, although theologically disturbing for some, is perhaps methodologically prudent. 'Christianity' as it is used in this paper refers to these variegated expressions of the conviction of faith in Christ. However, one can only admit that this definition may only be an operational one and not an essentialist, eternally valid definition.

'PLURALISM' should be understood as referring to the existence of varied and sometimes contending worldviews. This may be illustrated in the Zimbabwean context which has a climate of pluralism. This means that, 'the Christian church is one religious community among others, with its particular faith, cultus, and institutional forms.'[3] This factor brings with it religious *challenges*. Christianity finds itself existing alongside the indigenous religions, Islam, and other religions of the world.[4] In this religious economy Christianity has to jostle with other competitors for consumers, i.e., adherents. In this instance the term 'challenge' has to be understood in its everyday sense of referring to a hindrance or an obstacle. Religious challenges facing Christianity in this initial definition refer to the perceived difficulties posed by the existence of other players in the market. However, the term can also be appreciated in a more creative manner. 'Challenge' may also mean an opportunity for growth and chance for mutual fecundation. In this interpretation challenge need not be assigned negative connotations. Both applications of the term are used in this paper, the first as the general Christian understanding and the second as my own assessment of the implications of pluralism.

It may now be said that the task of this paper is to analyse how Christianity in its various expressions has responded to the pluralistic environment in which it finds itself in Zimbabwe. Due to the availability of several historical accounts on the implantation of Christianity in Zimbabwe,[5] this paper shall focus on the contemporary situation.

Christianity and African Culture

The relationship between Christianity and colonialism on the one hand and African culture on the other has been a major preoccupation of African intellectuals. At stake is the issue of African identity. Whilst considerable efforts have been undertaken in African theology,[6] African literature[7]and African philosophy[8] have also contributed to the debate. Given the central position occupied by the topic, it is clear that any meaningful discussion of the challenges facing Christianity in Zimbabwe should begin by looking at this important issue.

Discussing the centrality of African culture in post-colonial Africa is not an easy task. One common error has been to glorify a dead African past; the graveyard of the Negritude movement. The absence of specificity and analytical rigour on the part of African theologians in particular does not help matters. The prevalent reading of African culture has been to extol its allegedly unique features, such as the emphasis on the community and a high degree of religiosity. The presence of contending theories of culture and the feminist critique concerning some aspects of African culture imply that the term cannot be used simplistically. However, for the sake progress, I have chosen a minimum understanding of the term. As used in this paper, African culture generally refers to the life experience of black Zimbabweans. The experiences are by no means homogenous, mediated as they are by gender, class and other factors. Nevertheless, it seems for the sake of progress permissible to generalise and refer to a traditional worldview shared by many blacks. This encompasses the social and religious dimensions. Whilst traditional religion may be an important component of Zimbabwean culture, it is not the whole of it; hence the need for further amplification to include other traits.

If Zimbabwean culture is by no means homogenous as averred above, neither is Christianity. Here one has to delineate the various strands of the religion since their appreciation of local culture tends to vary. The Independent churches, Protestants, Catholics and Evangelicals all tend to perceive the relationship between Christianity and African culture differently. It is necessary to begin this rather sweeping survey by looking at Independent churches.

African Independent Churches and African Culture

Undoubtedly, one of the most pronounced features of African Christianity lies in the emergence of African Independent Churches or African Initiated

Churches. The latter term is gaining increased currency as some scholars feel 'Independent' is no longer applicable given that the colonial context has been passed and that many Protestant denominations are now, at least to a certain degree, also independent. Literature on African Independent/ Initiated Churches (AICs) has been produced copiously[9]. Regarding the reasons for the emergence and characteristics of these churches in Zimbabwe, Daneel's work remains informative.

The rationale for beginning the survey with AICs lies in my observation that they are being touted as paragons of indigenisation and contextualisation. A number of works portray them as 'the' example of how to relate Christianity to African culture. White missiologists and African theologians, strange bed-fellows at that, are in unison when it comes to an appraisal of AICs. J.S. Mbiti, an African theologian of note, makes the following observation:

> Whatever else be said in general about the independent Church movements in Africa, they are, in their own ways, attempts by African people to indigenize Christianity and to interpret and apply it in ways that, perhaps spontaneously, render Christianity both practical and meaningful to them.[10]

One can note that the reservations withstanding, Mbiti praises the AICs. A more unrestrained, positive evaluation is proffered by J.M. Lamola when he discusses them in the context of liberation. He argues, 'The AIC Movement is a symbol of African religious boldness and novel theological creativity, a step toward the construction of an authentic black religion for the Africa of the twentieth century.'[11] M.L. Daneel, a missiologist and the leading researcher in this field in Zimbabwe, regards AICs as offering their adherents 'havens of belonging' or 'places to feel at home.'[12] He considers their growth as having its basis in their willingness to seriously engage with the traditional worldview. Disputing the notion that the AICs are essentially reactionary movements, Daneel maintains that this theory obscures an important aspect of independent church leadership. This aspect is that of an unfettered, truly indigenous and imaginative response to the Christian Gospel, in which the Independent Church leader himself experiences his Missionary zeal as prompted directly by God irrespective of circumstantial factors.[13]

Many more examples could be provided to illustrate the valorisation accorded to AICs. With increased frequency, we are being told that these churches are the standard bearers of what African Christianity should be. Given this general consensus, any critique of the churches by an African scholar may be attributed to alienation or an unwarranted feeling of superiority. Fully aware of these dangers, one is still forced to ask: Has the study of independent churches been invaded by the spirit of romanticising the other? How do we account for the wholesome praise being given to these churches?

I do not want to down-play the achievements of AICs in Zimbabwe. To a considerable degree, they have grappled with African culture in a creative manner. They have had, and continue to have, marked success in the area of health and healing. A number of prophets have risen to national prominence due to their reputation concerning 'African types' of illness. The churches have provided an alternative therapeutic system and their interpretation of illness and disease closely parallels the traditional one. Their use of cloths, symbols and dances is inspired by the traditional concepts.

Whilst considerable progress has been achieved, I feel the AICs have been insulated from criticism due to ideological reasons, some of which I will allude to below. Admittedly, there are differences within these churches but one can detect a common attitude towards traditional culture. The majority of the Zionists and Apostles proceed on the ideology of 'elimination by substitution.' Ancestors, the different spirits, traditional medicine, and other facets of traditional culture are all seen as evils to be conquered. Here the concept of a challenge is essentially one of confrontation. Conversion is interpreted to mean a radical break with the past. A. Hastings notes, rightly in my opinion, that despite the undoubted fact that they represent a profoundly African response to Christian faith, their spirituality *vis a vis* their own past is often one of discontinuity rather than continuity, at least at the specific level of religion.[14]

Whilst AICs operate within the traditional worldview, they have radically reinterpreted it and only the power of the Holy Spirit has the right to exist. They, or at least the majority of them, proceed on the basis of rejecting the African past. African traditionalists are seen as pagans for whom Hell-fire is a certainty. They are described as *vakan'ora*, the unclean ones. This is in contrast to the spiritually clean adherents of AICs. African theologians, if I have understood their concerns correctly, emphasise the aspect of continuity. The culturalist thesis in vogue in African theology is predicated on the integrity of African culture. How do the African theologians propose to use the AICs as a source for theology, given their diametrically opposed views concerning the value of the African past? Have AICs adequately addressed the challenges posed by African culture? One is inclined to submit that the independent church response, like those of other branches of Christianity in Zimbabwe, has been partial. As long as most of them continue to adopt a confrontational attitude towards the indigenous culture, alienation is inevitable.

After having briefly looked at the attitudes of AICs towards local culture, the task left is to try to account for the incessant positive evaluation. A cursory historical glance will show that the earlier missiological evaluation was negative. Researchers tended to paint a negative picture and B. Sundkler's conclusion that 'the syncretistic sect becomes the bridge over which Africans are brought back to heathenism,'[15] captures the spirit at that time. G.C. Oosthuizen also regarded AICs as being too close to tribal religions and as leading to post-Christianity.[16] What occasioned the missiological 'conversion'? This is certainly a crucial question in the study of AICs, since in Southern Africa the discipline is dominated by missiologists. It is, however, difficult for one to fathom an answer to the question above. One possibility is that continued criticism on the part of missiologists could not be sustained in an age of African nationalism. Since the pioneers were white, negative evaluations could be easily attributed to racist superiority. Accusations of insensitivity and cultural arrogance would be difficult to parry. Hastings locates another possibility in the rise of ecumenically orientated white missiologists.[17] This however brings with it intractable problems. Is the involvement of missiologists in the activities of AICs 'innocent'? Through a hermeneutics of suspicion, one is bound to answer in the negative. For example, the major researcher in this field in Zimbabwe, Daneel, is also a sponsor of AICs in the southern province of Masvingo and he has led them in a number of activities.[18] As sociologists of knowledge have shown, there can be no neutral ground in the production and dissemination of knowledge. All works, this one included, are written from a particular stand-point. The interaction between missiologists and AICs influences their approach. However, Hastings considers this flirtation between AICs and white missiologists as 'little less than a kiss of death' for the latter. He elaborates, a little financial assistance and the prestige of entry into a local Council of Churches or even, conceivably the World Council were baits – however honourably offered – to entice independent leaders back towards 'orthodox' ways, the current norms of ecumenical Protestantism.[19]

Due to considerations of space, I cannot further pursue the politics of patronage, paternalism and territory – claims inherent in this interesting area of investigation.

African theologians, oblivious of the theological game being played, find themselves in a difficult position. Here are the AICs being put before them as the exemplars of African Christianity. African theologians are looking for a Christianity which has come to terms with African culture. It would appear a contradiction were the African theologian to be critical of AICs. The African theologian is thus forced to join in singing the songs of praise, extolling the authenticity of AICs. Whose authenticity?[20] This is done before the primary task has been undertaken, i.e. to explicate the conditions under which a movement may be regarded as being 'African.' In these days of subterranean cultural imperialism, AICs, for all their alleged revolutionary capacity, might be found desperately wanting. As matters stand, I feel AICs have generally been overrated, at least as regards their engagement with African realities. One is fully aware of the ripostes, but self-criticism remains the way to maturity. This however is not to denigrate the accomplishments of the AICs. They remain an important part in the never-ending search for a Christianity which drinks from African wells.

Protestant Churches and the African World-view

As was the case with the AICs, this section is also necessarily general. As we are often reminded these days, the starting point should not be an excoriation of the wrongs done by the early missionaries. Whilst generalisations are always dangerous, one might say that in the Zimbabwean context the Protestants were pioneers in trying to come to terms with the demands of the indigenous traditions. As W.J. van der Merwe notes of the Reformed Church Mission, missionaries and their black counterparts,' had to wrestle in their attempts to Christianise the culture and religious concepts of the Shona.'[21] For Protestantism in general, this has remained an uncompleted task.

Amongst some of the pressing issues to be handled were *kupira midzimu* (ancestor veneration),[22] *barika* (polygamy), *kugara nhaka* (inheritance), *kuzvarira* (giving of young girls in marriage), *roora* (bride price/wealth), brewing and drinking of traditional beer and many others. These issues were to confront both the Protestants and Catholics. After initial wholesale condemnation, most denominations began to see the value of some practices like the payment of bride price. Beer drinking and participation in traditional rites have remained officially proscribed. However, as most ministers of religion admit, some members still participate in these, albeit in the spirit of Nicodemus. Have the Protestants taken advantage of their earlier insights?

What has occurred in the political sphere in Zimbabwe has largely been replicated in the ecclesiastical circles. The personnel has changed but the structures have remained essentially intact. The same codes of conduct used by the missionaries are still applied in church discipline. Nowhere is this more clearly marked than in the issue of witchcraft belief. G.L. Chavhunduka makes the following observation: 'Many Shona people have a belief in the ability of certain people to harm others through some inherent power, or through the use charms and medicines.'[23]

It appears that in the theoretical presuppositions of Protestant theology in Zimbabwe witchcraft does not exist, despite the fact that most Africans are convinced otherwise. Here one has to refer to the AICs which have taken their followers' belief in the reality of witchcraft seriously. Without forsaking their denominations, many Protestants are taking their problems to traditional healers and prophets. This is indeed a serious challenge to the churches.

Protestant churches in Zimbabwe still have to come to terms with rites associated with death. Most members complain that the denominations, in their quest for orthodoxy, end up alienating them. The *nyaradzo* ceremony, which is held to console the bereaved, is a case in point. Some denominations are said to be discouraging this practice due to its close links with traditional rites. A trickier proposition has also emerged of late in the form of the unveiling of the tombstone. Whilst the practice is clearly a western one, it closely resembles the traditional *kurova guva* ritual. This ritual transforms the deceased into an ancestral spirit and Protestantism is bitterly opposed to it. Most church leaders regard the unveiling of the tombstone as a smokescreen. Admittedly, it is practised by the black middle class but it points to the tenacity of traditional values. It remains to be seen how the denominations will respond to these issues.

Whilst Protestantism in Zimbabwe has to be applauded for pioneering work in the translation of the bible into the vernacular,[24] as the above examples illustrate, there remains a lot of work to be done. There is need for more imagination within the different denominations. Instead of wishing away African realities, the onus is upon church leaders in particular to evolve a Christianity which reflects its context.

The Catholic Church and African Culture

In the early phase of missionary activity in Zimbabwe, the Catholic-Protestant division was hardly visible. Both expressions of Christianity had the overarching goal of winning the African to the faith. However, once the partitioning of the country into mission zones had been complete, the Catholic church was slow in adjusting. What Hastings notes of the period 1951–1958 largely applies to the preceding years. He maintains, 'It was not a period of creative thinking in Catholic mission circles.'[25] While the Protestants were localising personnel and were paying increased attention to African cultural realities, the Catholics lagged behind. This was however to change after the Second Vatican Council.[26]

For a movement which thrives largely on papal proclamations, the Second Vatican Council marks a watershed in the history of the Catholic Church in Zimbabwe. Terms like contextualisation and acculturation gained currency as the Church sought to make faith meaningful to the adherents. Political issues were not neglected as the Church played its part in the liberation struggle.[27] Although there was initial resistance, the Latin mass was gradually superseded by the vernacular. Drums and other indigenous instruments were employed in the liturgy. Unlike in the Protestant churches where the translation of hymns tended to be stiff, the Catholics have encouraged compositions in Shona and Ndebele.

Perhaps the area which best illustrates the sensitivity of the Catholic Church to local needs is that of burial and associated rites.[28] As members of other denominations often comment, the Catholics endeavour to bury an African as an African. This is because other churches follow European burial customs which they regard as being Christian. In the Catholic burial rite the ancestors are invoked to accompany the deceased to heaven. As in the traditional rite, relatives are allowed to play a leading role. Such has been the success regarding the integration that there have been accusations of the Church as having given in to traditional religion. Here, as in many other areas, where some see syncretism others see creativity.[29] Many other examples could be cited where the Catholic Church has sought to make Christianity truly African.

The above should not be misconstrued as implying that it is the Catholics who provide the paradigm for African Christianity. I tend to be quite suspicious of all attempts to locate examples of how Christianity should be in one place, as has been in vogue in the study of the AICs. One ready example of the limited nature of Catholic success has been in the area of celibacy. This practice contradicts the expectations of the local culture but the Church remains committed to it. Like its Protestant counterparts, the Catholic Church has promoted the physical-spiritual dichotomy and remains wary of claims of spiritual healing.[30] Like the Protestants, there is a long way to go before the Catholic Church adequately addresses the spiritual needs of the local people.

Evangelical/Pentecostal Churches and African Culture

The study of African Christianity often marginalises the Evangelical/ Pentecostal mode of Christian expression and tends to focus almost exclusively on the so-called mainline churches and the AICs. Most historiographies exclude this vibrant form of Christianity. As P. Gifford notes, the charismatic churches have become quite influential.[31] While it beyond the scope of this paper to characterise them in full, it is proper to note that in Zimbabwe they are mainly an urban phenomenon and have a marked following among the youth. They are evangelical in their drive to seek the spread of Christianity and Pentecostal in the role accorded the Holy Spirit.

In general, one may say that the Evangelicals are diametrically opposed to local culture. They preach the gospel of radical conversion and the imagery of the convert as a new creation is emphasised. The old passes away when one converts and local culture should no longer be entertained for it represents the state before salvation. One of their distinguishing features is the demonisation of traditional religion. Like the AICs, they see traditional religion as an opponent to be vanquished. J. Platvoet's observations regarding prophet-healing churches are equally applicable to them. He notes:

> They have often deviated from their Protestant background
> by introducing monarchical forms of church government, but

they have inherited the virulent demonisation of their major competitor, the African traditional religions, from the early pietist missionaries, which they equate traditional religion with witchcraft and alliance with the devil.[32]

While it is not possible for churches to completely avoid local culture, they want the barest minimum level of interaction. Any reference to the need for Christianity to have an African face is viewed with suspicion.[33] Based on a radical biblicism, the Zimbabwean Pentecostal churches have little time for local culture.

In practice, however, members are always negotiating their way between church doctrine and the demands of their context. This can be seen in the issue of recognising a marriage after the payment of the bride price. There has been tension, however, in some instances regarding weddings. Some pastors have gone ahead to officiate at weddings while the parents of either the bride or the groom would be having reservations. At the institutional level there has been a growing openness as evidenced by the seminars being run by the Zimbabwe Association of Theologians.[34]

Up to this point I have concentrated on how the different expressions of Christianity have responded to the challenges posed by the cultural realities in Zimbabwe. These evaluations were based on the integrity of the indigenous culture. This was necessitated by the observation that the host culture pre-dates religions like Christianity and Islam.[35] However this might give the impression that the various manifestations of Christianity are best evaluated in connection with their cultural sensitivity. This is not the impression intended and a different criterion would no doubt lead to another conclusion. It would also seem that the local culture is a passive object. African religions and cultures are dynamic and have left an indelible mark on Christianity in Zimbabwe. It is possible for another narrative to map out the extent of this influence. However, our task now is to review the challenge posed by Islam.

Christianity and the Challenges Posed by Islam

As was the case in the discussion on Christianity, the number of Muslims in Zimbabwe can only be approximated.[36] What cannot be debated is the fact that apart from population growth where children of Muslims take up the faith, Islam has made significant in-roads in Zimbabwe. While many accounts on religion in Zimbabwe tend to focus exclusively on Christianity, Muslim religion has been quietly growing. Islam has had a long history in Zimbabwe,[37]and is very much part and parcel of the religious scene. Unlike some of the religions of the world discussed below which are mainly based in urban areas, Islam is both an urban and rural affair. In the rural areas, particularly in the Masvingo constituency, it is practised by the Varemba people whose identity and conversion remains a subject of scholarly debate.[38] It is not the intention of this paper to pursue this issue, important as it is. What the numerical significance of Muslims serves to demonstrate is the fact that the challenges posed by Islam to Christianity merit separate treatment.

Muslim-Christian dialogue, if it refers to deliberate engagement on issues by representatives from either side, is virtually non-existent in Zimbabwe. The relationship between Christianity in its various forms and Islam has been characterised by indifference. Each religion has pursued its own issues to the exclusion of the other. The impression one tends to get is one of harmonious co-existence where everyone minds their own business. Superficially therefore it would appear as if the religions do not interact, thereby ruling out the concept of challenge. A more probing examination gives a different picture altogether. There are a lot of unresolved issues on either side.

Most church leaders in Zimbabwe are suspicious of the growth of Islam. Having enjoyed a monopoly of the religious economy, the presence of a determined competitor unsettles them. Like Christianity, Islam is a missionary religion which seeks converts. Zimbabwe, alongside other countries in southern Africa, is a target of Muslim missionary action. J. Hunwick makes the following observation: 'International Islamic organisations see sub-Saharan Africa as a field for missionary endeavour and an area where they may roll back the tide of Christianity'.[39] This is not surprising, given the fact that North Africa is already predominantly Muslim. However, is the indifference between the two religions healthy?

Peaceful co-existence can only be sustained to the degree where either party is convinced that its basic principles are not at stake. Once it becomes clear that there is more to be gained from adopting a tough stance, the fragile truce is flagrantly shattered. In Zimbabwe, religious war is seemingly a far-fetched possibility. However, it appears as if the era of indifference might now have culminated into one of verbal confrontation. This may be illustrated from the *halal* controversy which enjoyed much press coverage toward the end of 1996 and in early 1997. Some Christian leaders were at the forefront of a campaign to boycott *halal* products, i.e., meat which has been slaughtered according to Islamic custom. They considered buying such meat, as had been the case till then, a religiously loaded statement. For them this meant Christians were unwittingly acknowledging the superiority of Islam. In the past this would have gone unnoticed but the Muslim community was not intimidated. The Muslim Youth Organisation answered back, accusing the Christians of insensitivity and arguing that *halal* satisfied international hygiene standards. The controversy ebbed but it has become clear that the channels of communication are absent.

The Muslim community in Zimbabwe has become vocal. How Christians respond to this reality of another vibrant community faith cannot be charted easily. For too long only the opinion of Christians has held sway. Due to historical reasons, which saw Christianity come to the country in close association with colonialism, the religion has enjoyed a favourable relationship with the state.[40] On the other hand, Muslim states extended support to nationalists who now control certain African governments. In the difficult economic climate, Muslim states have often generously given donations through their embassies. It is clear that diplomatic ties with Muslim countries are favourable, in line with the policy of avoiding religious prejudices.

The confrontational approach which has been adopted by some Christian leaders is a result of their growing apprehension regarding the strides made by Islam in independent Zimbabwe. Islamic holidays and activities are receiving substantial coverage and some Christians feel threatened. They argue that the experience of Islam has been to dominate other religions. In this instance the challenge posed by Islam is interpreted as a call to arms. Is this the only way forward? It is important to realise that the constitution of Zimbabwe is religiously neutral. The notion that it is a Christian nation, fostered by the prominence accorded to Christianity, is a myth. It is therefore imperative for Christians to wake up to this reality. Conjuring images of oppression due to 'fundamentalism' and raising the issue of national security, no matter how legitimate, will not help. There is need for creativity and maturity on the part of Christians when dealing with the challenges posed by Islam. It is however not possible in a survey paper like this for one to try to map out the models open to this inevitable encounter. One can only point to the striking example: while the anti-*halal* drive was being mounted in Harare, some Christians in rural Masvingo were looking for a Muremba Muslim to slaughter their beast ahead of the Christmas festivities! Without deodorising the harsh realities of the rural scene, one can note how mutual respect and co-operation can be achieved. Nevertheless, how Christians and Muslims will relate is a large question with massive theological, political and economic implications. It requires a whole narrative to explore the ramifications.

Christianity and the Challenge of Other Religions

After having discussed how Christianity has interacted with African traditional culture and religion and with Islam, one would be forgiven for thinking that these three are 'the' religions of Zimbabwe. This however is not the case as many other religions have substantial following. These include Hinduism, Buddhism, Judaism, the Baha'i Faith, New Age Movements and many others which defy rigid classification.[41]Any reference to the 'triple religious heritage' of Africa obfuscates the radically plural religious climate prevalent in most African countries.[42]

A serious draw-back in the discussion of the challenges posed by other religions to Christianity in Zimbabwe lies in the paucity of material regarding the state of these religions. Much scholarly research has tended to focus on Christianity, African traditional religions and Islam. While it has to be admitted that, even when taken together, the other religions are still a minority, this does not justify their exclusion. There is a real danger that since religions like Judaism and Hinduism are tied to specific communities, any scholarly marginalisation of these religions might be translated on the political scene into a dictatorship of the majority. This is possible despite the prevalent disclaimers by academics that their work is 'objective' and hence has no political or other extraneous motives.

As noted earlier, the Constitution of Zimbabwe is religiously neutral and ideally this promotes religious pluralism. The syllabus on Religious and Moral Education also theoretically adopts a multi-faith approach. Each community is allowed to inculcate its own religious values in the Education Act. To this end there are many private schools in urban areas where specific religious communities are located. One can therefore say that there appears, on the part of the state at least, to be a commitment towards reflecting a pluralist ethos. On the ground, however, Christianity remains the dominant religion. In the debate on homosexuality, which involved the highest office in the land, traditional and Christian values were cited as reasons for condemning homosexuality. While it is beyond the confines of this paper to pursue the ideological use of religion and culture in the debate, it should serve to show that Christianity has become part of the Zimbabwean worldview, the generalisation permitting.

How does Christianity approach the other religions? Wielding so much power and influence, should it view them as last pockets of resistance to be conquered? Is the current spirit of indifference and arrogating superiority adequate? These questions require serious reflection in the Zimbabwean context. There is need for Christianity to reflect the fact that it finds itself amidst a plurality of religions. Thus far the tendency has been of proceeding with business, oblivious of the existence of the other. However, as the section on Islam demonstrates, there is need to shift from a plurality of religions to religious pluralism. At first glance this might appear to be a tautology, a mere play on words. However, there is a subtle difference. While the former may be seen as a historical accident, whereby different religions find themselves co-existing, religious pluralism is embedded in intentionality. This occurs when people living in a pluralistic environment consciously and deliberately undertake to deal with the existence of the 'other'. It remains to be seen whether Christianity in Zimbabwe lives up to the challenges posed by the pluralistic context in which, for better or for worse, it finds itself.

Atheism, Agnosticism and African Christianity

While the radically plural environment poses serious challenges, these may be regarded as external. Other challenges arise from within the religion itself. In the euphoria of celebrating the rapid spread of religion, one feature might go unnoticed. This is the phenomenon of some husbands who drop their wives and children for church while they pursue other 'manly' activities. The same pattern is replicated in the rural areas where the initial enthusiasm for Christianity is on the ebb. If (and this is debatable) atheism was unheard of in traditional Africa,[43] it is becoming a viable alternative for some. In some cases what is at stake is not so much the rejection of Christianity as it is a reduction in the level of expressing one's religiosity. In either case a difficult challenge is posed.

While African theologians insist that their Christian identity is African in every sense of the word, an increasing number of African intellectuals are distancing themselves away from Christianity. Fully aware of this challenge, Bediako makes the following observation: 'How African Theology responds to this African philosophical and intellectual atheism must certainly be one of the most crucial issues in the theology of the future.'[44] This attitude might have been prompted by a Christianity which understands itself in a model I have employed in this discussion, i.e., as an expressly 'religious' movement, having little to do with politics, economics and the milieu in which it finds itself. Realism forces one to question such a reading of Christianity and of religion in general. There are many challenges from the social, political and economic spheres with which Christianity must engage.

Social and Political Challenges

This section will necessarily have to be brief. It is not convincing to catalogue the religious challenges facing the religion and stop there, since Christianity, like every other religion, has to have a holistic perspective. In Zimbabwe, Christianity faces a plethora of social, political, and economic problems. It is however imperative to note that Christianity has no mandate to pose as the ultimate answer to social ills since in some instances Christianity itself is very much part of the problem. Nevertheless, through social analysis, self-criticism and bravery, Christianity could contribute towards the alleviation of human suffering.

Zimbabwe, like most other Third World countries, (I note the difficulties posed by the term) has embarked on Economic Structural Adjustment Programmes. While the name might differ from country to country or even within the same country, essentially this means an effort at reforming the economy. This is the wonder drug, the panacea prescribed by the International Monetary Fund and the World Bank. The result has produced enormous suffering for the common person. Unemployment has continued to soar and the prices of basic commodities are beyond the reach of the majority. The AIDS pandemic is decimating the youth and the economically active populace, whilst political apathy remains rife. One could go on listing all the evils. It is in this maze of confusion that Christianity is called upon to make life meaningful to the ordinary person. Hastings' comments on post-independence Africa are applicable to Zimbabwe and deserve to be quoted in full:

> The campaign for political independence had been sold to the common man as the road to something short of an economic and social millennium. That glittering prize was now found to be reserved to the small minority who could move into government jobs and settler farms, play ball with international capitalism, and become with every year that passed more alienated from the common man, whose smile turned slowly sour in the bewilderment consequent upon so great, if inevitable, a deception.[45]

In Zimbabwe, Christianity must address the issue of black economic empowerment and not avoid it. On the land question, the Church, in its Catholic and Protestant forms, has its hands tied. It owns vast tracts of land amidst landless peasants and in some cases even has forcibly evicted 'squatters'. Further challenges are to be found in the areas of gender and ethnicity. On the latter issue, some progress has been made, particularly in the issue of the ordination of women but further challenges await attention. Ethnicity remains Africa's nightmare as events over the past decade in the Great Lakes region have shown. Whatever foreign hands are at play, Africans remain culpable. In Zimbabwe the absence of a unifying nationalist cause has resulted in the solidifying and even creation of ethnic identities. Indeed there are many hurdles to be faced.

Conclusion

Christianity has had an indelible impact on the Zimbabwean national psyche. In its 'Independent', Protestant, Catholic and Evangelical forms, Christianity dominates the religious landscape. However, I have argued in this article that this Christianity must initially come to terms with local culture, broadly defined as the life setting of the ordinary black Zimbabwean. If the religion is to be meaningful, it must also creatively engage with the challenges posed by Islam, other religions, and the prevailing socio-political climate.

From a reflection on the issues raised above, it becomes clear that Christianity faces numerous challenges in Zimbabwe. Before any evangelistic campaigns are taken to the West, there is need for African Christians to grapple with pressing domestic issues. In particular, they should become more sensitive to the pluralistic context. They should endeavour to have a religion which radiates meaning in a world where their continent comes as an after-thought. In doing this they should no longer be willing prisoners of Western categories. This entails re-thinking key terms such as pluralism, used freely in this discussion. Failure to reflect on these issues would imply that the concept 'pluralism' would go the same way as terms like democracy, civil society, global village, and others: Western glamour concepts without an iota of relevance for rural Africa where, as Hastings accurately notes, 'most Africans live and die.'[46]

Notes

1. K. Bediako, 'Understanding African theology in the twentieth century', *Bulletin for Contextual Theology in Southern Africa and Africa* 3 (2): 8–9.

2. W.C. Smith, *The meaning and end of religion*, San Francisco: Harper and Row, 1978.

3. D.G. Dawe, 'Introduction', in G.H. Anderson and F.F. Stransky (eds.), *Christ's lordship and religious pluralism*, Maryknoll, New York: Orbis Books, 1981: 1.

4. This term is used in preference to the more popular 'world religions' due to the ideological problems inherent in the latter. See, T. Fitzgerald, 'Hinduism and the 'world religion' fallacy', *Religion* 20 (2), 1990: 101–118.

5. See, D.N. Beach, 'The initial impact of Christianity on the Shona: The Protestants and the southern Shona', in J.A. Dachs (ed.), *Christianity south of the Zambezi, volume 1*, Gwero: Mambo Press, 1973; N.M.B. Bhebe, *Christianity and traditional religion in western Zimbabwe, 1853–1923*, London: Longman, 1979; and C.J.M. Zvobgo, *A history of Christian missions in Zimbabwe*, Gweru: Mambo Press, 1996.

6. See, K. Bediako, *Theology and identity: The impact of culture upon Christian thought in the second century and modern Africa*, Oxford: Regnum Books, 1992; K.A. Dickson, *Theology in Africa*, Maryknoll, New York: Orbis Books, 1984; J.S. Mbiti, *Bible and theology in African Christianity*, Nairobi: Oxford University Press, 1978; M.A. Oduyoye, *Hearing and knowing*, Maryknoll, New York: Orbis Books, 1986; and L. Sanneh, *Translating the message: The missionary impact upon culture*, Maryknoll, New York: Orbis Books, 1989.

7. See, C. Achebe, *Things fall apart*, New York: Fawcett Crest, 1984; A.J. Chinweizu and I. Madubuike, *Toward the decolonisation of African literature*, Enugu: Fourth Dimension Publishing, 1980.

8. See, K.A. Appiah, *In my father's house: Africa in the philosophy of culture*, Oxford: Oxford University Press, 1992; A. Masolo, *African philosophy in search of identity*, Edinburgh: Edinburgh University Press, 1994; and K. Wiredu, *Philosophy and an African culture*, Cambridge: Cambridge University Press, 1980.

9. D.B. Barrett, *Schism and renewal in Africa: An analysis of six thousand contemporary religious movements*, London: Oxford University Press, 1968; M.L. Daneel, *The background and rise of southern Shona Independent Churches*, The Hague: Mouton, 1971; J.P. Kiernan, 'The African Independent Churches', in M. Prozesky and J. de Gruchy

(eds.), *Living faiths in South Africa*, Cape Town: David Phillip, 1995: 72–82; G.C. Oosthuizen, *Post-Christianity in Africa: A theological and anthropological study*, Grand Rapids: William B. Eerdmans, 1968; B. Sundkler, *Bantu prophets in South Africa*, London: Lutterworth Press, 1948.

10. J.S. Mbiti, *African religions and philosophy*, London: Heinemann, 1969: 233.

11. J.M. Lamola, 'Towards a black church: A historical investigation of African Independent Churches as a model', *Journal of Black Theology in South Africa* 2 (1), 1988: 5.

12. M.L. Daneel, *Quest for belonging: Introduction to a study of African Independent Churches*, Gweru: Mambo Press, 1987.

13. M.L. Daneel, 'Independent Church leadership south of the Zambezi' *African Perspectives* 2, 1976: 89.

14. A. Hastings, *African Christianity: An essay in interpretation*, London: Geoffrey Chapman, 1976: 53.

15. Sundkler: 297.

16. Oosthuizen, 1968.

17. A. Hastings, *A history of African Christianity, 1950–1975*, Cambridge: Cambridge University Press, 1979: 254.

18. Daneel is a major force in the Association of African Earthkeeping Churches (AAEC). See, for example, M.L. Daneel, 'The liberation of creation: African Traditional Religions and Independent Church perspectives', *Missionalia* 19 (2), 1991: 99–121; M.L. Daneel, 'Towards a sacramental theology of the environment in African Independent Churches' *Theological Evangelica* 24 (1), 1991: 2–26.

19. Hastings, *A history of African Christianity*: 254.

20. For a sharp critique of the notion of authenticity, see Jean-Marc Ela, *African cry*, Maryknoll, New York: Orbis Books, 1986: 121–134.

21. W.J. van der Merwe, *From mission field to autonomous church in Zimbabwe*, Transvaal: N.G. Kerkboekhandel, 1981: 108.

22. It remains a moot point whether what is involved is worship or veneration. Most African scholars favour the latter term for ideological reasons.

23. G. Chavhunduka, *Traditional healers and the Shona patient*, Gweru: Mambo Press, 1978: 14.

24. For the impact of the availability the bible in the vernacular, see Sanneh, 1989.

25. Hastings, *A history of African Christianity*: 119.

26. See Hastings, *A history of African Christianity*: 167–168.

27. See I. Linden, *The Catholic Church and the struggle for Zimbabwe*, London: Longman, 1980.

28. See J. Kumbirai, '*Kurova Guva* and Christianity' in M.F.C. Bourdillon (ed.), *Christianity south of the Zambezi, volume 2*, Gweru: Mambo Press, 1977: 123–130; P. Gundani, 'The Roman Catholic Church and the *Kurova Guva* ritual in Zimbabwe', *Zambezia* 21 (2), 1994: 123–146.

29. It remains debatable whether there has ever been an unadulterated Christianity. For a harmonisation of the terms, i.e. creative syncretism, see M.A. Oduyoye, *Hearing and knowing*, Maryknoll: Orbis Books, 1986.

30. See, E. Milingo, *The world in between: Christian healing and the struggle for spiritual survival*, London: Christopher. Hurst and Company, 1984.

31. P. Gifford, 'Ghana's charismatic churches', *Journal of Religion in Africa* 24 (3), 1994: 241.

32. J.G. Platvoet, 'The religions of Africa in their historical order' in J. Platvoet, J. Cox and J Olupona (eds.), *The study of religions in Africa: Past, present and prospects*, Cambridge: Roots and Branches, 1996: 63.

33. Bediako, 'Understanding African theology in the twentieth century': 6, refers to the preparedness of some Evangelicals to encounter African tradition in more positive ways.

34. Personal communication by Rev N. Pashapa, convenor of the Association in January 1997.

35. See Platvoet: 51–58.

36. Barrett projects that the number will be 140,000 in the year 2000 while Mandivenga put the figure at 61,000 in 1983. See D.B. Barrett, *World Christian Encyclopedia: A comparative survey of churches and religions in the modern world*, Oxford: Oxford University Press, 1982: 768; and E. Mandivenga, *Islam in Zimbabwe*, Harare: Mambo Press, 1983: 4.

37. See Mandivenga, 1983.

38. Some scholars maintain that some Varemba are Jews of Falasha origin while others insist on their Muslim orgins. See E. Mandivenga, 'The history and 'reconversion' of the Varemba of Zimbabwe', *Journal of Religion in Africa* 19 (2), 1989: 103–104; and J. Hellig, 'The study of Judaism in Africa: the case of the South African Jewry', in Platvoet, Cox and Olupona: 354.

39. J. Hunwick, 'Sub-Saharan Africa and the wider world of Islam: Historical and contemporary perspectives', *Journal of Religion in Africa* 26 (3), 1996: 251.

40. See C. Hallencreutz and A. Moyo (eds.), *The church and state in Zimbabwe*, Gweru: Mambo Press, 1988.

41. For figures and projections, see Barrett, *World Christian Encyclopedia*: 768.

42. See, for example, E.G.Parrinder, *Africa's three religions*, London: Sheldon Press, 1976.

43. It is striking that on the note on atheists in Zimbabwe, Barrett (*World Christian Encyclopedia*: 768) identifies only Europeans. This has serious philosophical implications regarding the possibility of atheism for blacks.

44. Bediako, *Theology and identity*: 439.

45. Hastings, *A history of African Christianity*: 140.

46. Hastings, *A history of African Christianity*: 184.

Part Three

CHRISTIANITY AND AFRICAN
NATIONAL IDENTITIES

Chapter Six
Church Life, Civil Society and Democratization in Malawi 1992–96
Kenneth R. Ross

Introduction: Midwives of Democracy

In Malawi's transition from dictatorship to democracy during two eventful years from 1992 to 1994 a remarkably prominent role was played by the Christian churches. By common consent it was the Catholic Bishops' Pastoral Letter of Lent 1992 which broke the spell of the Banda dictatorship and awakened Malawians to the need and possibility of radical political reform.[1] Thereafter the Presbyterian-launched Public Affairs Committee became the central engine of political renewal in the period leading up to the National Referendum held in June 1993 which introduced multi-party democracy to Malawi.[2] No wonder that, in his victory speech after the referendum, future State President Bakili Muluzi was quick to acknowledge the role played by the churches in the democratization process: 'In particular, I would like to single out the seven Catholic Bishops and the [Presbyterian] Blantyre Synod.'[3] The fact that the churches had pioneered and, to some extent, presided over the dismantling of the one-party system and the construction of a new political order is indicative of considerable change in the configuration of church, state and society in Malawi. At the last major political landmark of independence in 1964, the churches had occupied an ambiguous and even paradoxical position. The initiative lay with the nationalist movement (Malawi Congress Party) which was in several respects a product of the Christian missions and retained links with them, yet at the same time was constrained to distance itself from the churches which appeared to have been operating hand-in-glove with colonial rule. Events of the early 1990s revealed that the MCP had largely lost popular confidence while it was the churches which were able to voice the aspirations of the people. This reflects a social reality widely evident throughout Africa. As Terence Ranger has observed: 'Even while church leaders kept their heads down, their moral standing had grown indigenous. The churches came to be seen as the only surviving institutions which ordinary people still trusted. Political institutions have lost all credibility, but ecclesiastical institutions have been gaining it.'[4] In this context, churches in Malawi found themselves being expected to take a considerable degree of responsibility for the reconstruction of the political order. This paper attempts to assess their response to this expectation by considering the political engagement of the churches at three levels: 1) the structures, 2) the ethos, and 3) the spirit of democracy.

1) The Making of the Second Republic
The Prophetic Moment
The major political challenge facing Malawi in the early 1990s was that of how to peacefully remove the oppressive and decadent one-party system and replace it by a more just and effective political order. It was a challenge which was taken up in Lent 1992 when the Catholic bishops broke 30 years of silence with their devastating critique of the one-party system.[5] This was such a definitive moment that it is common to hear recent Malawian history divided into 'before the Pastoral Letter' and 'since the Pastoral Letter'! *Living our Faith* covered a range of issues but its most directly political point came in a section entitled 'The Participation of all in public life.' The Bishops drew on both biblical texts (Ephesians 4:7–16 and 1 Peter 4:10–11) and traditional African proverbs to argue that society can be strong only when it enjoys the participation of all its members. What this meant for Malawi was explained as follows:

> Human persons are honoured – and this honour is due to them – whenever they are allowed to search freely for truth, to voice their opinions and to be heard, to engage in creative service

of the community in all liberty within associations of their own choice. Nobody should ever have to suffer reprisals for honestly expressing and living up to their convictions: intellectual, religious or political. We can only regret that this is not always the case in our country .... Academic freedom is seriously restricted; exposing injustices can be considered a betrayal; revealing some evils of our society is seen as slandering the country; monopoly of the mass media and censorship prevent the expression of dissenting views; some people have paid dearly for their political opinions; access to public places like markets, hospitals, bus depots etc, is frequently denied to those who cannot produce a party card; forced donations have become a way of life.[6]

The Bishops went on to sketch the effects of all this on national life and consciousness, the dark tragedy which had overcome Malawi in the years since independence: 'It creates an atmosphere of resentment among citizens. It breeds a climate of mistrust and fear. This fear of harassment and mutual suspicion generates a society in which the talents of many lie unused and in which there is little room for initiative.'[7] First steps towards the restoration of a climate of trust and openness were proposed and these became Malawi's political agenda for the next two years: the establishment of an independent press, open forums of discussion, free association of citizens for social and political purposes, Government accountability, the establishment of independent, accessible and impartial courts of justice.[8]

The Political Contest and Religious Legitimation
When it came to the political process which would implement the vision of a just society and participative politics which had been set forth in the Pastoral Letter, the churches again proved to be key players. At the ideological level, religious legitimation all along played a critical role in the political contest. The MCP government had long been aware of the ideological power of religion in the political realm. Systematically and successfully over many years it had pressed the churches into service to supply it with religious legitimation. The extent to which the government was stung into serious over-reaction to the Pastoral Letter is a measure of how much it had depended on the unquestioning support of the church.[9] This was further indicated, after almost all churches had rallied behind the

work of PAC, by the importance which the government attached to the continuing support of the Nkhoma Synod – the Central Region section of the CCAP which had strong historical links with the MCP leadership.[10] As it struggled to retain an air of legitimacy it turned to ministers of the Nkhoma Synod to officiate at government functions and to generally show solidarity with the MCP. This they were willing to do especially during the early referendum period.[11] When even the Nkhoma Synod withdrew its unqualified support, the government was left even more bereft of the church endorsement on which it had depended in the past.[12] In desperation the MCP attempted to supply its own religious legitimation. When it launched its campaign newspaper, the *Guardian Today*, it was striking to note how many articles were devoted to portraying the MCP as having a divine mandate. This was epitomized by a cartoon series on the theme 'MCP Points to God!; Multi-Party – Horns of the Devil!'[13] Such desperate propaganda revealed how much the MCP government had depended on the legitimation which it had received from the churches in the preceding years. Once the churches had broken out of that ideological captivity, the MCP government faced a crisis of legitimacy which it was unable to surmount.

On the other hand, the emergent opposition was able constantly to appeal to the prophetic critique of the churches as justification for its political initiative. Indeed, the manifesto of the United Democratic Front, the first to be issued by an opposition party after the referendum, began with a quotation from the Lenten Pastoral Letter and stated that the movement for political reform had been initiated in response to the call from the Catholic Bishops.[14] In a country where the Christian faith is highly esteemed by a large proportion of the population, the legitimacy which the churches bestowed on the opposition movement, in face of government attempts to brand its leaders 'dissidents' and 'confusionists', was a considerable factor in enabling the forces of change to succeed. A notable feature of the ideological struggle was that the opposition began to argue that Rev John Chilembwe, a Baptist pastor, not *Ngwazi* Kamuzu Banda, was the father of Malawian politics.[15] There were good historical grounds for doing so since Chilembwe led an armed rising against British colonial rule in 1915.[16] It was notable that when the new government announced the public holidays for the 1995 calendar, Kamuzu Day was missing and Chilembwe Day had been introduced![17]

Making Democracy Happen

At a more practical level, the churches were active in education for democracy and in monitoring the conduct both of the referendum in June 1993 and of the General Election in May 1994. PACREM (Public Affairs Committee Referendum Monitoring) was an effective non-partisan watchdog which quickly drew attention to any abuses and gave people the confidence that they could vote freely. When interviewed many people have indicated that it was at church that they learned of the possibility of political reform and began to give their support to the multi-party cause.[18] Christian faith was worked out in terms of democratic participation. A survey of 420 church members in the Northern Region revealed that 71% affirmed that faith in Jesus Christ helped them to know how to vote.[19] 'Without Christian voting,' suggested one, 'the people would still continue dying under one-party government, there would be no democracy or freedom of speech in our motherland.'[20] A case study of southern Dedza likewise revealed that: 'Christian idioms and practices were … the most pronounced preoccupation on the eve of the referendum.'[21] It was through church life, by and large, that Malawians found the courage, resolve, information and resources necessary to secure a 63% vote in favour of multi-party politics. In the subsequent run-up to the General Election of 17 May 1994 the churches remained by far the most effective organisation in civic education and election monitoring and contributed significantly to the Election being a very peaceful and highly efficient exercise.[22] Anastasia Msosa, the Chairperson of the Electoral Commission, commented that: 'When you use the church, usually it is very effective. During the elections, if you appealed through the church it produced quick and effective results. The political change was positive in a short time because it came through the church.'[23]

With the General Election of 1994 the Second Republic was inaugurated. The new constitution was implemented, initially on a provisional basis for one year before being ratified by Parliament, with minor amendments, in May 1995. The full machinery of democracy is now in place. The Life President has been replaced by a State President elected to serve for five years with a maximum of two terms. The executive authority of the Presidency is balanced by a careful separation of powers in which serious attempts have been made to secure the integrity of the legislature and the judiciary. There is a parliamentary opposition which offers vociferous criticism of the government. There is a free press and, while some newspapers remain highly partisan, others are achieving an impressive level of independence and impartiality. All political detainees have been freed and all exiles are permitted to return. Churches and civil rights groups publicize alleged abuses of human rights and any failure to meet the requirements of the constitution. An Ombudsman has been appointed to whom appeal can be made by citizens who believe that their rights have not been duly respected. Compare this with the situation of two years earlier when one individual enjoyed absolute power, Parliament was a rubber stamp, the law courts were politically manipulated, the press was government controlled and used as an organ for propaganda, any suspected dissident was detained or assassinated, and the witness of the churches was silenced. At one level, the democratic transition is complete.[24] Yet for democracy to flourish, more is needed than formal constitutional provisions.

2) The Promotion of Civil Society
The Public Affairs Committee
In the democratization process, as will already be apparent, many of the functions of civil society fell to the churches. Integral to the success of the Public Affairs Committee was the fact that it gathered together surviving fragments of civil society. Its membership was made up not only of the churches themselves but also the Malawi Law Society, the Associated Chambers of Commerce and Industry, the Muslim Association, and the emerging pro-democracy political parties. This alliance covered a sufficiently broad range of non-governmental associational life to embrace a truly national constituency and to be able to negotiate with government on that basis. At this point the churches could be seen to be galvanizing civil society and injecting a totally new dynamic into Malawian political life simply by bringing into play groups and associations which were outside the party/government structures. PAC's mobilizing of civil society, however, was undermined, paradoxically, by the success of the pro-democracy movement which took many of the lawyers, business people and putative politicians into government. The situation then tended to revert to one where associational life was very much concentrated in the churches. A series of British and American researchers passing through the University of Malawi have gone out looking for civil society and have found nothing but church life! The churches occupy this influential position partly by default. The one-party system which prevailed from

1964 to 1992 systematically suppressed or co-opted all other organisations which might play a positive role in civil society. The churches, on the other hand, though restricted in their witness, had grown prodigiously during this period, both in numerical strength and in public confidence. In the absence of other forms of associational life, the churches were the only nationally organised institutions which could mount a challenge to the one-party system. However, the fact that they were able to do so to such remarkable effect cannot be explained entirely by negative factors. Neither the prophetic power of the Catholic Bishops' Pastoral Letter of 1992 nor the organizational genius behind the Public Affairs Committee can be explained without reference to the vitality of contemporary Christianity in Malawi. There was a moral and spiritual force in the pro-democracy movement which drew deeply on Christian convictions regarding justice, truth and human dignity. This gave resonance to its message amongst a predominantly Christian population and broke through the web of deceit woven by the propaganda of the one-party system so that a new political dispensation became possible.

In post-1994 Malawi the churches have continued to play an important civil society role in a situation where almost all initiative comes from government. They have attempted to make clear their distance from government, e.g. in August 1995 when PAC sent an open letter to the President criticising the government for being accountable to international institutions rather than its own people and, in particular, for resisting World Bank recommendations to trim the cabinet while agreeing to remove the subsidies on fertilizers;[25] or when the Catholic Bishops issued a Pastoral Letter in September 1996 which offered critical analysis of the problem of government corruption.[26] At the same time powerful forces operate to secure the churches' collusion with government and they will not retain their independence without a struggle, especially since government patronage will always hold a strong appeal for impoverished church leaders. Yet the experience of having been compromised and silenced has sharpened the sensitivity of church leaders to the importance of maintaining critical distance in relation to government. The churches are preparing themselves to play the role of watchdog in relation to national political life, exposing any corruption which creeps into the exercise of government and detecting any imbalances in the separation of powers. The challenge for government is whether it will be prepared to tolerate and encourage such critical engagement in the interests of healthy democracy or whether it will act out of narrower self-interest to subvert it by means of patronage.

Church Congregations and Civil Society

A deeper challenge for the churches is whether they can take their mobilizing of civil society a step further so that it takes effect to a much greater extent on the ground. The individuals and organisations which participated in the Public Affairs Committee were drawn from among the elite. Apart from encouraging people to vote, there is little evidence that the churches have been effective in promoting pro-active participation on the part of the population at large. Malawi may be a model of democratization so far as the formal constitutional and political structures are concerned but anyone expecting that these automatically lead to a flourishing civil society will be disappointed. With rare exceptions, the vast rural population remains passive so far as the political process is concerned. John Minnis suggests that 'There is a vicious circle at work here: a genuine democratic transition requires the mobilization of a demanding civil society, yet how can the poor and the illiterate organize and participate in such a mobilization when they are ignorant of their political rights?'[27] The churches, with their parish networks and their record of success in mobilizing the rural population for electoral participation, may be the only means of breaking through this vicious circle. Whether they will do so will depend to a great extent on how far they are prepared to face in church life itself the implications of a demanding civil society.

This is a challenge which the churches must meet not primarily in their upper eschalons but, rather, at a much more grassroots level. In the watchdog function of the church, the top leadership is necessarily prominent. Committees, Councils, Conferences, Synods and Assemblies have access to the public arena and top church leaders can address national issues through the mass media. This gives the opportunity to engage with national politics when required. It was through statements issued at this level that the churches were effective as the midwives of democracy. When it comes, however, to the consolidation and deepening of democracy, attention turns to the church at the level of the local congregation or base community. Surveying the African scene as a whole, Terence Ranger has observed that: 'The opening of the second revolution takes place at the centre and the combined church hierarchy can play a critical role. But sustainability will be won or lost in the regions, the localities and at the grass roots. The mark of the first phase is the making of constitutions; the mark of the second must be the achievement of local autonomy.'[28] This indicates the limits of the kind of activity which in Malawi has been channelled through PAC. When doing research on Christology among rural people in Northern Malawi I found that quite often respondents would cite PAC as evidence for the connection between faith in Christ and political action.[29] However, it is seen largely as an elite organisation for top church leaders. The question is whether the churches can make the transition needed to be effective in Ranger's 'second phase', i.e. to be an organization operating at local level to promote democratic participation and empowerment. Here the question is whether the church has the kind of *congregations* which can be forces for democratisation. The most exalted vision and the sharpest prophetic witness offered by individual church leaders can very easily be completely undermined by what Peter Walshe has described in another context as 'timid local clergy and phlegmatic parishes.'[30]

One difficulty for the churches is that a movement of grassroots empowerment will raise questions about ecclesiastical polity. This is something that has already begun to be evident. In the Roman Catholic Church younger priests were ready to point out that the very Bishops who had championed democracy in the political arena operated in their dioceses on a basis of dictatorship![31] It is said that in the new Malawi you can freely criticize the State President but you dare not criticize the Bishop or General Secretary of your church! It was partly the same concern which moved women of Blantyre Synod to march to the Administrators' Conference in January 1995 with a petition on 'Justice and Peace *in the Church*.'[32] In so far as the churches simply mirror a hierarchical, authoritarian and exploit-ative political ethos they will tend to inhibit civil society activism rather than promoting it. On the other hand, in so far as the churches are open, participative and justice-oriented they will be likely to have a 'knock-on' effect in the life of the community at large which is positive in terms of promoting civil society. The critical ecclesiological question is whether the prevailing model will be the church 'from above' or the church 'from below.' This question of polity reaches deep into the identity of the church and, depending on the kind of answer it gives, determines the extent to which it can be a significant force in Malawi's democratization at the deeper level of promoting a vibrant civil society.

3) The Spiritual Roots of Democracy

In understanding democratization it is helpful to distinguish between democratic procedures and institutions on the one hand, and democratic norms and values on the other.[33] The former can be constructed through writing constitutions, passing laws and holding elections – matters which can be settled by a dominant elite. The latter cannot be achieved without the participation of the people as a whole. However 'politically correct' may be the structures and mechanisms of representative government, there will be no democracy if the popular imagination is not captured by the democratic vision and if the people do not sense that the system genuinely gives them power to have a say in their own destiny. In Malawi there was a tremendous sense of empowerment among the rural people when they were able to exercise their vote to elect a President and MP of their own choice.[34] Today the popular suspicion is that the rhetoric and the processes of democracy are just a smokescreen to conceal what has been, in effect, a palace revolution amongst the small dominant elite which has no intention of disturbing the fundamental social structures from which it benefits. Although everyone appreciates the democratic freedoms which so recently were unimaginable, disillusionment has set in because so much more was expected. While most Malawians celebrate the freedom from fear which once was an unreachable paradise, their welcome to democracy is tempered by the fact that 'the system' still seems to be an alien reality which works in interests other than their own. Democratic government in Malawi has largely been constructed 'over the heads' of the ordinary people which explains why there seems to be such a gap between the rhetoric of democracy and the reality. The weakness of the constitution is that, however well constructed it may be, it has not been sufficiently internalized by the people and can easily be disregarded or manipulated by those holding political power. As F.F. Kanyongolo has pointed out: 'The constitution articulates values whose validity in the context of Malawi has never been tested by popular referendum or any other means. In the end violations or opportunistic amendments of the constitution do not have a degree of moral blameworthiness sufficient to act as a deterrence or basis for mass political action.'[35] The democratic procedures and institutions are in place but they will remain alien, elitist and very vulnerable so long as they are not founded upon norms and values which are cherished and nurtured among the people at large.

For democracy to be effective it is not enough to establish a certain legal and constitutional system. There is need for the inner drive and motivation to make the system work. It is when democracy is considered at this deeper level that religious considerations arise, especially in a context where the worldview and behaviour of the people is greatly influenced by religion. Democratization will remain superficial if it fails to take into account the religious understanding of political power and authority which prevails in African societies.[36] Where there are issues of democratization to be addressed, it is unlikely that these will be fully understood without reference to the underlying religious understanding of politics and power. Hence the churches as religious communities engaged with their social reality at a religious level have a considerable influence – for good or ill – on the evolution of the political order around them. It is not coincidental, then, that the churches were integral to the democratic transition in Malawi nor that the struggle for religious legitimation was at the heart of the political contest. It is a pattern to be expected where the political order is understood to repose, ultimately, upon religious realities. The challenge for the churches is whether they allow themselves to be used as ideological support for a predetermined political agenda or whether they can relate their biblical message to the political life of the nation in a critical and creative way. It is as the churches represent the non-dominating, serving love of Jesus that they have their deepest impact upon the process of democratization. Inasmuch as the churches can enable the 'love of power' to be replaced by the 'power of love'[37] at the heart of political behaviour, they are in a position to give to a young democracy the moral and spiritual impetus which it requires if it is to succeed. 'This,' as John de Gruchy notes, 'is not something which democracy itself can produce; it is a spiritual value of redemptive love which no political system can manufacture.'[38] The challenge here to the church is one which cuts much deeper than the issue of whether it can raise a prophetic voice in relation to the politics of the day. For it reaches to the heart of the church's own life and calls it to be the community which manifests such outgoing and redemptive love.

Presidential Power and Patronage

At this deeper level there is less evidence of successful church engagement. In fact, what impresses many observers in Malawi today are the many characteristics of the oppressive one-party system which have been carried over into the democratic era.[39] While the President has adopted a much more realistic and down-to-earth style than his predecessor, he has also displayed a tendency to imagine that he can rule simply by decree. This was evident as early as the day he assumed office when he announced to a packed stadium that a number of prisons were to be closed and that the New State House in Lilongwe was to be converted into a Parliament building.[40] The latter pronouncement was made without Parliament itself being consulted and proved to be quite impractical. Another Presidential decision which aroused serious concern was his appointment of Chakufwa Chihana as 2nd Vice-President at a time when there was no constitutional provision for such a position.[41] He evidently imagined he had authority to act in this way and was challenged only by a small group of concerned citizens who decided to take him to court for breach of the constitution.[42] The idea of the separation of powers has been taking root only slowly and tendencies to authoritarianism and unaccountability in government have by no means been eradicated. It is striking to notice that the 50 resolutions passed at the National Constitutional Conference held in Lilongwe from 20 to 24 February 1995 were mostly concerned to limit the powers of the President and to strengthen the Legislature. Yet this popular concern was brushed aside in Parliament which took no heed of the Conference's rejection of the office of 2nd Vice President and its call for a Senate or Upper House of Parliament to be established.[43] A strongly Presidential system, in a context where politicians are accustomed to ruling by means of patronage, is likely to consolidate power at the centre rather than promoting democratic participation on the part of the people at large.[44]

A particular disappointment is that, rather than opting for the simplicity and austerity which would have signalled a contrasting approach to the use of political power, President Muluzi took over the palaces, the private plane and much of the pomp and circumstance of the Banda regime. Much popular concern has been focused on the conspicuous consumption and suspected corruption of government ministers and others entrusted with high office. Democratization has evidently done little to challenge the 'gravy train' mentality inherited from the colonial and one-party periods in which access to resources was centrally controlled and political involvement a matter of bettering oneself through the patronage of the powerful. The most common complaint against the Muluzi government is that its members are using the resources of the state to enrich themselves and to entrench their own position by means of patronage. John Lwanda has observed that the concentration of economic power in the office of the President 'enables the leader to establish a core group of the elite, whose responsibility in turn is to establish secondary patronage groups, all owing loyalty to the centre. In this scheme of things the rural and urban poor ... are at the bottom of the heap.'[45] A serious question for the democratization movement is why it has failed to dislodge or even challenge this anti-democratic system of political control. The particular challenge to the churches is whether *their* organisational life provides an alternative pattern or whether it simply mirrors the politics of patronage practised within the structures of the state?

Personality Politics

A further major disappointment of the democratic era has been the extent to which 'personality politics' still prevails, albeit in a more open and freely contested public arena. The messianic idiom in which Kamuzu Banda presented himself has not been abandoned but rather transferred to the new leadership.[46] John Lwanda has noted that 'opposition groups showed the same tendency to define ... the leadership first and then build parties around the leadership.'[47] This explains the weakness and vacuity of political debate as noted by John Minnis: 'Political discourse, as evident in newspaper accounts and public utterances of various kinds is narrow in focus, sensationalist, and largely preoccupied with the day-to-day machinations and exploits of particular politicians .... Political leaders spend an inordinate amount of time jockeying for position in ways which promote their personal ambitions. Changing party allegiance is commonplace in the quest for self-aggrandizement. Thus the major parties appear to be monopolizing not only the political space, but are defining the very parameters of political discourse in sectarian terms when they should be doing just the opposite.'[48] The redefinition of politics required in Malawi has not yet addressed the problem of the political messianism and the concomitant personality politics which inhibit popular participation and the emergence of authentic democracy. If the political leadership remains authoritarian, arrogant, self-interested, corrupt and nepotistic then Malawians are entitled to ask whether the so-called democratization has been anything more than a game of musical chairs. There is need here for what might be called an evangelization of politics, an addressing of the biblical message to the understanding of the exercise of power. It is striking that even the very word used for politics – *ndale* – is a term which suggests intrigue, craftiness and chicanery. It stands, as Augustine Musopole has suggested, for 'an anti-human understanding of politics.'[49] Though it is difficult to quantify, the evidence suggests that in the first two years of the democratic era the churches have made little impact at the level of challenging destructive, exclusive and anti-human tendencies which have for too long prevailed in Malawian political life. A searching question is how far the affairs of church life are moved by personality issues rather than theological, missiological or national matters of concern.

Economic Inequalities

Prominent in popular consciousness in 1995–96 was the realization that the radical political reforms which have taken place since 1992 have scarcely disturbed the profound economic inequalities which were bequeathed to Malawi by the colonial system and further entrenched under the Banda regime. Both the 1992 Pastoral Letter and the WARC/CCAP Letter of that year had called for the disparity in living conditions between the rich and the poor to be addressed. It was this part of their critique which was most neglected. The advent of multi-party democracy brought little tangible change. Indeed, the new constitution was marked by the conspicuous absence of any provisions which might allow for affirmative action in favour of those who were dispossessed by the colonialism and neo-colonialism of the past. As F.F. Kanyongolo has argued: 'The constitution does not articulate any principles to guide the solution of major social and economic *problems of inequalities* resulting from culture and tradition, internal government policies and the adverse positioning of Malawi in the international political economy. The significance of the constitution is therefore diminished in the eyes of a society which finds that it does not clearly address their concerns on matters such as equitable distribution of wealth, the transformation of the relationship between labor and capital, and the balance of power among the various cultures.'[50]

Scepticism about the prospects of the new dispensation promoting a more equitable economic order has been heightened by the conduct of the Muluzi administration. Though the UDF government was elected on a ticket of poverty alleviation, it was not long before the popular joke was that it was actually 'PPA' – personal poverty alleviation – as government ministers were manifestly using their new positions for personal economic advantage![51] In light of such popular concern it was surprising that in April 1996 government saw fit to award pay rises of 300% to cabinet ministers and 88% to principal secretaries but only 12% to junior workers.[52] Now people are wondering whether their sense of political empowerment is delusory as they see the benefits continuing to flow to the wealthy elite while they remain in deepening poverty. In early 1995 the popular Kwathu Drama Group's play *Tisaiwale* had a bishop telling his people that if you were married to a husband who provided you with food and clothing but was constantly beating you and you decided to remarry only to find that, while your new husband was very kind and never beat you, he was unable to provide food and clothing, then you would think twice if at all the change was worth it![53] A sense of disillusionment compounds the hopelessness and lack of initiative inherited from the colonial and one-party periods. Until this situation is addressed and there is a genuine empowerment of the rural population, the exercise of power in Malawi is going to be skewed in favour of the small but dominant middle class. The churches, with their 'preferential option for the poor', should be in a position to pursue this question with vigour unless their own leadership is too enmeshed in the existing exploitative structures. Furthermore, it is the churches which may be best placed to take up this issue at the global level. For the impoverishment of the majority in Malawi has to be understood in relation to the world economic order and the point has to be made that, ultimately, there will be no authentic democratization without a serious endeavour to address the gap between rich and poor at a global level. The church, with its ecumenical vision, may have to take responsibility for developing a world-wide engagement with this issue.

Tribalism and Regionalism

Part of the legacy of the Banda years is the regional fragmentation brought about by Kamuzu's attempts to establish a hegemony of his own Chewa people of the Central Region.[54] In crude regionalistic terms the multi-party movement of 1992–94 can be interpreted as the North and the South striking back against the Centre! Moreover, while the two powerful opposition parties sought to be national movements it soon became apparent that Aford was predominantly a northern party while the UDF was predominantly southern. This was borne out in the results of the 1994 General Election when each of the three regions gave overwhelming support to the party with which it identified. In the presidential election, Chakufwa Chihana of Aford took 85% of votes in the Northern Region against his 8% in the Centre and 7% in the South; Kamuzu Banda of the MCP took nearly 70% of the votes in the Central Region against his 16% in the South and 9% in the North; Bakili Muluzi of UDF took 75% of votes in the Southern Region against his 23% in the Centre and 7% in the North.[55] It could be argued that UDF won the election simply because the Southern Region is the most populous! The problem of national unity now came into the open as an urgent political issue.[56] So much so that Aford and the MCP, sworn enemies hitherto, were able to justify their sudden and short-lived alliance on the grounds of the need to secure national unity.[57] It was the same concern which convinced President Muluzi that he must have a Vice-President from each of the other regions and led to the controversial creation of the office of 2nd Vice President for Chakufwa Chihana. There was a real danger that politicians would regard their accountability in regional terms. National political life in the post-election period often appeared to be no more than a contest between competing regional power blocks. It is possible to regard this as a strategy more or less cynically adopted by the ruling elite to create politico-economic borders which make control easier. Wiseman Chirwa, e.g., has suggested that in Malawi ethnicity and regionalism are, in fact, ideological tools used by 'the country's bourgeoisie and petit bourgeoisie to inherit the state as a class for purposes of accumulating political power and economic resources.'[58]

The churches, through PAC, had earlier provided a rallying point for a united national movement. However, the churches themselves were seriously compromised by regionalism. This was most apparent in the Presbyterian Church where the Nkhoma Synod of the Central Region took a line which suggested that its political loyalty came before its ecclesiastical unity with the other Synods.[59] In 1992, when the other church leaders were making their risky and costly prophetic social witness, the Nkhoma Synod acted in solidarity with the MCP government. The other churches felt betrayed that Nkhoma appeared to be lining up against them in the struggle for justice and truth in Malawi. This led to the Nkhoma Synod being suspended from membership of the Christian Council of Malawi in November 1992.[60] Clearly the churches had not been immune from the regional fragmentation which was the legacy of the Banda years. Nevertheless, however imperfectly, the churches had also been able to act as the custodians of national unity. It was notable that the Pastoral Letter of 1992 drew its power in part from the fact that the Bishops were able to appeal to the need to 'guarantee the progress of *the nation*.'[61] Likewise PAC was concerned to explain to the government that it was concerned with '*national* issues affecting all aspects of the lives of the citizens of this country.'[62] The churches had the capacity to affirm a sense of national identity and to establish a sense of national accountability.

The extent of the churches' ability to contribute to the resolution of this problem may well be determined by the success or failure of their own struggle for unity among themselves in the Gospel. One important crucible in which the attempt to move beyond regionalism might be made is the General Synod of the CCAP. It is more than coincidence that the Blantyre, Nkhoma and Livingstonia Synods are identified with the regional power-blocs which have brought a dangerous political fragmentation to Malawian national life. For reasons of mission history the southern Blantyre Synod is ethnically composed of predominantly Yao and Mang'anja, the central Nkhoma Synod is composed of predominantly Chewa, and the northern Livingstonia Synod is composed of predominantly Ngoni and Tumbuka. Presbyterian Christians have to face the question of how far these tribal and geographical divisions inhibit the development of a real centre of ecclesiastical unity in the General Synod, which is widely considered to be 'very ineffective'.[63] It may be that the CCAP can give a lead to the nation by implementing the recent recommendation of the visiting team from the World Alliance of Reformed Churches: 'The process of closer cooperation and unity among the Synods calls for the writing of a constitution for the General Synod which will make it effective and empowering it in the life and mission of the CCAP.'[64] It is regrettable to observe, however, that at the very time when inter-regional tension is at its height the three member Synods of the General Synod are drawing further apart rather than closer together. The long-drawn out Dwangwa border dispute between Livingstonia and Nkhoma Synods has flared up to such an extent that Livingstonia has suspended its active participation in the work of the General Synod. By settling for a federalism which is based on inter-regional suspicion the CCAP has failed to achieve a unity which could withstand political pressures which play up ethnic and regional differences. The struggle within the CCAP at this point may prove to be the make-or-break of Malawi's endeavour to sustain a viable sense of national identity and unity. If the CCAP were able to discover and put into practical effect a spiritual unity, then it would act to counter the tendency for regionalism to inhibit the formation of a truly democratic outlook.

Indigenization of Democracy

Where churches and other religious institutions may have a particularly critical contribution is in the 'indigenization' of democracy. The democratic system will have limited impact so long as it is confined to language and structures imported from elsewhere. There is need to make connections with the vernacular understanding, to find for the new democratic institutions points of resonance with the African tradition. Otherwise democracy, paradoxically, becomes the mechanism by which the educated elite entrench their supremacy and alienate the rural majority. The need for a reappropriation of the African tradition is heightened by the way in which 'culture' was manipulated by Kamuzu Banda as a source of legitimation for his regime.[65] Peter Forster has observed that whereas Banda focused on the authoritarian elements in African tradition, the 'rebel' ministers who split with him in the 'Cabinet crisis' 'were prepared to some extent to take pride in traditions, but where they saw virtue in the past, it was in terms of egalitarianism rather than hierarchical authority.'[66] Now is the time to recover these very powerful currents in traditional Malawian life on which a democratic ethos and consciousness may be developed. David Clement Scott, one of the early Scottish missionaries at Blantyre made the observation in 1881 that: 'The African if he is anything is constitutional – no change or step of importance is taken without first open *mlandu* in which *the opinion of all is fully sought and expressed.*'[67] Having identified this strongly democratic tradition among the people of Malawi, Scott moved quickly to incorporate it into the life of the church. In 1894 he ordained seven deacons from among the early converts and these formed the effective governing council of the young church. Scott had no hesitation about their capacity to fulfil this responsibility by drawing on the resources of their own tradition: 'One could wish for no weightier justice than that of native *mlandu*-power Christianized into a Church Court.'[68] An important question for the church is how far the indigenous democratic traditions which it incorporated in its own life from this early period have survived sufficiently to be reappropriated by the state at a time when it is emerging from a period of despotism and striving to find solid foundations on which to build a democratic order.

The potentially strategic role which the churches occupy at this point is that they have been engaged in a long-running indigenization project as their once-exotic faith has been planted in African soil. It is instructive to compare the current expansion of the churches which is popular, vernacular and spontaneous with the democratization which appears elitist, foreign and contrived. Could the powerful drive behind the indigenization of Christianity be tapped as a means of enabling the Malawian people to discover the democratic norms and values which will provide the true foundation for a viable democratic political order?

Conclusion

Surveying the three levels of democratization which we described as the structures, the ethos and the spirit of democracy, it has been apparent that the effectiveness of the churches' engagement with political life progressively diminishes the deeper one looks. The churches were highly effective at the first level – mounting a challenge to the Banda dictatorship and acting as the midwives to the birth of the democratic Second Republic. They were effective up to a point in promoting civil society – mobilizing extra-statal associational life and securing massive popular participation in voting yet failing to facilitate at local level the generation of the self-motivated groups which would constitute a demanding civil society. They were least effective at the level of the spirit of democracy – exposing the surviving anti-democratic tendencies which would tend to corrupt the new political order and addressing a biblically and religiously inspired message to the heart of political behaviour. Ironically, the churches have done well when they have formed a political opposition, been fairly successful as civil society activists, but least effective at being *churches*!

Furthermore, to put this analysis fully in context it is necessary to notice that the international pressures being brought to bear on Malawi by 1992 were such that some kind of democratization process was all but inevitable. While it *was* courageous and radical in the domestic context to issue the Pastoral Letter and form the Public Affairs Committee, it was done in an international context where the momentum behind the democratization movement was practically irresistible in a country like Malawi which is obliged to dance to the tune of the 'donors'. To some extent the churches rode the crest of that wave. Where there is much less evidence of progress is in the infinitely more challenging area of the spiritual values needed to make democracy effective. Judgement here should not be too harsh. The Pastoral Letter did grip the nation at a deep, spiritual level and stands, at the end of 1996, as, according to John Lwanda: 'an as yet unsurpassed high point in its demands for economic, political and moral welfare for Malawians.'[69] The whole movement which subsequently led to the formation of PAC and the National Referendum did draw on the religious and moral commitment of many key participants. Yet democratization has taken relatively little effect among the ordinary people who remain as impoverished, powerless, exploited and marginalised as they were under the one-party system. Their participation in church life has not, by and large, given them the spiritual vision and moral impetus necessary to achieve a meaningful participation in the political process. The churches' failure to confront such issues as economic inequalities, patronage, personality politics, and regionalism raises the question of how far church life simply reflects prevailing social and political trends rather than challenging them. It may be that the next stage in the democratization process will depend to a significant extent on the form of associational life which prevails in parish churches.

Afterword: Theological Institutions and Malawi's Democratization

Though not usually so immediately and directly involved as the churches, theological institutions have been engaged with the process of political reform in Malawi from 1992 to 1996. Conscientized seminarians within the Catholic Church held discussions which some have considered influential in the background to the famous Bishops' Pastoral Letter *Living our Faith*.[70] The Catholic seminaries therefore may have played a certain formative role in the preparation and issue of the Letter as well as in providing centres for the dissemination and discussion of the Letter in the decisive mid-1992 period. The Protestant Zomba Theological College also played an important role at that point since, following student action, the staff issued a statement offering their support for the critique expressed in the Pastoral Letter.[71] This was the first public response on the Protestant side and played a part in the process that led up to the formation of the Public Affairs Committee in August/September 1992. Meanwhile the University of Malawi Department of Theology and Religious Studies had since 1988 been thrust into a political struggle arising out of the MCP government's opposition to the introduction of a theology degree programme in the University.[72] This had made theology a highly sensitive area within the University and staff members were often subject to considerable pressure. Some observers have seen significance in the conference of ATISCA (The Association of Theological Institutions in Southern and Central Africa) which was hosted by the Department of TRS at St. Peter's Major Seminary at the end of 1991.[73] The exiled Catholic Bishop Patrick Kalilombe addressed this conference on the subject of ministerial formation and emphasised the social and political context within which the church's witness is offered.[74] This was at least some further fuel on the fire that would ignite in the form of the Lenten Pastoral Letter a few months later. Two years later, in December 1993, the Department hosted another conference at the same venue under the auspices of ATISCA and the newly launched African Christianity Project, based at the University of Edinburgh. At this particular time, between the National Referendum and the General Election, an international conference on 'The Role of Christianity in Development, Peace and Reconstruction' had unmistakable relevance.[75]

Meanwhile, the Department of Theology and Religious Studies, in collaboration with the Department of Law, was the first organise an academic response to the Pastoral Letter. This took the form of a seminar at Chancellor College on 13 March 1992 which had to be held 'underground' since the Pastoral Letter had been banned by the police two days earlier. This initiative was sustained in the more open climate which followed the calling of the National Referendum and from early 1993 a series of seminars under the title 'Social Change in Malawi' was held at the University, co-sponsored by the Department of Law and the Department of Theology and Religious Studies. The atmosphere in the seminars was often quite electric as academics, for the first time, were able to freely express their views. The material generated was finally published as *Church, Law and Political Transition in Malawi 1992–94*, edited by M.S. Nzunda and K.R. Ross and published by Mambo Press, Gweru, as the first book in the Kachere Series. The seminars continued in 1995–96 and the material generated is presently being edited so as to produce a further volume, provisionally entitled *Democratization in Malawi: A Stock Taking*, with grant support from the National Endowment for Democracy in Washington DC.

Partly as a result of this work, in May 1994 the Department of Theology and Religious Studies was invited by the World Council of Churches Unit III (Theology of Life Programme) to carry out an intensive case study on Malawi under the theme 'all exercise of power is accountable to God'. This provided stimulus and resources in 1994–96 to hold a series of conferences, consultations and interviews with both key players in the political process and with those who had reflected on it in original ways. The provisional results of this case study, which were quite critical of the democratization process, were published as a pamphlet in November 1995.[76] Seven thousand copies of the pamphlet were distributed across a wide section of Malawian society and provoked a considerable response. One Cabinet Minister was reported to have remarked: 'These theologians! Do they want to start another revolution?' Included in the pamphlet was an invitation to the public to participate in an essay competition in which responses could be offered to the points advanced. The winner of the competition was a prisoner in Zomba Central Prison who had been held on remand, on a murder charge, for six years without his case ever coming to court. He was released on bail shortly after winning the competition. The final results of the study project were published in January 1997 as *God, People and Power in Malawi: Democratization in Theological Perspective*, edited by K.R. Ross and published by CLAIM, Blantyre, in the Kachere Monograph series.

Although at times theological institutions may have come close to playing a pro-active role in political affairs, in general the attempt has been made to remain a step back from direct involvement and to offer rather a nurturing of the spiritual roots of democracy by advancing critical perspectives from a religious basis. At a fairly basic level, academic institutions have contributed to social and political change simply by documenting and reflecting on events as they have unfolded. The Public Affairs Committee, e.g., expressed gratitude to the Department of Theology and Religious Studies for its documentation of PAC's contribution to political reform.[77] At the level of civil society, theological institutions have sought to promote incisive critiques of political behaviour and, through publications, members of staff addressing public meetings and students returning to their communities, these have been disseminated. Through an in-depth study process such as that which produced *God, People and Power* the attempt has been made to reach the areas in which the spiritual roots of democracy may be nurtured and strengthened. As that process revealed, a difficult dilemma for theological institutions is how far they should take up a pro-active role to the point of becoming directly participant in the political process or how far they should maintain an academic reserve in order to keep their critique concentrated at the deeper level.

Notes

1.   See *Living our Faith*, Pastoral Letter from the Catholic Bishops of Malawi, 8 March 1992; also published as *The Truth Will Set You Free* (Church in the World No. 28), London: CIIR, 1992.

2.   See K.R. Ross, 'The renewal of the State by the Church: The case of the Public Affairs Committee in Malawi', *Religion in Malawi* 5, 1995: 29–37.

3.   *UDF News* 1 (21), June 1993: 17–24.

4.   T. Ranger, 'Conference summary and conclusion', in P. Gifford (ed.), *The Christian churches and the democratisation of Africa*, Leiden: E.J. Brill, 1995: 19.

5.   See K.R. Ross, 'The truth shall set you free: Christian social witness in Malawi 1992–93', *Journal of Theology for Southern Africa* 90 (March), 1995: 17–30.

6.   *Living our faith*: 9.

7.   *Living our faith*: 9.

8.   *Living our faith*: 9–11.

9.   Tapes of the MCP emergency convention of 11 March 1992, which plotted the assassination of the bishops, have been widely circulated. See, e.g., *The Nation* 1 (12–21), 2 Sept.–4 Oct. 1993.

10.   For the history of the Nkhoma Synod see C.M. Pauw, 'Mission and Church in Malawi: The history of the Nkhoma Synod of the Church of Central Africa Presbyterian 1889–1962', D.Th., University of Stellenbosch, 1980.

11.   See, e.g., *Daily Times*, 6 November 1992.

12.   *Daily Times*, 30 April 1993.

13.   See, e.g., *Guardian Today*, 19–25 May 1993.

14.   *UDF Manifesto*, July 1993: 1.

15.   See, e.g., *The Monitor*, 28 April to 4 May 1993.

16.   A full account of the rising is found in G. Shepperson and T. Price, *Independent African*, Edinburgh: Edinburgh University Press, 1958.

17.   For discussion of the political importance of the 'Chilembwe myth' see K. Fiedler, 'Joseph Booth and the writing of Malawian history', *Religion in Malawi* 6, 1996.

18.   See G. Chigona, Research Notes on Political Transition in Malawi, conducted at Ntaja, Mwanza, Dowa and Nkhata Bay, November–December 1994.

19.   K.R. Ross, 'Current Christological trends in northern Malawi', *Journal of Religion in Africa* 27 (2), 1997: 160–176.

20.   K.R. Ross, 'Current Christological trends in northern Malawi'.

21.   H. Englund, 'Between God and Kamuzu: The transition to multi-party politics in central Malawi', unpublished paper, 1995: 28.

22.   PACREM was replaced by PACGEM – Public Affairs Committee General Election Monitoring. See Public Affairs Committee file, November 1993.

23.   Anastasia Msosa, Chairperson of the Electoral Commission for 1994 General Election, interview by Isabel Apawo Phiri, 29 December 1994.

24.   For studies of the 1992–93 period see T. Cullen, *Malawi: A turning point*, Edinburgh: The Pentland Press, 1994; L.B. Dzimbiri, 'The Malawi referendum of June 1993', *Electoral Studies* 13 (3), 1994: 229–334; *Kirche und Gesellschaft in Malawi: Die Krise*

von 1992 in historischer Perspektive, Hamburg: EMW Informationen No. 98, 1993; J.L.C. Lwanda, *Promises, power, politics and poverty: Democratic transition in Malawi (1961–1999)*, Glasgow: Dudu Nsomba, 1996; *Malawi: A moment of truth*, London: CIIR, 1993; J. Newell, "'A Moment of Truth?" The Church and political change in Malawi, 1992', *The Journal of Modern African Studies*. 33 (2), 1995: 243–262; C. Ng'ong'ola, 'Managing the transition to political pluralism in Malawi – Legal and constitutional arrangements', *The Journal of Commonwealth and Comparative Politics* 34 (2) 1996: 85–110; M.S. Nzunda and K.R. Ross (eds.), *Church, law and political transition in Malawi 1992–94*, Gweru: Mambo Press, 1995; K.R. Ross, 'Not catalyst but ferment: The distinctive contribution of the churches to political reform in Malawi 1992–93', in P. Gifford (ed.), *The Christian churches and the democraatisation of Africa*, Leiden: E.J. Brill, 1995: 98–107; J.K. van Donge, 'Kamuzu's legacy: The democratisation of Malawi. or searching for the rules of the game in African politics', *African Affairs* 94, 1995: 227–257.

25. *The Nation*, 24 August 1995.

26. Catholic Bishops of Malawi, *Walking together in faith: Our journey towards the year 2000: Pastoral Letter*, September 1996.

27. J.R. Minnis, 'Can civil society be a force for political change in Malawi? Paper presented at Conference on Social Change in Malawi, Chancellor College, 30 June 1995: 13.

28. T. Ranger, 'Conference Summary and Conclusion': 26.

29. See K.R. Ross, 'Current Christological Trends in Northern Malawi'.

30. P. Walshe, *Prophetic Christianity and the liberation movement in South Africa*, Pietermaritzburg: Cluster Publications, 1995: 143.

31. Unattributable interviews.

32. See *The Independent*, 19–24 January 1995, my italics.

33. See J.W. de Gruchy, *Christianity and democracy*, Cambridge: Cambridge University Press and Cape Town: David Philip, 1994.

34. This could be witnessed at the polling booths in even the most remote areas as long queues of people waited for hours under the hot sun in good order and good humour to cast their votes.

35. F.F. Kanyongolo, 'State and Constitutionalism in Malawi', Paper presented a Conference on Social Change in Malawi, Chancellor College, 28 June 1996: 16.

36. See B. Bujo, *African theology in its social context*, Maryknoll, New York: Orbis Books,, 1992: 18–21; cf. P. Tempels, *Bantu Philosophy*, Paris, 1959: 63.

37. See J.M. Lochman, *The faith we confess: An ecumenical dogmatics*, Edinburgh: T. & T. Clark, 1985: 96–97.

38. De Gruchy, *Christianity and democracy*. 244.

39. See, e.g, Lwanda, *Promises, power*.

40. *The Nation*, 23 May 1994.

41. *Daily Times*, 29 September 1995.

42. *The Nation*, 14 November 1994.

43. See Jande Banda, 'Aspects of current constitutional change debate in Malawi', Paper

presented at Social Change in Malawi Conference, Chancellor College, 1 July 1995: 12–13.

44. For the instructive comparison of the Zambian situation see C.J.J. Mphaisha, 'Retreat from democracy in post one-party state Zambia', *The Journal of Commonwealth and Comparative Politics* 34 (2), 1996: 65–84.

45. Lwanda, *Promises, power*: 71.

46. See K.R. Ross, 'The transformation of power in Malawi 1992–95: The role of the Christian churches', *The Ecumenical Review* 48 (1), 1996: 38–52.

47. Lwanda, *Promises, power*: 69.

48. Minnis, 'Can civil society be a force for political change in Malawi?': 12.

49. A.C. Musopole, 'A vision for theology in Malawi', *Religion in Malawi*. 6, 1996.

50. F.F. Kanyongolo, 'State and Constitutionalism in Malawi': 12, author's italics.

51. See, e.g., *The Weekly Chronicle*, 29 August–4 September 1994.

52. *The Nation*, 30 April 1996.

53. *The Nation*, 2 May 1995.

54. See L. Vail and L. White, 'Tribalism in the political history of Malawi', in L. Vail (ed.), *The creation of tribalism in Southern Africa*, London: James Currey and Los Angeles: University of California Press, 1989: 151–192.

55. *Daily Times*, 20 May 1994.

56. See, e.g., *Daily Times*, 19 May 1994; *The Enquirer*, 21–24 May 1994.

57. See, e.g., *The Monitor*, 29 June 1994; *The New Express*, 30 June 1994.

58. C.W. Chirwa, 'The politics of ethnicity and regionalism in contemporary Malawi', *African Rural and Urban Studies*, 1 (2), 1994: 94. Cf. D. Kaspin, 'The politics of ethnicity in Malawi's democratic transition', *The Journal of Modern African Studies* 33 (4), 1995: 595–620.

59. The Nkhoma Synod grew out of a mission established in 1889 by the South African Dutch Reformed Church. There have always been tensions between Nkhoma and the Synods of Scottish Presbyterian origin – Blantyre in the south and Livingstonia in the north – but they have been ecclesiastically united in the Church of Central Africa Presbyterian since 1926.

60. *Daily Times*, 6 November 1992.

61. *Living our faith*: 8, my italics.

62. Rev M.E. Kansilanga to Hon B. Bisani, 12 October 1992, my italics.

63. See, e.g., comments of Synod representatives to WARC representatives, July 1995, Report of Pastoral Team Visit to the Church of Central Africa Presbyterian (CCAP), Malawi, 30 June–3 July 1995, Geneva: World Alliance of Reformed Churches, 1995: 3.

64. Report of Pastoral Team Visit: 5.

65. See P.G. Forster, 'Culture, nationalism, and the invention of tradition in Malawi', *The Journal of Modern African Studies* 32 (3), 1994: 477–497.

66. Forster: 489.

67. *Life and Work in British Central Africa* (Blantyre Mission newspaper), November 1891, my italics.

68. *Life and Work in British Central Africa*, November 1894.
69. Lwanda, *Promises, power:* 104.
70. J. Divala, class presentation, TRS350, Chancellor College, University of Malawi, June 1995.
71. Very Rev Dr Silas Ncozana, interview, Blantyre, 28 June 1995.
72. See K.R. Ross, 'Theology and Religious Studies at the University of Malawi 1988–1993', *Religion in Malawi* 4, 1994: 4–5.
73. See, e.g., Lwanda, *Promises, power:* 91.
74. See ATISCA *Bulletin* No. 1 (1992).
75. See I.A. Phiri, K.R. Ross and J.L. Cox (eds.), *The role of Christianity in development, peace and reconstruction: southern African perspectives*, Nairobi: AACC, 1996.
76. K.R. Ross and F.L. Moyo, *Udindo Wonse*, Zomba: University of Malawi Department of Theology and Religious Studies, 1995.
77. Meeting of Bishop Joseph Bvumbwe, Vice-Chairman, Rev Misanjo Kansilanga, Secretary, and Mr Charles Mapapa, Administrative Secretary, Public Affairs Committee with Department of Theology and Religious Studies, held at Zomba Theological College, December 1995.

Chapter Seven

Christianity and National Development in West Africa: Dilemmas and Possibilities

Gustav H.K. Deveneaux

Introduction

It is particularly instructive to note the importance now attached to the role of religion in nation-building in the emergent nations of Asia, Latin America and Africa. For hitherto, nation-building had largely been considered in political, economic and perhaps sociological terms. As the complex, moral, psychological and sociological factors important to successful nation-building are better understood, an examination of the role of religion – in our case Christianity – in nation-building becomes useful in the West African sub-region.

Background

Historically, the importance of religion in the transformation of states leading to economic development and social revolutions has been recognised. Studies in English history, particularly the consequence of the Protestant and Puritan revolutions in the sixteenth and seventeenth centuries, clearly confirm the significant role religion played in contributing to the socio-political development of England during that period and subsequently.[1] It is, therefore, perhaps not surprising that from the earliest, European expansion into the wider world commencing with the Spaniards and the Portuguese in the fifteenth and sixteenth centuries and ending with the English, French, Italian, German and Dutch in the nineteenth and twentieth centuries were all conceived by the imperial and colonial powers not only as economic and political enterprises but also as religious enterprises.[2] For it was widely believed and assumed that colonial and imperial enterprises would either remain unfulfilled or incomplete without religious content.

This is evidenced by the leading role which the Church and other religious organisations played in the Age of the Enlightenment from the fifteenth to the eighteenth centuries. Indeed, as records show, explorers, priests, administrators, statesmen and soldiers served the empire for 'God, gold and glory'.[3] Although frequently, economic and other motives masked the religious justification for the colonial wars between Spain and Portugal, Spain and the Netherlands, and subsequently Britain, France and Denmark and other European countries, it nevertheless remains true that religion was advanced as the main reason for disagreement and conflict. It was through this route that the global dominion enjoyed by Spain, and Portugal, originally sanctioned by none other than the Pope himself, was quickly broken as France, Britain and Holland acquired imperial territories in North and South America, the Caribbean, Africa and Asia.[4]

To a large extent, therefore, it was through early colonial expansion that Christianity was introduced into these parts of the world and during the nineteenth and twentieth centuries, with modern imperialism, the process continued. European imperial and colonial expansion and domination in the last century was equally characterised by a strong religious drive, although unlike the earlier periods, in the face of stiff resistance from Islam, Hinduism and other religions. In North America, Arabia, the Western Sudan, India, Indonesia, Malaysia and China, for example, the colonial enterprise was ultimately compelled to moderate its religious mission.[5] The net result was that after the Second World War, in most places Christianity of one sort or another had either become important in the organic structure of the successor independent states, or an embattled minority religion against large Muslim, Hindu or Buddhist majorities. This, therefore, accounts for the fundamental importance of religion, whether Christian, Islam, or Buddhism, in the development of the new nation states of the world.

West Africa

This is no less true of West Africa than other parts of the world. Within a few years of the triumph of Islam in Arabia, by 640 C.E. it had arrived in Egypt, from which it radiated westwards into the Maghrib, reaching Morocco by the tenth century, and southwards into the Upper Nile even earlier.[6] In Egypt and the Maghrib, the Arabs had converted Tuaregs and Berbers, and those who followed the traditional religion were exiled into the Western Sudan, so that from the tenth century onwards, Islam became very important by virtue of the number of adherents it had won and the status it had achieved. An example of this is the collapse of one of the earliest Sudanese empires, Ghana, which was brought about by conflict between traditional religion and Islam at the level of the monarchy. Thereafter, it was not uncommon for some of the Sudanese monarchs in Mali and Songhai not only to be Muslim but also to make the pilgrimage to Mecca, one of the obligations of a good Muslim. Mansa Musa perhaps was the most famous of them.[7]

There was also a division in society between those who continued to adhere to traditional African religious practices and beliefs and those who committed themselves to Islam. Indeed, this division was a factor which contributed to the collapse of the Songhai empire, following the Moroccan invasion and attack of 1591. A civil war ensued which further ruptured Sudanese society.[8]

Among other things, it was this state of uneven balance between Islamic and traditional African religious practices and beliefs which set the stage for Islamic religious revival and reforms in the region in the eighteenth century in Segu, Kaarta and Macina, and in the nineteenth century in the Fulani/Hausa states beginning with the Osman Dan Fodio *jihad* of 1804, stretching into the Senegal and Niger valleys from the 1850s with the *jihad* of Al Haj Omar Taal and ending with those of Ahmed and Samori Toure in the 1880s.[9] Even this Islamic revival and revolution failed to completely Islamise the Western Sudan, however, as traditional African religions firmly stood their ground. Nonetheless, it is important to note that during this period, Islam had finally succeeded in penetrating the forest regions and reaching the coastal regions of West Africa. Islam was present in Kumasi for example, the seat of the *Asantehene* of the Ashanti Confederacy, and in Oyo, following the fall of Ilorin in 1818.[10]

Another indication of the spread was that quite a number of the slaves who were transported across the Atlantic to the New World were Moslems. Some were even lucky enough to return to their native land from bondage in the Americas.[11] It is, therefore, clear that by the time Europeans started penetrating West Africa from the coast, Islam was already significant as a religion among its peoples.

Christianity

While there is biblical evidence to demonstrate the presence of Christianity in Egypt and Ethiopia, as far as West Africa is concerned, its presence is associated with the arrival of the Europeans, in the fifteenth century,[12] penetrating from the coastal settlements, bases and trading posts into the interior. Initially, it was Portuguese priests of the Catholic Church who, by the end of the fifteenth century, converted Africans from Cape Verde to the Congo. The process continued in succeeding centuries with the arrival of other nationalities on the scene, such as Protestant missionaries from other religions who continued the earlier efforts of the Portuguese.[13] The Protestant impact, however, was largely a nineteenth century phenomenon which continued into the twentieth century as European rule consolidated its hold in the region. The abolitionist movement of the late eighteenth century in which Britain assumed leadership in eradicating both the slave trade and slavery in Africa, provided the inspiration for colonisation, the spread of legitimate commerce and Christian evangelisation across the continent.[14] As was to be expected, the sub-region of West Africa became the scene of various missionary activities which continued in the colonial period.

From the colony of Sierra Leone, which was established in 1787 by humanitarians and abolitionists with the support of the British government, the Church Missionary Society (CMS) from England radiated along the West Coast, reaching the Gold Coast and Nigeria by the 1830s and then spreading into the interior of the sub-region by the second half of the nineteenth century.[15] It was not only the British who were engaged in such missionary enterprise. The French also, from their bases and posts in Senegal, Guinea Francaise, Côte d'Ivoire, Dahomey, and Gabon, extended their economic, political and cultural influences, including their religion, into the interior.[16] The Germans too had established their presence in West Africa in the 1880s and in accordance with traditional colonial practice encouraged Christian missionary activities in their spheres of influence.[17] By the end of the century, Christian missions had proliferated all over West Africa reflecting various denominations. Catholicism, Anglicanism,

Presbyterianism, Methodism, Lutheranism and other sects all took root in the region during this era.

As was the case with the spread of Islam, the penetration of Christianity encountered opposition both from Islam and traditional African religions. In almost every place where the Europeans had established a recognised presence and where Christian missionary activity had taken place, such opposition occurred (although it was frequently subsumed in political or economic terms). Frequently, however, missionaries blamed Islam for the resistance of Africans to Christianity, but if the case of Sierra Leone is anything to go by, exemplified by the experience of the CMS in Northern Sierra Leone during the nineteenth century, resistance to the spread of Christianity came more from the traditional beliefs of the Temne than Islam.[18]

In the end, Christian missions had to adjust and live with Islam in several parts of West Africa and persevere with the conversion of Africans from their traditional faiths, although with varying degrees of success. It is, however, important to note that as long as Islam accepted the political suzerainty of the colonialists and co-operated with them in commerce and in preserving law and order, then the Islamic sects were allowed to live in peace and even grew as in the case of the *Mourides* in the Senegal.[19]

By the end of the nineteenth century, therefore, when colonialism was formally established in the region by France, Britain, Germany, Portugal and Spain, Christianity had become an important moral, social, political and economic force in shaping its history. The initial confrontation between Islam and Christianity had given way to accommodation between the two while sectarianism and conflict with indigenous and traditional African beliefs continued with Christianity.

Colonialism

The surge of imperialism in Europe in the 1870s, which culminated in the rise of world-wide colonialism by the 1880s, saw the transformation of centuries of informal relations between Europeans and Africans in the sub-region into formal ones characterised by the imposition of colonial rule.[20] The process was frequently slow, encountering stiff resistance from the West African traditional political and religious authorities as well as intellectual challenge from African élites.[21] Nonetheless, by the end of the First World War, it had been completed with the whole of the continent, including West Africa, partitioned. The new states were now colonies of France, Britain, Germany, Portugal, Italy and Spain.

The formality of colonialism imposed new responsibilities on the colonial governments which had hitherto been informally discharged largely by Christian missionary societies. Such responsibilities included the welfare of the colonised inhabitants within their respective colonies. Apart from the fundamental necessity of promoting conditions and institutions supporting law and order, welfare included such things as education, health, trade, employment and finance. For peaceful governance, systems concerned with law and order were instituted in collaboration with traditional authorities, whether Moslem or traditional, along with the construction of roads and other infrastructures to facilitate communication. It must be strongly emphasised, however, that this agenda represented the ideal, the *raison d'etre* for the imposition of European colonial rule in West Africa in the nineteenth and twentieth centuries, namely the spread of Western civilisation. As we all know, the degree to which each colonial power fulfilled this agenda varied depending on both local and international circumstances.

The Germans are generally thought to have had a bad record, for example in Togo and the Cameroons, while the French were relatively impressive, particularly in the area of infrastructural development, especially in the period after the Second World War. However, French colonial rule was more autocratic and repressive with less regard for African traditional authorities.[22] The British, on the other hand, are thought to have been more progressive on social matters such as education and health, and liberal in political affairs, such as granting concessions to aspiring African élites and reforming traditional authorities through education.[23]

The debate on the benefits and disadvantages of colonialism to West Africans will long continue with great passion on all sides of the argument. What there seems little argument about – and this is central to our focus – is that what little was achieved in the discharge of the social and political agenda can be attributed largely to the work of Christian missions. The colonial governments frequently lacked the financial and technical resources to promote education and public health in the colonies and therefore decided either to leave these matters entirely in the hands of missionaries or assist with funds and other services. It was in the prosecution of this policy during the colonial era that Christian missions came to assume a large role in the development of the colonies, quite out of proportion to the numbers of missionaries present in them.

The work of spreading Christianity to Africans during the pre-colonial era thus continued in the colonial period with an even larger mandate in countries ranging from Senegal in the extreme north-west to Nigeria and the Cameroons in the south-easternmost tip. Through the hundreds of schools which the missionaries established, they were able in time directly to transform the lives of their pupils and students by importing both practical skills and universal ideas springing from Europe and America, ideas such as freedom, common humanity, Christian morality, law and government and business and finance. In the area of public health, too, it was missionary societies which pioneered in many African countries in the sub-region a practice which has continued even in the post-colonial period.

In Sierra Leone, for example, missionaries were instrumental in the establishment of schools like the CMS Grammar School (1845), the Methodist Boys High School, the Methodist Girls High School, Christ the King College in Bo, St Francis Secondary School in Makeni, the Albert Academy in Freetown, the Annie Walshe Memorial School (1849) and the St Joseph's Secondary School, the St Edwards Secondary School, the Bumpe High School, the Wesleyan Methodist Secondary School in Segbwema, Jaluahun Secondary School for Girls and Hartford Secondary School for Girls in Moyamba.[24] At the pinnacle of the educational establishment was Fourah Bay College, originally founded in 1819 for the training of men for the CMS Ministry, but later expanded into a liberal arts college, affiliated to Durham University in England, and developed to train the Western educated élite from not only Sierra Leone but throughout West Africa.

In the area of public health, the missionaries came to realise very early on the importance of the promotion of public health among Africans as part of their evangelical mission, and frequently clinics came to be attached to schools and mission homes. For example, there was a clinic attached to the St Joseph's Primary (now St Anne's) School at Howe Street in Freetown. At a higher level, missionaries established full-scale hospitals in Magbesseneh (Catholic), the Nixon Memorial Hospital (Protestant) in the Port Loko District Segbwema, the Serabu Hospital by the UMC missions in the eastern and southern provinces, the Eye Clinic and the Princes Christian Maternity Hospital in Freetown by the CMS.

The case of Sierra Leone demonstrates the vast role which Christian missions came to play in the development of the colonial state in West Africa, and this was true of almost every colony, whether French, English, Portuguese or German. It is important, however, to be aware of three factors arising from this role. The first is that almost without exception, the number of African converts to Christianity in each colony was small compared to the number converting to other religious affiliations, such as Islam and traditional African beliefs. Indeed, the disparity was sometimes so overwhelming, as in the case of Senegal, Niger or Nigeria, that the impact of Christianity in these countries was almost imperceptible.

The second is that during the colonial period, because of the enlarged mandate of the Christian missions and because the nationality of missionaries was frequently European, they came to be identified with colonial authority in West Africa.[25] Further, it is not hard to understand why in a colonial context strongly infected with racist undertones and overtones, the largely African colonial subjects came to perceive the missions, in spite of all their selfless work, as part of the white colonial structure. Christian missions became identified with authority, reflecting the fear and respect Africans developed for the colonial *imperium*. Further, they were perceived as privileged because of their European and Western origins and close association with the white colonial authorities.

The third factor – and again very significant – is that the impact of the Christian missions on the lives of West Africans during the colonial period cannot be measured simply by the number of converts to Christianity, nor in the numbers of Africans who directly received either education or medical attention from missionary institutions. A sort of multiplier effect was at work which rapidly brought thousands more into the web of Christian influences. Those who received Christian and Western education either became teachers themselves, thereby extending Western influences to distant areas, or spread ideas which undermined traditional practices and beliefs. Even more striking is that the services offered by the missions came to be appreciated for their moral or utilitarian worth by all Africans regardless of faith. Thus many Moslems not only ensured that their children acquired Qur'anic education but also attended Western orientated schools, achieving the greatest heights at local and metropolitan universities in Europe and America.

Traditional African devotees accepted the reality of the colonial presence and sent their children to missionary schools for education or to clinics and hospitals for cures for all sorts of ailments and diseases which traditional African institutions were unable or ill-equipped to provide. However, while more Africans converted to Christianity because of the evangelistic and social work of the missions, nonetheless, the numbers who committed themselves to Islam and traditional African faiths grew faster. Herein lies the source of the frustration and agony frequently expressed by Christian and Muslim missionaries both during the colonial and post-colonial periods: the dogged persistence of the worship of 'idols and other forms of heathenism' by their followers.[26] In a very real sense, though, Africans responded to the work and evangelisation of Christian missions in a pragmatic and spiritual manner.

It is evident that from pre-colonialisation to the present, Christianity has played a very important role in nation-building in West Africa. In critical sectors, such as education, health, government and business, Christian missions have been pivotal in laying the foundations for independence and development in the post-colonial period. This role, it must be emphasised, was not always played without opposition from the secular state, Islam and traditional African beliefs.

Independence and the Post-Colonial Period

The day the Gold Coast attained independence, 6 March 1957, marked a significant turning point in the political history of West Africa for it heralded the beginning of the end of colonial rule in the region.[27] In rapid succession, one colony after another achieved independence from France or Britain, so that by 1965 when the Gambia became independent from Britain, virtually all the French and British colonial possessions had recovered their political sovereignty. Only the Portuguese colonies had yet to become free, a process that was violent, bloody and tortuous and which ended in the 1970s for Cape Verde and Guinea Bissao following the collapse in a revolution of the Caetano dictatorship in Portugal.[28]

Independence was achieved in West Africa as a result of the nationalist struggle. There were, however, other significant and related factors, such as the exhaustion of the colonial powers after the disasters of the Second World War, the international complications of the Cold War, and the liberal spirit in the West which had emerged as part of the agenda of the Atlantic Alliance in their fight against Fascism.[29] While the retreat by the colonial powers may have been strategic, compelled more by the unmanageable economies of the colonies in West Africa, as Professor Hargreaves has recently suggested, there still remains the undeniably critical role which the African nationalists played in this process.[30]

Again, it is important to stress here that Christianity had been directly and indirectly involved in not only providing the leadership in this struggle but the moral and religious logic of it as well. For in almost every African country, nationalists had either attended missionary schools or had become ministers of the Church itself. Kwame Nkrumah, Herbert Macaulay, Robert Mugabe, Dr Milton Margai, Dr Siaka Stevens, Julius Nyerere, Tom Mboya, and Albert Margai come to mind in this regard.

Thus from the very beginning, Christianity was closely involved in the nationalist movement which led to independence. The new African governments then naturally assumed the responsibilities of the previous colonial authorities and, being African, were under even greater pressure to discharge these social, economic and political responsibilities to their people. The logic of independence then meant that the post-colonial governments had to assume more responsibilities for education, medical services and the development of infrastructures.

To the credit of the post-colonial West African governments, it must be admitted that initially such responsibilities continued to be discharged admirably but by the late 1970s and into the 1980s, a crisis situation had arisen. Discharging these social and economic responsibilities had become difficult, and in some cases impossible, largely because of the financial and technical costs involved, costs which the African govern- ments found difficult to bear as one after the other, their economies fell apart.[31] Furthermore, political turmoil, civil strife and wars compounded the situation so that sadly, a large proportion of national expenditure had to be diverted to meeting political and defence requirements rather than social responsibilities. The early years of independence had been marked by a continued partnership between Church and State, with the Church continuing to promote the spiritual and material welfare of their followers and those needing its services. Thus, missionary schools, hospitals and clinics continued to function and even expand in the post-colonial period in West Africa.

A new dimension in the work of missions had developed by the 1970s which put even greater emphasis on economic development. Economic development, which promoted the welfare of the people, whether Christian or heathen, was accepted as part of the Christian mission. As a consequence, the Church acquired an even greater and more critical role for itself in the governments of newly independent countries of Africa, who heartily welcomed development projects which, in many instances, they on their own either lacked the resources or the political will to undertake. In my view, the role of Christian missions in West Africa became greater than at any time since the introduction of Christianity in the region because they accepted the responsibility of contributing to economic development. The missions were in a position to call on large resources, financial and otherwise, from Europe and America which were used for both the spiritual and material needs of people.

In a few instances, however, the story was not always a happy one. The partnership between Church and State was ruptured as result of tension and misunderstanding over political, moral and educational issues.[32] Further, the close association between Church and State during the colonial period, to which earlier reference has been made, tended to taint the missions in the eyes of radical nationalist leaders such as President Sekou Toure who regarded the Catholic Church with great suspicion as part of the neocolonial menace which faced his besieged country, Guinea. Mission schools were taken over by his government and the Catholic Church and its adherents were persecuted.[33] Similar developments marked relations between Church and State in Ghana under Kwame Nkrumah, and in the Cameroons where the Catholic Church was thought to be supporting reactionary and opposition forces.[34]

However, the moral dilemmas between the new nation states of West Africa and the Church were even more agonizing. For in a very real sense, the leadership of these new countries at every level, commercial and financial included, soon found itself caught up in the conflicting and tortuous demands of African nationalism, political expediency and cold war international politics, all of which confounded their aspirations to conform to Christian precepts.

Whereas in the colonial period, the question of political legitimacy was not an issue, since, after all was said and done, colonialism depended/relied on force to maintain control, independence in West Africa made the issue of legitimacy central to governance. To satisfy the most basic requirements of legitimacy to rule by popular consent, many African leaders, many of whom had either Christian backgrounds or an educational training and therefore knowledge of Christian values of morality, resorted to all sorts of devices, some ingenious and others undemocratic, that were brutal and ultimately self-defeating. One by one, therefore, many of the African governments abandoned the inherited parliamentary systems bequeathed to them by their former colonial rulers in favour of either single party régimes or imposed military régimes, characterised by corruption, suppression of fundamental human rights and economic mismanagement. In such a climate, when the moral decline so widespread in society was criticised and denounced by the Church, the leaders of the new nation states yielded easily to the temptation of enforcing secularism over religious tolerance and freedom.

It seems, however, unfair in the circumstances to lay the blame squarely at the feet of the Christian leadership of these countries, as many critics are wont to do. It is important to understand that in almost every African country in the sub-region, these Christian political, social and business leaders were operating within a highly-charged political atmosphere dominated by Muslim and other African groups larger than themselves whose moral values did not always accord with Christian ones, but whose views and values of necessity had to prevail in a democratic society with pretensions to satisfying the wishes of the majority. Sadly therefore, political expediency contributed considerably to the expression of West African nationalism during this era and the sharpening of the moral dilemmas between Church and State.

In general, however, Christianity and the State collaborated in the tasks of nation-building in the post-colonial period, because both institutions needed each other. By the 1980s, however, perhaps it was the State that needed the Church more as the tide rose for political reform and single party régimes were dismantled to be replaced by pluralistic democratic governments committed to human rights and free-market economics. Most African governments had become financially bankrupt by then and wracked by the political turmoil of the transition to democracy, a process that has been characterised more by frustration and pain rather than hope. African governments accepted the logic of their predicament and began to solicit the missions once more to play an even greater role in education, social welfare and public health. In some instances, as in Sierra Leone, mission schools which had been taken over by state authorities were handed back as the State recognised it was unable to run them for lack of financial and technical resources.[35]

The 1990s witnessed a continuing and expanding role for Christianity in West Africa. Church relief work, for example, is now crucial in the areas of refugee resettlement and rehabilitation as Africa becomes a strife-torn continent with the unenviable record of having the second highest number of refugees, over 6.5 million, in the world. For example, the outbreak of civil war in Liberia which spilled over into Sierra Leone as a rebel war from 1990 onwards, created over two million displaced persons and refugees whose care would never have been as adequately met without the charitable and selfless support of Christian missions, both Catholic and Protestant. The Church has, therefore, played a positive role in nation-building in West Africa particularly in the post-colonial period. Nevertheless, areas of tension between Church and State remain.

Dilemmas and Possibilities

The task of nation-building is complex, embracing economics, politics and ethics, so that those West African countries which acquired sovereign status before nationhood face a daunting task in welding their congeries of ethnic or tribal groups within their national territorial boundaries into integrated and developed nations. At independence in almost every African country, it was soon recognised that in some cases, where the state comprised a multiplicity of ethnic groups for whose loyalties ambitious political leaders vied for narrow personal or regional benefits, these groups would have to be contained by whatever means possible if the nation state were not to disintegrate and collapse. It is this struggle between the centripetal forces of nationalism and centrifugal forces of ethnocentrism and tribalism which is the source of widespread civil strife in the continent leading to political instability and underdevelopment.[36]

In addition to this, illiteracy on the part of the masses leading to political inertia on the one hand and sycophancy and cynicism on the other, poverty and greed, corruption and limited political vision, coupled with a generally hostile international economic and political climate, have all made the task of nation-building in West Africa an extremely difficult, explosive, dangerous and expensive proposition, but which of necessity must be accomplished. It then becomes easy to understand why, in a generally poor economic environment, fragmented along ethnic lines and with high illiteracy rates, the determination of political élites to cling to power at all costs has created a very sensitive climate in which nation-building has been taking place. As a result of this sensitivity, the Church and the State have frequently run into conflict.

One of the strongest appeals of the gospel, after the possibility of salvation to those who accept Christ as their Saviour, is the message of the equality of humanity before God. Undoubtedly, this has been one of the most important factors favouring the spiritual growth of Christianity in Africa. The offer of equality and freedom to Africans who convert to the faith has been most attractive. The Church, since its inception in West Africa, has endeavoured to live up to this ideal. The observance of the biblical injunction to Christians to render unto Caesar the things that are Caesar's and unto God the things which are God's has not always prevented clashes between God and Caesar in West Africa. For where the Christian Church has become convinced of political suppression and oppression by secular political authorities, it has not only protested vigorously but also encouraged its followers to stand up to the oppressors in the interest of equality, freedom and justice. For precisely this reason, therefore, sensitive political leaders under pressure to attain their goals have frequently tended to regard the Christian Church as either unnecessarily meddlesome or as an agent of Western European imperialism. This explains why, in almost every country in West Africa where there has been a movement recently for dismantling the single party state in favour of a multi-party democracy, Christians have played a prominent role, much to the anger and dislike of the secular political authorities.

The second area of conflict has been the application of Christian morality and ethics in civil society. The promotion and practice of values such as honesty, accountability, fairness and equality based on the Bible, are accepted as conducive to the growth of a God-fearing and morally healthy society. Those individuals, however, who wish to be greedy, corrupt, wicked, callous, selfish and dishonest will find Christian morality obstructionist. Since independence, in West Africa in particular, and Africa as a whole, it is common knowledge much to the sadness of all patriots, that vices such as corruption, greed, selfishness, dishonesty and callousness have become quite widespread among holders of public offices as well as ordinary citizens.

The Church in turn has accepted the responsibility for combating these vices and the various Christian missions which have multiplied in the sub-region since independence have decided to meet the challenge head on. Not unnaturally, this combative attitude is deeply resented particularly by powerful African leaders in the political, economic and social sectors of society.

Yet a third cause of tension which Christianity faces in West Africa comes from other faiths such as Islam, and from other Christian sects. The opposition which Islam posed to the spread of European colonial rule in West Africa in the nineteenth and twentieth centuries has already been re-counted. Equally significant is the fact that Islam collaborated with colonialism after this bitter episode, all the while naturally jealous of the privileged place which Christianity occupied in the colonial establishment.

With independence, however, Islam became more assertive in several West African countries, especially in those where followers of the faith were in the majority, such as Nigeria, Senegal, Mali, Cameroon and Niger. This new assertiveness was also facilitated by the growth of world-wide Islamic movements, of which many African states soon became members, giving them a feeling of confidence which they had hitherto lacked under colonialism. Perhaps, the single most important factor which contributed to this assertiveness of Islam was the newly-acquired oil wealth from the Arab States and the determination of the leaders of most of these states, such as Saudi Arabia, Iran, Kuwait and Libya to use their wealth to promote Islamic and Arab causes in the world, including West Africa.

Islam as a religious force, therefore, was elevated to a powerful position where it could compete effectively with Christianity not only in the propagation of its faith, but in the promotion of social welfare and economic projects for the well-being of converts to Islam. Herein lies the new sense of confidence which Islam has enjoyed in West Africa in the last fifty years but which, unfortunately, has occasionally led to intolerance on the part of other faiths, particularly Christianity. This attitude partly explains the frequent religious clashes which have occurred in Northern Nigeria in recent years between Muslims and Christians, resulting in the deaths of hundreds of supporters of both religions.

The example set by countries like Iran, Saudi Arabia, Libya and Sudan where religion and state are one and where, as in the case of the Sudan for instance, *Sharia* law has been imposed, are very attractive to some Islamic followers in West African society who would wish to reproduce similar legal situations in their own regions. From this source stems the opposition to secular politics in modern Africa, which are perceived as threatening both orthodox Islam and Christianity.

It is significant in this regard to note that since independence, Christian sects have multiplied in the sub-region. Apart from the main-line Churches such as Anglican, Methodist, Catholic and Presbyterian, we also now have the Pentecostalists, various African spiritual Churches, in addition to the old and established Church of the Lord, Aladura, the New Apostolic Church and the Church of the Latter Day Saints. In the light of the proliferation of such Christian groups, sectarianism can develop and lead to conflict within the Christian community. In Sierra Leone, and reportedly in other countries in the sub-region where these groups, whose adherents are generally known as "born-again Christians", have expanded, their zeal in the propagation of the faith and their tendency to interpret the Bible literally have tended to foster intolerance and tension within and without the Christian community.

The current Christian revival in West Africa, Africa and other parts of the world nonetheless undeniably owes its inspiration to these sects. Fundamentalist preachers and healers like Rheinhardt Bunke, on visits to African countries such as Nigeria and Sierra Leone in the early 1990s, attracted very large crowds at their revival meetings, many of whom were either Muslims or adherents of traditional African beliefs. West Africans, it seems, are impressed by the fundamentalists' direct and rather literal approach to Christianity rather than the conformist and staid approach of older Christian traditions. No doubt the lively form of worship, character-ised by loud, melodious singing, clapping of hands, inspirational trances, into which supposedly true believers lapse and then speak in tongues, and communal togetherness, all have a strong appeal to their followers.

It is precisely these appeals, however, which arouse the resentment of not only traditional, non-fundamentalist Christian sects, but also other religious bodies, such as orthodox and fundamentalist Islamic sects. Their evangelisation is perceived as threatening and consequently a danger to the religious balance which various bodies have tried to maintain in their communities. It is, therefore, not surprising that in places like Nigeria with a large Muslim population, following the departure of Reverend Bunke after one of his revivalist meetings, violent clashes occurred, leaving a significant number dead. Since the tendency is for non-Christians to attribute the activities of Christian fundamentalists in general to all Christians in society, it therefore becomes the responsibility of all Christian denominations to treat the matter as a common challenge.

The fundamental problem, however, remains: the critical factor of African traditional beliefs with which both Christianity and Islam have to contend. Whereas in the past, Islam tended to co-exist more easily alongside traditional African beliefs rather than with Christianity, increasingly in recent times, militant and fundamentalist Islamic sects have been sounding more uncompromising about traditional African religious practices, especially devotion to secret or esoteric societies. Briefly put, they are regarded as incompatible with both the theology and practice of orthodox Islam.

Christianity, on the other hand, although displaying disdain for some of the more devilish practices of these esoteric societies and cults, has looked rather favourably on other aspects considered to enhance social well-being. Some would argue that the proliferation of esoteric African cults in the sub-region actually enhances African culture, which in turn can only be a positive factor in the process of nation-building. The debate will continue, but there is no doubt that Christian morality and values, which are fundamental to the creation of a healthy nation, will encounter difficulty in an environment suffused with African secret cults rooted in traditional religious beliefs.

Conclusion

Over twenty years ago, the late Dr Kwame Nkrumah, President of Ghana, identified Africa's three religions, traditional African, Islam and Christianity, as forming the base for a lasting African political and moral philosophy. He expressed this thought in the following way:

> On balance, we might say that political toleration in Africa is best exhibited first among believers in traditional religion, who are prepared to accept Muslim or Christian as leaders without too much bitterness. Political toleration is next exemplified by Muslims in Africa, who have established both in Senegal and in Tanzania a capacity to follow a Christian leader without blaming him for his religion. Political toleration in this sense in Africa is least exemplified among Christians, whose capacity to follow leadership other than their own is often relatively limited.[37]

Continuing further, he observed:

> the related factors emerging from this analysis imply that tra-
> ditional African religion is socially conservative but politically
> tolerant; that Islam is socially conservative but politically radi-
> cal; and that Christianity is socially innovative and progressive
> but inclining towards political conservatism. All these are over
> simplified but they provide traffic indicators in our long journey
> towards [understanding] the role of religion in African life and
> experience.[38]

It is clear from these comments that the range of influence exerted by these three beliefs far exceeds the purely spiritual or even political arenas, reaching extensively into virtually every area of African life.

Some fifteen years ago, drawing on the historical scholarship of Professor Jackson Turner, the American historian, concerning the significance of the frontier in American history, I applied the frontier theory to the study of African history.[39] The frontier, in this conception, incorporated religion, trade, militarism, philosophy, food and a whole range of aspects of life from the three fundamental cultures which have shaped African historical and cultural experiences: indigenous African, Asian (Arab) and European (Caucasian). Viewed from this standpoint, religion becomes only one of the many variables which impact on the African in a very complex 'frontier' process which is unending and dynamic.[40] As we have clearly demonstrated, the purveyors of religion in Africa have never limited themselves to importing or introducing mere spiritual or philosophical concepts but a lot more, spanning culture, language, economics, politics, clothing, architecture, food and so on.

The role of religion, particularly Christianity, in nation-building in West Africa is therefore best understood within the context of the 'frontier' in Africa. From the very beginning, Arab and European invaders, explorers, adventurers, traders, and missionaries, reinforced the importance Africans themselves attached to religion by introducing their own faiths, Islam and Christianity. Then, in the colonial period, Christian penetration and status expanded, though in a spirit of tolerance and co-operation with Islam, allowing the latter in the process, to increase its own following in the continent. Finally, in the post-colonial period with religion having thus played an important role in the evolution of these West African colonies into independent states, it continued to exert an even more significant impact on the development of these states.

As I have demonstrated, Christianity's influence on nation-building in West Africa spans religion, education, philosophy, economics, trade, health, infrastructural development and finance. What is clear, however, is that the other religions will not allow Christianity to exercise dominance over the lives of West Africans. Islam is engaged in a fierce competition for converts while traditional African religions doggedly continue to attract the loyalty and devotion of even those avowedly professing to be Muslims and Christians. In order to preserve a healthy and stable balance between the faiths in the post-colonial situation, it seems to me that no faith should have a state monopoly. Even in pre-colonial West Africa, it is clear that when state cults demanded a monopoly from other local cults, this frequently led to social instability. Similarly in the colonial period, the attempt initially by the European colonialists to suppress local cults and Islam only led to hostility, tension and political instability.

All the faiths must now draw lessons from the past to avoid mistakes which could not only deter nation-building but lead to social and political instability. The temptation is great for either Islam or Christianity to seek a monopoly over the state in particular countries, but this would be fraught with danger. The secular state in West Africa, therefore, appears to be the most appropriate constitutional framework in which Christianity or Islam can contribute to nation-building. Whether the country has more Muslim, Christian or traditional African religious followers should therefore make no difference as to the basic constitution of the state.

In a world in which there is ever-growing respect for the fundamental civil liberties of the individual, African political leaders will have to accept the role of Christianity in insisting on respect for human rights. This is not only because their constituencies contain large numbers of Christians or that the Christian world has much to offer towards the development of West African countries, but because upholding and sustaining respect for human rights is intrinsically good for stable and healthy growth.

Christianity definitely has a positive role to play in nation-building in West Africa. The possibilities are enormous for Christianity to make contributions to the spiritual, political and social development of the continent. It must be remembered, however, that because development and growth in Africa should always operate under conditions of the "frontier" Christianity must continue to find ways to live with Islam and traditional African religious beliefs.

Notes

1. R.H. Tawney, *Religion and the rise of capitalism*, with a new introduction by Adam B. Seligman, New Brunswick, New Jersey: Transaction Publishers, 1998 (first published in 1926, New York: Harcourt, Brace and Company); C. Hill, *Irreligion in the Puritan revolution*, London: Queen Mary College, 1974. Max Weber, *The Protestant ethic and the spirit of capitalism*, translated by T. Parsons, with an introduction by A. Giddens, (Routledge classics series), London: Routledge, 2001.

2. J.H. Parry, *The age of reconnaissance: Europe and the wider world 1415–1715*, London: Weidenfeld and Nicolson, 1963.

3. K.S. Latourette, *A short history of the Far East*, New York: Macmillan, 1964.

4. R.R. Palmer, *A history of the modern world*, New York: A.A. Knopf, 2002 (9th ed.), especially chs iv, vi, xiv and the monumental work of Paul Kennedy, *The rise and fall of great powers: Economic change and military conflict from 1500 to 2000*, London: Unwin Hyman.

5. J.E. Goldthorpe, *The sociology of the Third World: Disparity and development*, Cambridge: Cambridge University Press, 1986: chs 3 and 10; E. Burns, *World civilizations*, New York: W.W. Norton, 1974: chs 23 and 31; and P. Mason, *Patterns of dominance*, London: Oxford University Press, 1970: 81–124.

6. Roland Oliver and J.D. Fage, *A short history of Africa*, New York: New York University Press, 1962: 77–91; H.A.R. Gibb, *Mohamedanism*, London: Oxford University Press, 1961.

7. E.W. Bovill, *The golden trade of the Moors*, London: Oxford University Press, 1958; J Spencer Trimingham, *A history of Islam in West Africa*, Oxford: Oxford University Press, 1962; N. Levtzion, *Muslims and chiefs in West Africa: A study of Islam in the Middle Volta Basin in the pre-colonial period*, Oxford: Clarendon Press, 1968; P.F. Moraes Farias, 'Great states revisited, Review article of *Ancient Ghana and Mali* by N. Levtzion, London: Meuthen, 1973 in *Journal of African History* 15 (3), 1974: 470–488.

8. L. Kaba, 'Archers, murketeers and mosquoitos: The Moroccan invasion of the Sudan and the Songhai resistance 1591–1612', *Journal of African History* 22 (4), 1981: 457–476.

9. B.O. Oloruntimehin, *The Segu Tukulor Empire*, London: Longman, 1972; M. Hiskett, *The sword of the truth: The life and times of Shehu Usuman dan Fodio*, New York: Oxford University Press, 1973; M. Klein, *Islam and imperialism in Senegal: Sine-Saloum, 1847–1914*, Edinburgh: Edinburgh University Press, 1968; A.S.K. Forstner, *The conquest of the Western Sudan: A study in French military imperialism*, London: Cambridge University Press, 1969; R.A. Adeleye, *Power and diplomacy in northern Nigeria 1804–1906*:

The Sokoto Caliphate and its enemies, Harlow: Longman, 1971; J.D. Hargreaves, *West Africa partitioned*, 2 vols, London: Macmillan, 1974–1985.

10. S.A. Akintoye, *Revolution and power politics in Yorubaland 1840–93: Ibadan expansion and the rise of Ekitiparapo*, New York: Humanities Press, 1971; T.E. Bowdich, *Mission from Cape Coast Castle to Ashantee*, London: Griffith and Farran, 1873.

11. D. Grant, *The fortunate slave: An illustration of African slavery in the early eighteenth century*, London: Oxford University Press, 1968.

12. The Book of Exodus for example in the Bible confirms the presence of Christianity in West Africa, see J.W. Blake, *European beginnings in West Africa 1454–1578*, London: Longmans, 1937.

13. For the beginnings of Christianity in West Africa, see J.W.Blake, 1937.

14. R. Coupland, *The British anti-slavery movement*, London: F. Cass, 1964; D.B. Davis, *The problem of slavery in Western culture*, Ithaca, New York: Cornell University Press, 1966; E. Williams, *Capitalism and slavery*, Chapel Hill: University of North Carolina Press, 1944.

15. J.F. Ade Ajayi, *Christian missions in Nigeria, 1841–1891: The making of a new elite*, London: Longmans, 1965; E.A. Ayandele, *The missionary impact on modern Nigeria 1842–1914, A political and social analysis*, London: Longmans, 1966.

16. R.L. Delavignette, *Christianity and colonialism*, London: Burns and Oates, 1964.

17. For example in Senegal, see, Delavignette: Ch VI.

18. G. Deveneaux, 'The political and social impact of the colony in northern Sierra Leone 1821–1896', Unpublished PhD dissertation, Boston University, Boston, 1973: chs VII and VIII; M Klein, 1968; A.S.K. Forstner, 1969.

19. D.L. Cruise O'Brien, *The Mourides of Senegal: The political and economic organization of an Islamic brotherhood*, Oxford: Clarendon Press, 1971: 163–304. Delavignette notes a p. 84 that colonial armies favoured Islam: 'Muslim feasts were celebrated by the military who showed little concern for Christian festivals and still less for animistic rituals. It looks as if the colonial armies of all the European countries were haunted by the memory of the Indian mutiny in 1857, which was carried in part by the European officers disregarding or forgetting a prescription in the *Qur'an* that affected their Muslim troops. The watchword of colonial armies was respect for Islam and great importance was attached to securing psychological harmony between the Christian centurion and the Muslim legionary'.

20. H. Brunschwig, *French colonialism: 1871–1914: Myths and realities*, London: Pall Mall Press, 1966; J.A. Hobson, *Imperialism: A study*, London: Allen and Unwin, 1938; M.E. Townsend, *The origins of modern German colonialism: 1871–1885*, New York: Columbia University, 1921.

21. G. Deveneaux, 'Public opinion and colonial policies in the nineteenth century Sierra Leone', *The International Journal of African Historical Studies* 2, 1976: 45–67; F.J.A. Omu, *Press and politics in Nigeria 1888–1937*, London: Longmans, 1978; C. Fyfe, *Africanus Horton, 1835–83: West African scientist and patriot*, New York: Oxford University Press, 1972; H. Lynch, 'The native pastorate controversy and cultural ethnocentrism in Sierra Leone 1871–74', *Journal of African History* 31, 1964: 395–413.

22. J. Suret-Canale, *French colonialism in tropical Africa, 1900–1945*, London: C. Hurst, 1971; M. Crowder, *West Africa under colonial rule*, London: Hutchinson, 1968.

23. Crowder: 198–216.

24. D.L. Summer, *Education in Sierra Leone*, Freetown: Government of Sierra Leone, 1963: 64 notes: 'It is significant that at the beginning of the first Secondary School in Sierra Leone, there should have been representatives from both the colony and the hinterland. This shows that not only healthy contacts had been established with the hinterland by the people of the colony, through the medium of the Church and school, but also that these relations had been reciprocated by the people in the hinterland. Of the fourteen boys admitted from the Fourah Bay Institution, five were from the Gallinas country; three were from Kissy, two from Kent, two were Freetown boys: and one was from Port Loko. These were under the principalship of the Rev Thomas Peyton'. Also, at p. 134, Summer adds, 'In 1900, there were some 31 Protectorate mission schools; 12 were in the Ronietta District, belonging to the Home Frontier and Foreign Missionary Society of the United Brethren Church in America. There were 498 pupils with an average attendance of 391.' See also, C. Fyfe, *A history of Sierra Leone*, London: Oxford University Press, 1962: 128–31; 251–3; 288–294; 317; 318; 327; 353; 358; 359; 405; 408; 435; 498–9. On Bo School see Summer:139; 140; 227; 243; 265. J.R. Cartwright, *Political leadership in Sierra Leone*, London: Croom Helm, 1978: 42 notes the impact on political development in another area which bore directly on the future prospects for persons from the two regions: 'Education in the north was even further behind, with 3291 children in primary schools against 11,466 in the southern provinces. In part this disparity could be attributed to the fact that the southern province had been penetrated earlier by missionaries but it appears also that the Mendes tended to be more receptive to western education, possibly because Islam was less widespread.' Also C Fyfe (ed.), *Sierra Leone inheritance*, London: Oxford University Press, 1964 on pp 304–307 describes the Bo School and at pp 156–157 refers to the prospectus of the CMS Grammar School.

25. Delavignette: 66, 73. A Memmi, *The colonizer and the colonized*, Boston: Beacon Press, 1967.

26. Lamin Sanneh writes in 'Muslim in non-Muslim societies in Africa' in *Christian and Islamic contributions towards the establishment of independent states in Africa* edited by K.W. Bechold and E.J. Tetsch, Tübingen: Laupp and Göbel, 1979: 'Levtzion in his detailed description of Islam in the Middle Volta region of Ghana shows how, in one area, the Muslim clerk found himself in keen competition with the priests of the powerful medicine shrine and unable to match their strength abandoned Islam and joined them. In many other examples, Islam survives only by taking shelter under the buoyancy of traditional religious vitality. It is not so much the flexibility of Islam that we are witnessing as the regenerative capacity of the African religious environment. It is by that factor alone that we can explain the cockeyed phenomenon of Islam seeking to rivet the chains of orthodox conformity on people and also contenting itself with nothing more than a mere lip-service to its tenets'.

27. D. Austin, *Politics in Ghana*, London: Oxford University Press, 1964.

28. Crowder: VII; T Hodgkin, *Nationalism in colonial Africa*, London: Frederick Muller, 1956.
29. J.D. Hargreaves, *Decolonization in Africa*, London: Longman, 1996 (2nd ed).
30. R. Sandbrook, *The politics of Africa's economic stagnation*, Cambridge: Cambridge University Press, 1985; S. George, *A fate worse than debt*, New York: Grove Press, 1988.
31. Ladipo Adamolekun, *Sékou Touré's Guinea*, London: Methuen, 1976: 133, 139.
32. On Nkrumah's Ghana and conflict with the Church, *West Africa*, January 6, 1962: 11; *West Africa*, August 18, 1962: 95 which reports under the heading, 'Ghana Expels Churchmen': 'Ghana Government this week expelled the Archbishop of West Africa, the most Reverend Cecil J. Patterson and the Bishop of Accra, the Right Reverend R.R. Roseheare. In addition it expelled also Mary Dokenoo, the Scottish wife of Mr. Ben Dokenoo. All three had been criticized by the official Ghana papers, the *Ghanaian Times* and *Evening News*. All of them, particularly the Bishop of Accra had condemned some of the activities of the Young Pioneers, shock troops of the CPP and the late president as 'ungodly'. However, in November, the magazine reported that permission had again been given by the Ghanaian government for the Bishop of Accra to return to his diocese: *West Africa*, November 10, 1967: 1251. See also, *Africa Confidential* 17 (24), August, 1962: 2–3 on the religious background, particularly Catholic, of Kwame Nkrumah and other African leaders such as Abbe Youlou, Julius Nyerere and Tom Mboya.
33. A government commission under the late Dr E.T. Mondeh in 1991 made such a recommendation.
34. Sandbrook: 63–82.
35. A. Mazrui, 'The sacred and the secular in east African politics', *Cahiers D'Etudes Africaines* 52 , 1973: 667.
36. Mazrui, 1973.
37. G. Deveneaux, 'The frontier in recent African history', *International Journal of African Historical Studies* 11 (1), 1978: 63–85.
38. Deveneaux, 'Frontier in recent African history': 68.
39. Deveneaux, 'Frontier in recent African history': 77.
40. Deveneaux, 'Frontier in recent African history': 84.

Chapter Eight

Christianity, Nation-Building and National Identity in Ghana: Religious Perspectives

Elom Dovlo

Introduction

During the 1990s, the political organisation of various countries experienced profound changes. West Africa is no exception to this with its strong current towards multi-party parliamentary democracy. In my own country, Ghana, these changes ushered in the Fourth Republic, which in turn inspired many expectations. Such expectations involve a yearning for a new deal for African countries and for Ghana, a new deal of political and economic stability, social cohesion and general prosperity. It is as if we have been offered a second opportunity after Independence to take off. The atmosphere seems different from previous occasions when *coup d'etats* and subsequent republics were seen as a fresh start. This is because the current wind of change is not blowing in isolation but within the context of an international wave of change triggered off with the collapse of the Soviet Union and Socialism. The end of the 20th century and the dawn of the 21st century add a sense of urgency to our desires. It is as if inability to make a breakthrough as a nation would mean being left behind in the 20th century.

To say we have a sense and feeling of a new beginning suggests that independence, which marked our first beginning as a state within internationally recognised boundaries, had not quite succeeded in building a viable nation. However, I would rather say that since nation-building is an ongoing process we cannot declare that in the past no efforts were spared towards this end. We must grant that even genuine attempts at nation-building are bound to involve levels of error that may need to be corrected. As a process, therefore, we can simply say that we have reached a new point, a point at which we can re-assess our achievements after over thirty-five years of independence and at which we must decide what our generation can do to forge ahead more positively. And when we say a new deal, we must not assume that it is something that we passively accept from Western powers or our elected rulers. We have to make the deal ourselves and in so doing provide the basis for even better building efforts by the next generation. It is a task that cannot be finished, but towards which we must not shirk a duty to make invaluable contributions.

It therefore becomes incumbent not only on individuals but also recognised bodies within the country to put their shoulder to this task. Religion is one of the main bases of community and organisation within the country. It therefore has an essential role to play in this task. This means that we must be able to define what nation-building is, what its major concerns are and how religion fits into its scheme in the country. In doing so, in this article, I hope to centre mainly on only three of the multi-faceted aspects of our topic. These relate to nation-building and integration, economic development and education. Along the line, I shall draw on international historical examples to make the case that the religions of Ghana can with full confidence also contribute towards the process of nation-building.

The Nation as an Integrated Unit

Nation is a term that has several definitions. The main definition and European understanding of the term has ethnic overtones. The Chambers Twentieth Century dictionary renders a nation as 'a body of people marked by common descent, language, culture or historical traditions'. Thus, the Scots, the Welsh, the English and the Irish in the United Kingdom have regarded themselves as nations. Though the Europeans reserved the word nation for its 'ethnic groups' and 'tribes' for African ethnic groups, one would say that the definition of nation may apply to the Ashanti, Ewe and Gonja in Ghana. These are ethnic groups which have been thrown together by history and, rather than blending together, have tended to look inward for their survival. The consequence of this attitude has often been rivalry and disunity within the country. Indeed, one of the banes of true nationhood in West Africa is ethnic divisions. The havoc that inter-ethnic rivalries pose cannot be denied as they have exploded into violence on several occasions. Though the various ethnic groups may not crave for the fragmentation of the state, there is a subtle struggle by the major ethnic groups to have a stranglehold on power to the disadvantage of other groups and this divides the nation.

Clearly, a people living within internationally accepted boundaries do not make a nation. For when we talk about a nation we mean more than a superficial common identity of being Ghanaian. It takes more to make a nation than simply being thrown together. A nation in the African context must reflect a real unity of the body politic within the territory, bonded not by rules and constitutions alone but by a feeling of unity, fellowship, a state of peaceful co-existence, the spirit of common purpose, mutual reliance and goodwill, all geared towards a common goal and the preservation of that goal.

It is within the context of this definition that the operative word nation-building becomes relevant. For this reason, I agree wholly with Gaba that

> a fundamental concern of Nation-building therefore is with integration ... Nation-building implies integration, national in-tegration, territorial integration, value integration, ruler – ruled integration. It is the maintenance or establishment of social order within territorial framework.[1]

In other words, the quest of the pre-fabricated states of West Africa such as Ghana should be how they can be turned into united progressive states in which people can live a human life; be able to live in peace and with a sufficient material basis through sound integration.

Various sociologists have noted the integrative power of religion. This, it is acknowledged, is mostly the case when a single religion finds adherence among a people. Unfortunately, apart from the ethnic centred nature of traditional religion, we know that religion in Ghana is pluralistic. Moreover, various religions have become what Assimeng refers to as 'surrogate tribal units'.[2] At times also political affiliations are made along religious lines. The situation is made complex because of a North-South divide across the West African region that associates the North with Islam and the South with Christianity. What Trimingham calls 'Ethno-religious cleavage' has become part of national politics.[3] This use of religion to create factions within the state naturally does not augur well for integration. How then can the various religions contribute effectively to the process of national integration?

In response to this question, I wish to handle the discussion by raising three broad issues. The first relates to the issue of the integration of persons as individual citizens; the second, the integration of people of various ethnic groups and the third, the integration of people of various religious persuasions through the forging of religious tolerance.

I will raise the first of these three issues rather briefly in an exploratory manner hoping that it will invoke further discussion. By the integration of individuals to have a sense of self identity that binds them to the nation, I wish to exhume for post mortem the old argument that religious pluralism leads to disintegration not only of communities but also of individual personalities. In our African and Ghanaian context it has often been argued that Islam and Christianity (especially the latter) in Africa sowed seeds of doubt in the African 'self identity' by demonising the African's heritage. There is therefore the need for the recovery of the African self in whatever religion the African belongs so that 'self identity' becomes the common denominator of various religious people that can be stimulated towards their common good.

Probably the quest for the inculturation of Christianity in Africa may enable this. But on the part of Islam it may be argued that most scholars feel that its present drive is to rid itself of its African elements and therefore it is moving away from this common denominator. However, I doubt if what Lamin Sanneh refers to as the 'domestication' of Islam in Africa can ever be fully reversed. For while scholarship seems to a assume that there is a process of reform in Islam that seeks to rid it of 'mixing', recent investigations reveal that the process is not that simple and it has been revealed over and over again that Ghanaian students who study in the Middle East are confronted with the dilemma of projecting themselves as Muslims while retaining their cultural identity as Ghanaians. For example, those who bear

Arab names are asked if they have no authentic Ghanaian names. The issue of 'self identity' therefore remains to be fully explored.

For my second and third discussion (which I will combine), I refer to an argument I advanced in the early 1990s at a meeting of the West African Association of Theological Institutions at Cape-Coast in a paper entitled 'Religious pluralism and Nation-building'. At that meeting I was criticised for being idealistic. However, it is our ideals that inform reality. I also think my argument calls for believers to practice their faith while those of my critics are inadvertently insisting that some doctrinal beliefs and teaching cannot be observed in practice. In that case it will be the religions rather that would be idealistic.

My contention is that the impact of social transformation should be an adequate genuine test for religion so it should be possible taking into account the universal claims of most of the religions in West Africa to foster and facilitate integration of different peoples. The Christian faith teaches that 'There is neither Jew nor Gentile, slave nor free, male or female for you are all one in Christ'. (Gal 3:28, cf. Col 3:11). This implies that there should be no discrimination among Christians on the basis of ethnic identity. In other words, to use current parlance, tribal blood should not be thicker than baptismal water.

Islam also upholds the notion of the equality and brotherhood of all believers. This position is reinforced by Qu'ran chapter 49:13:

> O people, we created you from male and female and made you into clans and tribes so that you may know each other. Verily, the most honoured among you in the sight of Allah is the most pious of you.

It may be argued that these are injunctions to be blind to race, colour and tribe. In both the case of Islam and Christianity it may be maintained, though not without some difficulty, that the peace and unity envisaged here is meant only for the body of believers. Even if this should be the case, a true observance of this injunction cannot but lead to respect for people of other ethnic groups who may not share one's faith. I cannot simply see how a Ewe Christian may respect a Gonja Christian without that respect eventually being extended to all Gonja Christians and without that respect eventually being extended to all Gonja as part of God's creation. If the principle is applied, it would mean that with time we could have nations where negative ethnic identities are reduced. I must emphasize that by this I do not advocate the erasure of ethnic identity but the eradication of its prejudices and negative tendencies, on the one hand, while stressing on the other that the positive assets of various groups may be harnessed for the common good. This will naturally lead to the sort of integration that is fundamental to a sound social, political and economic life.

I acknowledge that this is not an easy task, since the various religious bodies must first put their own houses in order. First of all, they must eschew all internal ethnic rivalries, as there are ethnic cleavages within some religious bodies. In an earlier article, I noted how some Christians have attitudes towards northern converts in the south that may be considered to be mean and derogatory.[4] As Ghanaian Christians, we are acutely aware that ethnic divisions often rear their ugly head in leadership elections in the church, at times even leading to threats of schism. Often churches sweep ethnic problems under the mat, but probably it is time that the whole question of ethnicity and the church is discussed and addressed. This problem is not peculiar to Christianity. Ghanaian Muslims are organised in ethnic enclaves in the south and rivalries, especially for leadership, often operate along these lines.

If religion should be able to help effect the integration and unity of the people of our countries in their ethnic diversity, then charity must begin at home. Religious ideals of tolerance must be made concrete in practical situations. This means that the various religions must take it upon themselves both individually and in dialogue with each other to inculcate in their adherents a sense of nationhood. They must encourage and educate their members to look forward to a common social, economic and political destiny. We must realise that once we are bound territorially, such a destiny is unavoidable. The question that we must seek to answer is whether it is better to build a good common destiny together or to remain adrift on an ocean of woes because of differences in faith and ethnicity.

Forging the essential unity can be done by the various religious traditions by engendering trust among their members of various ethnic groups on the one hand and between the various religions themselves on the other. Trust is an essential element in nation-building especially where diverse people are thrown together within the same territory as is the case with most African countries. Thompson, tracing some classical thought on nation-building, posits the role of the Romans in antiquity as exemplary nation builders and, among other virtues, says that the Romans themselves believed that nations grow and achieve greatness due to 'fides' – trust, in the sense of keeping faith, keeping one's word in one's relationship with one's fellow human beings and in the sense of implicit belief that all are governed by the same code of conduct.[5] This is possible only if there is a high level of dialogue and consensus, and that is only certain if religions encourage, uphold and defend democratic principles. I want to reiterate in this context that the forces that make for integration may not be laws but the voluntary inculcation of values, such as trust, faith, consensus-building and shared values. This is an area in which religion can wield much influence.

Religion and Socio-economic Development

Development and modernisation have been seen, at times narrowly, as the essence of nation-building. Both, however, are also allied with a world of increasing secularisation. As Jules-Rosette points out, citing Shiner, most social scientists argue that development and modernisation are not reconcilable with religion. It is assumed that the structures of modern industrialisation trigger religious change which bring about '1. Desacralization, or decline in the role of religion in defining the social order, 2. The process of structural differentiation by which religious and secular institutions become distinct and autonomous and 3. The transposition of religious knowledge and activities in the social domain'.[6]

Can religion therefore play a role in this context of the building process? My response is that in the African situation and in Ghana in particular we believe that religion still wields much influence in both modern politics and indeed the economic life of the people.

Religion wields much power in the politics of self identity and the maintenance of political power. For example, in spite of attempts at secular ideologies, Kwame Nkrumah had to rely on religious symbolism to promote his image as a leader. We are aware that many politicians turn to religious leaders and functionaries for prayers and more practical spiritual aid often to maintain their hold on power. In fact, it is well known that during the Acheampong era in Ghana there was a proliferation of new religious movements of all shades because of his personal search for security. Generally, contrary to the above position, westernisation and commercialisation rather than bringing about the decline of religion in Ghana engendered new waves of spirituality, even if not strictly on orthodox lines.

In Ghana, most governments try to sell their policies of change and modernisation through the medium of the pulpit. In effect this amounts not only to a recognition of the informing and educating medium of religion but also the sanctity that may be attached to validity and veracity of messages transmitted through the channels of religious organisation.

Our electoral process on several occasions has also demonstrated that religion cannot be ignored. It has been recognised over and over again that there are religious constituencies that must be lobbied especially at times of election. It will not be an over-exaggeration to say that the religious communities in Ghana have virtually formed themselves into security communities, similar to the ethnic groups as far as political matters are concerned. The last elections in Ghana, for instance, generated a lot of religious controversy. From the superficial to doctrinal debates, the elections were coloured by religious considerations. Party songs were popular hymns and choruses with political lyrics; various religious groups were courted and a whole national argument was generated on the fear of God and the Love of God. After all has been said and done, the Ghanaian politician knows that the average person retains a level of religiosity even if it is folk religiosity and he seeks to exploit this to attain his ends. He is aware that his constituency is also made out of congregations, Muslim, Christian, Traditional, Hindu, Buddhist, and so on. The question is whether the religious persons and organisations are ready to let the process of governance and nation-building end at casting their vote or if they wish to assist in such governance and nation-building on the basis of their religious persuasions.

Since religion undergirds the cultural values of a people and it is a medium of organising the people, it cannot stand by and let the regeneration process pass by without adding its wisdom. Often this has been the case as governments have a narrow concept of nation-building that sees the process simply in terms of developing physical infrastructures. They think only in terms of external and quantitative development ignoring the human value and qualitative aspects of development or at best seeing them as appendages to their plans. In the particular case of building the economy I totally agree with the following comment of E.B. Idowu:

> In a building, the foundation is of vital, paramount importance. If the foundation is not properly laid – and that refers to the ground on which it rests, to planning, workmanship and choice of materials – however artistically and skilfully executed the superstructure, it will sooner or later fall into ruins. This is a point to be watched with particular reference to nation-building, which is more of a spiritual undertaking than it is of material things.[7]

In agreeing with Idowu, I do not mean that religions should draw up economic strategies, but that they should provide the right philosophy to underpin such strategies. To put it another way, they should contribute a vision for the socio-economic development that would enhance the process of nation-building. This vision must address what development should mean in the context of our times, our country and our culture. Certainly, fundamental differences due to religious pluralism may suggest that this would be an impossible task. But it is difficult to accept that religions are so diametrically opposed to each other that they cannot reach consensus on anything. Actually, values and this-worldly soteriological goals are often similar (at least conceptually) though the means to their attainment and contextual descriptions and expressions may vary. If this is the case, then it is possible that beyond mutual respect, religions in dialogue can look out for common values that seek the improvement of humanity and strive to arrive at a confluence of such values as a common vision for the nation. They may then urge their adherents to apply the means they (the religions) individually teach towards the realisation of such a vision.

Further, it is also well known that in Ghana and West Africa, certain occupations and professions are associated with various religious commitments. Organised religion can therefore serve as a medium to sensitise such people to new philosophies of nation-building along economic lines by encouraging them to let go of negative practices that impair the economy while inculcating positive attitudes that would enhance it. We all know that religion can enhance the work ethics of people. This has been exemplified for instance by the protestant ethics which enjoined hard work and prohibited all manners of extravagance and frivolity, instead advocating thrift. This, as Max Weber maintains, was the basis of European capitalism. Various scholars have also given the example of Japan where post war economic success has been partially attributed to the inculcation of transcendental values that they used to underpin their industries. We are also aware that one of the main reasons for success of new religious movements in Japan has been to instil a sense of diligence and fidelity in business affairs as part of their moral code. This augured well for the new religious movements and also the entire country.

Education and Nation-Building

It will be difficult for various religions to make an impact in any attempt to contribute towards nation-building without sensitising the people of the country through education. By education, I mean more than the continued contribution to the accumulation of 'the three Rs' by Ghanaian children, though this is still necessary to nation-building. Beyond this, however, I believe that there should be a process of sensitising the government, adherents, and indeed the formal and informal educational systems that prevail today. It means that religious bodies must take the initiative of spreading their vision to government through sponsored seminars, lobbies and public meetings. They must use their normal process of creating awareness among their members to the task of nation-building and help them to inculcate the virtues they require. Then they must try and influence not simply the curricula but also the mode of education in the country to enable a better foundation for the next generation that would take over and continue the task of nation-building.

Conclusion

The task of nation-building is not simply a mundane task as may be assumed by some. Essentially it is a task that demands a high level of faith. Faith in a system engenders voluntary effort towards the realisation of goals. Where such goals are seen within a religious framework, faith fosters hopes and aspirations even in seemingly mundane matters. The values that the religious person strives for may be elevated above the secular framework and given a more enduring and sacral dimension through religion. That is why religion is important to the task of nation-building: it can inform, transform and strengthen social, economic and political life as well as enhance the cultural values of the nation.

Yet in our religiously plural country, religious traditions have to harness all resources towards this task to be up to it. This calls first of all for individual examination of the task and secondly for dialogue towards the common good of the nation. This should not be interpreted as a selective process of choosing one religious tradition as having the exclusive vision for the nation. Such a view would be unrealistic. Rather, it is time for the various faiths to share their ideals and ideas and generate a competitive spirit of how best to live by these towards the realisation of the nation-building goals of this generation. Each must give the best it has to offer in a spirit of tolerance and understanding.

It is possible for various religions to work together to build a nation. Already, in Ghana we are experiencing an ecumenical spirit in political and social matters. When there was a peace march at the height of our election campaigns in 1992, it was led by clergymen of the Christian faith and leaders of the Baha'i faith among others. During the ethnic conflict in the north which occurred in 1993, various religions came together to issue a joint statement calling for peace. In recent times, for instance, the Ahmadiyya Mission in Ghana has been partners with the Christian Council of Ghana and the Catholic Secretariat in addressing the matters of national interest. On the social front we find Muslim Women groups working closely with counterpart Christian groups in many charitable works. At the local congregation level, recently a church in Tema sponsored a peace seminar addressed by people of different faiths. What we must note is that often such social collaboration is initiated by government or secular non-governmental organisations to serve their own interest. If such co-operation is possible, then the avenues it has created must be explored further through a type of dialogue that penetrates to levels where serious discussions are conducted among a variety of religious groups on the future of Ghana.

Notes

1. C.R. Gaba, 'The African traditional way of nation-building', *Orita: Ibadan Journal of Religious Studies* 9 (1), 1975: 7–8.
2. M. Assimeng, 1991, 'Historical legacy, political realities and tensions in Africa', in Lutheran World Federation, *Encounters of religions in African cultures*, Geneva: Lutheran World Federation: 6.
3. J.S. Trimingham, *The influence of Islam upon Africa*, London: Longman, 1968: 115.
4. Elom Dovlo, 'Religious pluralism and Christian attitudes', *Trinity Journal of Church and Theology* 1 (2), 1991: 40–52.

5.   L.A. Thompson, 'Some classical thoughts on nation-building,' *Orita: Ibadan Journal of Religious Studies* 8 (2), 1975: 114–123.

6.   W. Benetta Jules-Rosette, 'Tradition and continuity in African religions: The case of New Religious Movements', in J.K. Olupona (ed.), *African Traditional Religions in contemporary times*, New York: Paragon House, 1991: 149–166.

7.   E.B. Idowu, 'An introduction: Nation-building', *Orita: Ibadan Journal of Religious Studies* 8 (2), 1974: 89.

Chapter Nine

Christian Missions and Nation-Building in Ghana: An Historical Evaluation

Robert Addo-Fenning

Introduction

In 1454 a Papal Bull granted Portugal the monopoly of the Guinea trade with an exhortation to proselytise the native population. In compliance with this exhortation the Portugtuese carried out their first act of conversion when they baptised the King of Fetu (in the Cape Coast hinterland) in 1503. The effort at proselytisation was not sustained, and by 1576 the fitful endeavours of the Portuguese had come to an end![1] Subsequent efforts by the French Capuchins at Axim and Komenda (1638–1640), the Moravian Mission at Accra and Elmina (1737–1773) and the Society for the Propagation of the Gospel (1752–1800) achieved insignificant results. By the end of the eighteenth century Christianity had made hardly any impact on Ghana.[2]

In the early decades of the nineteenth century a host of European missionary societies arrived in Ghana to resume proselytising activities. Leading the field was the Basel Mission which began its work at Osu in Accra. By the turn of the century the Basel Mission was the dominant mission in the Eastern Region with stations at Akropong-Akuapem (1843), Aburi (1847), Krobo-Odumase (1849), Kyebi (1861) Anum (1865) Ada (1867) Begoro (1875) and Abetifi (1877).

The Wesleyan Mission had its main base at Cape Coast (1835), from where it extended its activities inland to Dunkwa and Manso. By 1912, it was the leading mission in the Central Region. Sharing the region with the Wesleyans were the Roman Catholic, the Society for the Propagation of the Gospel and the American Methodist Episcopal Zion Missions.[3] The Seventh Day Adventist Mission established its headquarters in Sekondi (Western Region) in 1898. In the Volta Region the main missionary society was the Bremen (North German) Missionary Society. Its first station was established at Peki in 1847. By 1893 it had six stations in the region including those at Keta (1853) Waya (1856) and Ho (1857).

Asante and Northern Ghana were without mission stations by 1900. In the former, the Wesleyan efforts of 1841–1850 produced no satisfactory results and the region was completely abandoned in 1872. As for Northern Ghana, official hostility prevented the establishment of a missionary presence there before the formal declaration of the region as a British Protectorate in 1901.

The missionary movement has been described as 'a child of the Evangelical revival' which swept 18th century Europe, especially in the last decade.[4] Members of this Evangelical revival, known as the Puritans and the Pietists in Great Britain and on the Continent respectively,[5] held the conviction that God spoke directly to each one of his children 'in the events' of their lives, 'in the words of the Bible, and especially in (their) feelings' as they prayed and read the Bible. They also believed in divine intervention in their lives to correct them. Based on these beliefs, they emphasised a life of stricter puritanical behaviour 'than that of their non-pietist neighbours' as well as of 'intensive individual piety and Bible study'.[6]

To bring their dream to fruition, the Pietists attempted to establish in their native land communities that would be 'like islands in the broad seas of their non-pietist neighbours'. In such communities they hoped to live their lives outside the ambit of state control.[7] The separatism of the Pietists became a source of annoyance to many European governments and to escape discrimination and persecution, many pietist groups migrated to places 'where they could live in freedom and without persecution'.[8]

Missionary Work in Ghana

Many of the missionaries who worked in Ghana in the nineteenth century were natives of Württemberg with pietist connections. Württemberg typified the central European traditional village, largely self-sufficient in food and versatile in village crafts such as carpentry, basketry and masonry. The 'Württembergers' were fully committed to a life close to the soil and their ambition rose to establish in Ghana prosperous farming and industrial communities firmly rooted in the Christian faith.[9]

At the headquarters of the Basel Mission in Akropong-Akuapem, a Christian community was established on mission land as early as 1843. It comprised European missionaries and about six West Indian families (numbering twenty-four) besides others such as Clerk, Robertson, John Rochester and his sister, Anna Rochester. In September 1854, the Basel Mission established another Christian community of thirty persons at Abokobi on land bought by the mission about 1844. The settlers were mainly poll-tax resisters fleeing British bombardment of Osu. Plans to reinforce the settlement with a colony of German Christian farmers and craftsmen were aborted by the death of Zimmermann's colleague Steinhauser, in 1857.[10] In Akyem Abuakwa the Basel Mission bought land for the resettlement of converts from the 1860s.[11] By 1889, all Christians of Asiakwa and Sadwumase were living on mission land. At Kyebi all Christians 'apart from a few Christian women married to heathen husbands' had relocated their homes on mission land.[12]

These suburban Christian settlements, variously known as 'Salem', 'Mission', or 'Oburoni Krom' (white man's town), were intended to insulate the mission's 'fledgling' converts from heathenish contamination. By the 1890s Salems with their distinctive architectural designs and well-laid streets had become noticeable landmarks on the missionary landscape of the Eastern Region. In the Central Region, the Wesleyans also established at least one self-supporting Christian community (Beulah) near Cape Coast between 1842 and 1856.[13]

Agriculture formed a vital part of missionary work in Ghana. Indeed, 'the first missionary command' was: 'Be fruitful and multiply, and fill the earth and subdue it'.[14] This biblical injunction was understood to mean the right of every human being 'to possess land, to raise a family and build a homestead'.[15] Both the Wesleyan and Basel Missions encouraged their converts to become economically self-reliant by engaging in agricultural activity. To this end they introduced a new range of cash and food crops to members of their congregations.

The Wesleyans ran coffee and cotton plantations at Dominase and

Abura in the Central Region in the early 1840s. In 1842, T.B. Freeman purchasing F. Swanzy's coffee and cotton plantation near Cape Coast called 'Napoleon' and re-named it Beulah. Until 1857, when Freeman resigned as head of the Wesleyan Mission, Beulah flourished as an agriculture training centre for Wesleyan Christian farmers.[16]

Like the Wesleyans, the Basel missionaries encouraged the cultivation of cash and food crops by their converts. The West Indian colonists recruited from Jamaica for evangelical work at Akropong-Akuapem in 1843 were under obligation to promote agricultural activity. Under the terms of their recruitment, the mission undertook to provide them with houses 'as well as lands for gardens' on which they were to 'work at least one day of the week'.[17] Accordingly the West Indian recruits brought with them fruits such as mangoes, pears and oranges, as well as potential cash crops like tobacco and coffee. David Rochester, one of the recruits, introduced an edible variety of cocoyam into the country, which soon became a leading staple in the people's diet.[18]

The cultivation of coffee and mangoes spread rapidly among Christian congregations in the Eastern Region. By the end of 1864, the school farm of the Kyebi Boarding School had 500 coffee trees. The trees numbered between 600 and 800 in 1867 and yielded 200 pounds of coffee. Christians and non-Christians alike cultivated small coffee farms for themselves and by 1869, 'every big village' in Akyem was reported to be growing some coffee. Mango trees were also to be found growing in many places.[19]

Another new crop promoted by the Basel Missionaries was cocoa. Johannes Hass, a trained agriculturist unsuccessfully attempted to nurse cocoa seedlings imported from Surinam in 1857. Bishop Auer's imports from Cape Palmas the following year appear to have fared better and by 1861, about 10 small cocoa trees were reported to be growing on the Mission's farm at Akropong.[20] Only one tree survived by August 1863 and from this tree the first ripe pods were harvested by J.J. Laing and distributed to other mission stations.[21] A small cocoa plantation at Akropong survived the departure of Laing from the country in 1868.[22] In 1879, a Basel Mission-trained locksmith, employed as a seaman, smuggled into the country a few pods of cocoa from the Spanish island of Fernando Po. His cocoa plantation at Mampong-Akuapem furnished a quantity of pods that were supplied to prospective cocoa farmers at the cost of £1.00 per pod.[23]

By the turn of the century, the cocoa industry had spread through New

Dwaben into Akyem Abuakwa. Some of the earliest seeds planted in the state were from pods imported from the Cameroon or West Indies in 1890 by the Mission and distributed to Akyem farmers at 2/6d (25p) per pod.[24] Governor Nathan was 'glad to see ... that there was a good deal of cocoa plantations' in Akyem Abuakwa as he passed through Kukurantumi on his way to Kyebi in February 1901.[25] By 1903, cocoa was already 'bringing much money to the people of ...Akim ...'[26]

Besides agriculture, the Christian Missions encouraged their converts to take to trade. The Basel Mission, for example, showed the way by establishing a Basel Mission Trading Factory at Christiansborg in 1855 to buy agricultural produce: coffee, rubber and cotton. Similar trading establishments were set up at Anum and Ho. The Basel Mission's trading establishments provided a ready market for the produce of Christian converts. In 1864, for instance, the Mission arranged shipment to Liverpool of 440 cwt of cotton grown in the Trans-Volta area.[27] The example of the Mission encouraged many a convert to take to private trade as retailers or brokers for Accra-based European firms.

Agriculture and trade were but only two dimensions of missionary work. As declared by the Rev E. Schrenk in 1865, missionary work was a package including 'industrial schools or shops, schools and preaching'.[28] The potential of 'the school' as a nursery for Christian converts had been recognized early in the history of missionary work. As early as 1529, the Portuguese attempted to set up a school at Elmina.[29] When the Dutch opened a school at Elmina in the 1640s, their purpose was 'to teach children to read, to pray and to live pious lives'.[30] The Rev Thomas Thompson, Anglican Chaplain at Cape Coast, also started a school in the 1750s.

By 1844 the Basel Mission was running a school at Akropong-Akuapem. The Wesleyans had schools in 18 towns mainly in the Central Region and also at Accra and Winneba.[31] The North German (Bremen) Mission also established its first school at Peki in 1847.[32] By 1850, when the Gold Coast Colony became independent of Sierra Leone, the main educational effort was coming from the Wesleyan and Basel Missions. Between them the two Missions had about 1,000 pupils in their schools.[33]

Kimble had emphasised that the main purpose of Christian missionary education was to propagate the Christian faith in Ghana.[34] In the early days of evangelization the Christian missions had relied heavily on public (street) preaching to win adult souls. In 1877, for example, the Rev David

Asante of the Basel Mission at Kyebi, between himself and his Catechists, travelled 190 days preaching in 50 towns and villages in Akyem Abuakwa.[35] The results of such exertions, however, remained incommensurately small up to the late 1870s.[36] Street preaching was little patronised. An audience of 10 people was a good attendance. Not infrequently there were no listeners at all.[37] Most free-born adults showed little interest in Christianity and often demanded pecuniary inducement as a condition of becoming Christians.[38]

From about 1868, the Basel missionaries in Akyem Abuakwa began to focus attention on two main target groups: bondsmen and school pupils. Slaves and pawns were bought from bondage by individual missionaries and liberated after working for their benefactors for an agreed period of time. Some were lent money from the Basel Mission's Emancipation Fund to purchase their freedom. The beneficiaries almost invariably became converts to Christianity.[39] Indiscriminate conversion of royal slaves provoked the hostility of the Abuakwa political authorities, culminating in a church-state controversy that led to the arrest, trial and exile of Okyenhene Amoako Atta I to Lagos in 1880.[40]

It was school pupils who held out the highest hope of victory for the Christian Missions. In 1866, 19 of the 26 pupils enrolled at the Kyebi Primary Boarding School were baptised Christians.[41] In 1887, 190 out of 330 members of the Kyebi congregation were children; at Apapam 50 out of a congregation of 87 were children; while at Asiakwa 89 out of a congregation of 150 were children.[42] The pupils were not only available for conversion; they were also used as part-time evangelists. A discerning, un-named *Okomfoo* (fetish-priest) of Kyebi importuned the Kyebi Court in 1867 to close down the Kyebi school because its pupils were 'spreading the seed' during their vacations.[43] At the end of the school year of 1886, the 18 pupils of the Kyebi Boarding School undertook 'a 17-day preaching tour of West Akim.'[44] It was to insulate the young fledgling Christians from pagan influences that the Basel Mission conceived the idea of boarding schools in the late 1850s.

The curriculum of the Christian mission schools provided for academic, moral and industrial training. For their intellectual development, primary and middle school children were exposed to a wide range of academic subjects: General Geography, Natural History, World History, Greek, English, Arithmetic, Geometry, Local Languages, Spelling, Music (harmonium playing) and memorization of proverbs and songs.[45] A high academic performance was expected of the pupils and the less academically-gifted ones either dropped out of school or were expelled for failing their examinations.[46]

The moral development of the pupils was ensured by the study of Biblical History, religious instruction and strict discipline. Misconduct or lateness was severely punished either by flogging or by expulsion. In 1885, for example, two pupils were expelled from the Begoro Middle Boarding School for misbehaviour, one of them for drunkenness on the occasion of his mother's death.[47]

Christian mission schools provided agriculture and limited industrial training for their pupils. The White Fathers opened a school and carpentry workshop at Navrongo in 1907 with 26 youths. The Basel Mission made agricultural, industrial and manual work an essential part of their education. Indeed for Kimble, the Mission's 'most original contribution' to this country's educational system was its combination of 'practical work with book-learning'.[48]

Pupils of the Akyem Boarding Schools at Begoro and Kyebi spent at least two hours a day working on their schools' coffee and maize farms, on their school buildings, on roads and streets in the Salem, or on rainy days, on sewing. By 1877, older boys were still making their own clothes.[49] Academically weak pupils who were unable to continue their education at the Middle School, were given opportunity to learn a trade.[50] C.H. Armitage, Chief Commissioner, Northern Territories, privately invited the Basel Mission to open a 'factory' at Tamale for 'training trade apprentices'.[51]

Meaning of 'Nation'

In the eighteenth century, a German pastor and philosopher, Johann Gottfried Herder (1744–1803) argued that every people had their own distinctive spirit and genius which they expressed through their culture and language.[52] From the time of the French Revolution and the Napoleonic Wars, groups of Europeans began to view themselves as separate from others. Such groups sought to establish themselves as separate, autonomous political entities based on their perceived cultural unity. The emerging political societies possessing 'real or imagined cultural unity manifesting itself especially in a common language, history and territory',[53] came to be described as 'nations'. Historically then, the modern nation, or nation-state, developed out of certain objective conditions among which were language, history and culture. Their emergence was a consequence of conscious efforts by their citizens to turn their cultural unity into a political reality by ensuring that their territorial and state boundaries coincided.

An historical evaluation of Christianity's contribution to nation-building in Ghana ought to focus on the ways in which the activities of the Christian Missions contributed, in the long-term, to the process of converting the multiple 'ethnic nationalisms' of the past into the single Ghanaian nationalism of to-day. It must attempt to show how Christianity prepared the Ghanaian youth morally and intellectually, to deal with challenges of twentieth century nationalism.

Christianity and Nation-Building

Christianity's greatest contribution to the development of the Ghanaian nation was in the sphere of socio-cultural integration. By the first half of the twentieth century, Christian congregations existed in every nook and corner of Ghana. The Presbyterian Church, (formerly Basel Mission), boasted a total congregation of over 8,000 in Akyem Abuakwa in 1926. The Wesleyan (Methodist) Church had 18,000 converts by 1912.[54] The Christian congregations, though they constituted a small percentage of the country's population, became the yeast that slowly leavened the whole lump, championing and propagating new values, attitudes, beliefs, habits and new notions of discipline.

The Christian community waged war on traditional cultural norms and practices that they deemed to be inconsistent with Christian morality. The new moral code propagated by Christianity frowned on moral laxity of all kinds: sexual permissiveness, polygamy, alcoholism, gambling and loose living. Converts to Christianity adopted monogamy. Basel Mission Evangelist, Emmanuel Yaw Boakye, father of Nana Sir Ofori Atta I and Dr J.B. Danquah, gave up four of his five wives on becoming a Christian.[55] Ordinance marriage was gradually substituted for the traditional form of marriage, an expensive affair that was an important factor in rural indebtedness.[56]

A high moral tone was set within the Christian community through the firmness with which acts of immorality were punished. The Church spared no one: leaders, members of congregations, school teachers and pupils. Fornication, drunkenness and adultery were punished with expulsion or suspension. German Missionary, the Rev Baum, was suspended from missionary work at Gyadam on a charge of allowing a woman to sleep in his room for four nights.[57] In the 1870s, several teachers and catechists were dismissed or suspended for adultery.[58] School pupils were expelled for drunkenness at relatives' funerals.[59] Fines were imposed for disobedience of presbyters and for gambling.[60] Abstention from alcohol, the ban on trade in spirits and ordinance marriages saved many Christians from being placed in pawn as a result of indebtedness;[61] while Christian marriages introduced a significant modification in the traditional pattern of inheritance of property.[62]

Christianity also helped to generate a new sense of egalitarianism, through the biblical message of equality before the Creator and through its relentless fight against slavery and pawning. Converts of slave origins were admitted to membership of the presbytery and given self-esteem.[63] The new self-esteem was given its clearest expression at the Kyebi Boarding School in 1876 when an ex-slave pupil, ordered by another pupil from a royal family to fetch water for the dining table, retorted: '*Kosaw nsu bra afei yen nyinaa yé pé*' (You go and fetch water for the table. Now we are all equal).[64]

The emancipation of slaves and pawns in which Christianity played a crucial role fostered a veritable social revolution. Hundreds of emancipated slaves and pawns from all over the country were re-united with their families. In Akyem Abuakwa an estimated 1000–2000 liberated pawns returned to their families.[65] Many of the liberated slaves became Christians 'out of gratitude to God'.[66] At Kyebi the first leader of the congregation, Joe Bosompem, brought most of the ex-slaves that he had inherited from his uncle to live with him at the Salem where they were given lessons in reading.[67] Alien ex-slaves who did not return to their people, became domiciled in other parts of the country and gradually became culturally assimilated to the local community.[68] The abolition and emancipation of slaves and pawns marked the first step in the progressive loss of social prestige and economic power by the traditional ruling elite, and in the evolution of a new social structure. Even more significant was the opportunity which emancipation afforded the ex-slave children to receive education. Barely six months after the Slave Emancipation Laws were promulgated, the Revs Asante and Mohr reported that they had had to turn away twenty ex-slave children from the Kyebi Boarding School for want of places. They asked for more schools to be opened.[69] For the first time in 1882, the list of candidates from the Kyebi Primary Boarding School being considered for admission to the Akropong Middle School included an ex-slave boy from Salaga, John Ayebinim, whose fees the Basel Mission offered to pay as he had no relatives.[70]

Until the 1852 Education Ordinance, the Wesleyans in the West and the Basel Mission in the East were the chief providers of education.[71] By 1858, the Wesleyans had 29 day schools (most of them mixed), spread along the sea-board from Dixcove to Prampram with a total enrolment of 1130. The Basel Mission had 13 day Schools and 4 Boarding Schools in Christiansborg, Aburi, and Akropong Districts. The total enrolment was 250 with boys and girls enrolled in separate schools. As against 42 schools run by the two Christian Missions, the Government had about 10.[72] By 1881 the Basel, Wesleyan, Bremen, and Catholic Missions owned 136 out of the existing 139 schools in the country. The Mission Schools between them enrolled 4,500 odd pupils as against 507 enrolled by the 3 Government schools. They also employed about 200 teachers as against 16 by the Government.[73]

It was again the Christian Missions which led the way in the provision of higher education. By 1913, the Government did not own a single Secondary School in the country.[74] Mfantsipim School (1876) and St Nicholas Grammar School (1910) were owned by the Wesleyan and Anglican Missions respectively.[75] Until Mfantsipim was established, post-primary education could only be obtained overseas.[76] The only institution providing formal training for teachers in the country by the turn of the century was the Akropong Akuapem Seminary owned by the Basel Mission. Other Missions relied on external examinations for certificated teachers.[77]

The campaign for expanded opportunities for post-primary education in the late nineteenth and early twentieth centuries was led by enlightened, public-spirited Ghanaians including mission-educated ones. John Mensah-Sarbah and Egyir-Asaam, pioneer students of the Wesleyan High School at Cape Coast, helped to found private secondary schools in Cape Coast.[78] In Accra, educated Ghanaians founded the Accra Grammar School in 1905 with the Rev S.R.B. Attoh Ahuma as principal.[79] In the hinterland, the initiative of mission-educated schools was also very much in evidence. At the instance of the Akyem Abuakwa Scholars' Union (founded in 1916), Nana Sir Ofori Atta 1 and J.B. Danquah, products of Basel Mission education, set up the Abuakwaman National Fund for education. In October

1937, Abuakwa State College grew out of the private initiatives of prominent members of the Abuakwa Scholars' Union, including Charles E. Okai and K. Adarkwah.[80] The Christian missions also recognized the importance in any society's development of female education. The Wesleyan Mission tried to go beyond primary school education for women by establishing the first Girls' Secondary School at Aburi in 1895. The venture, however, turned out to be short-lived.[81]

By the turn of the twentieth century, Christianity was becoming synonymous with literacy, enlightenment, civilization and good, purposeful leadership. In 1890 the oman of Kwabeng petitioned Governor Griffiths to persuade John Oware, a member of the Kwabeng royalty, to accept election to the Kwabeng stool,

> in hopes that he would as an educated Christian young man bring more civilization (sic) to the country, and also give all necessary advise (sic) to King Amoako Atta II who is still illiterate ... that we also might enjoy the benefit of education and Christianity.[82]

In December 1900, the Amantoomiensa, which had spearheaded the persecution of Christians in Akyem in the 1870s and 1880s, made the proper 'care of the Christians' a condition of deposed King Amoako Atta's reinstatement.[83] Indeed, from 1900 there was a clear tendency to prefer educated and or Christian candidates for stools in the Colony.[84]

The leadership role of the mission-educated elite was not confined to stool occupancy. Mission-educated men provided leadership in the church, in commerce, in education and in national politics. The roles of John T.A. Martin, Solomon and T. Laing in the Methodist Church and of Theophilus Opoku and David Asante in the Basel Mission work, are too well-known to be recounted here.[85] In politics, mention may be made of Konor Mate Kole, Nene Azu Mate Kole, Nana Sir Ofori Atta I, Dr J.B. Danquah, Casely Hayford, Van Hien.

There can be no doubt that Christian education contributed immensely towards the evolution of modern Ghanaian society. It endowed the country with a core of literate, skilled, morally sound, and far-sighted men whose modern outlook, drive and progressive ideas influenced the course of Ghana's political and social development. The structure of Christian education, especially its syllabus, curriculum, the Boarding House system and its routine, remained important landmarks on the Ghanaian educational landscape well into the 1980s. The attention paid to the study of vernacular languages by missionaries such as J.G. Christaller, J.B. Schlegel and J. Zimmermann, resulted in the production of dictionaries for the Twi, Ewe and Ga-Adangme languages that are still in use to-day.[86] The suburban Christian settlements, the-Salems, with their well-laid streets, were a model of improved sanitation; their novel architectural styles influenced building and planning techniques in the indigenous townships.

The Christian Missions, by helping to popularise scientific medicine and improve sanitation, contributed significantly to the growth in rural population between 1920 and 1930.[87] By the 1890s, Basel missionaries in the interior were treating wounds and minor ailments without asking for payment beyond the cost of the drugs.[88] Christians and non-Christians alike visited the Mission stations to ask for help. The Rev Bauer of the Begoro station of the Basel Mission spent part of his time working as a dispenser.[89]

No less significant was Christianity's contribution to the economic foundations of Ghana. Between 1860 and 1882 Christian missionaries urged their congregations to grow the oil palm tree as an economic crop. The Basel Mission did not only contribute directly to the genesis of the cocoa industry, it also contributed to the expansion of the industry by exhorting their African agents, congregation members and 'graduates' of their schools to take to cocoa farming.[90] In 1916, the District Commissioner for Birim District described the farms of mission-educated Akuapem migrant farmers in the Densuagya area and at Anyinam as being 'better tended' than those owned by their uneducated Akyem counterparts.[91]

Before the missionary penetration of the interior, land alienation as a commercial proposition was hardly known. The numerous purchases of land by the Christian missions for the construction of mission stations and missionary emphasis on agriculture production in the era of Legitimate Trade, stimulated an influx of migrant farmers into the forest country of Akyem Abuakwas and Asante from the 1860s, and made land a most valuable economic asset and a saleable commodity.[92]

Emancipation of slaves and pawns afforded equal opportunity to all to participate individually and privately in the expanding trade in palm oil, gum-copa, monkey-skins, parrots, kola nuts and rubber. Participation in trade gave rise to a new class of *noveaux riches* in the interior. Mission-trained entrepreneurs formed a substantial proportion of the new class in the Ghanaian hinterland. They included James Kwaku Ashmore of Asamankese, John Yaw Boafo of Abomosu and Kofi Johnson of Abampe. By 1901, Kofi Johnson, a dealer 'in rubber and spirits', had accumulated a considerable private fortune estimated at £3,000 in silver coins and £1,000 in gold. By 1909 he was worth a total of £4,890.00.[93]

Was the Missionary Impact Wholly Positive?

It is generally agreed among historians that the greatest flaw in the work of Christian missions in Ghana was the inflexibility of their attitude towards African ways of life. Paul Jenkins comments:

> The missionaries ... had great difficulties everywhere with tradition and custom. Their congregational rules were very exact and very western. They wanted to build up model villages, *just like ones at home*; with African ... Christians living *in the kind of marriages and households* they themselves had grown up in, seeing the world through *European Pietist eyes* ...[94]

This obsession with casting African societies in a European mould had serious implications for the political and cultural unity of traditional societies. From the point of view of traditional authorities, politics was inseparably linked with religion. To them religion's role was to sanction political authority and provide solace for the community as a whole. By contrast, the Christian missions regarded church and state as separate and insisted on freedom of worship and conscience for subjects irrespective of their duties to the state. The seeming irreconcilability of the two views led to polarization and mutual suspicion between church and state.

In the privacy and security of their Salems, the Christians disregarded the customary taboos cherished by their non-Christian compatriots in the main townships. Indeed, the Salems became an *imperium in imperio* of sorts, conferring immunity from customary prohibitions. The Rev Mohr indeed confirmed that the reason why some people at Osiem became Christians and relocated their domicile in the Salem was that they were 'not allowed to keep goats in Osiem, and working on the farm is also forbidden on specific weekdays, both of which prohibitions would not apply if they lived on mission land ...'[95]

The Church-state dichotomy undermined social and political cohesion. In 1904, the Chief of Tumfa summed up the situation thus: 'You missionaries make two towns out of each town and bring division among us, who are brethren'.[96] Nana Sir Ofori Atta I, in a memorandum to the Presbyterian Synod of 1941, criticised the Basel Mission for its segregation of Christians into 'a separate community in each town' and for its general antagonism 'towards African ways'.[97]

On the coast, Christian denigration of African culture created frustration that expressed itself in the Mfantsi Amanbuhu Fekuw of the last decade of the nineteenth century.[98] In February 1902, the Gold Coast Aborigines, the mouthpiece of the Aborigines Rights Protection Society, called for the country's system of education to be re-orientated to foster respect for the people's culture. It demanded:

> We want Educated Fantis not Europeanised natives. We simply want our education to enable us to develop and improve our native ideas, customs manners and institutions.[99]

Governor Guggisberg was worried by the long-term harm that was likely to result from the attempt to make Europeans out of Africans. In 1920, he remarked:

> One of the greatest mistakes of education in the past has been this, that *it has taught the African to become a European instead of remaining an African*. This is entirely wrong and the Government recognises it. In future our education will aim at making an African remain an African and taking interest in his own country.[100]

Guggisberg's hopes remained a dream because the Christian missions which controlled education remained uncompromising in their resolve to implant European cultural norms in the minds of their pupils.[101]

The Christian Missions also failed to sustain their initial enthusiasm for manual labour. By a cruel twist of fate, Christian education which set out to teach the dignity of working with one's hands, ended up alienating its products from the soil. As early as 1888 the Rev Sitzler reported that:

...the people say that when someone has been to school they are no good for the ordinary way of life. They are too idle to farm and do other form of manual work ...[102]

The revulsion against manual labour continued into the 1920s. In 1922 Governor Guggisberg, in a speech at Kyebi, expressed regret that 'nearly all educated young men think it's a disgrace to work with their hands'.[103] The Trade Schools established by him in the 1920s at Kyebi, Asante-Mampong, Asuantsi and Yendi were intended as a corrective measure. The impact of the four schools was, however, too limited and the prejudice has persisted to this day.

Conclusion

Nation-building connotes calculated efforts by a people to create for themselves and their posterity a sovereign state culturally integrated, politically united, economically viable and socially just, which gives scope for their genius to be expressed and for individual talents to be developed to a degree limited only by people's ambition, initiative and drive. By providing Ghanaian youth with opportunities for education and stressing the need for good character and training, by equipping them with entrepreneurial skills and instilling in them the spirit of self-help, industry and a sense of patriotism, mission work laid the foundation on which the superstructure of Ghanaian nationhood could be built.

The racial prejudice and arrogance of some Christian missionaries caused Ghanaian native ideas, customs and institutions to evolve along pre-determined lines instead of being allowed to evolve spontaneously in response to changing circumstances. This criticism not withstanding, one cannot help agreeing with Adu Boahene that 'the missions on the whole did more good than harm'.[104]

Notes

1. Tufuor, 'Relations between Christian mission: European administrators and traders in the Gold Coast 1824–74', in O.U. Kalu (ed.), *The history of Christianity in West Africa*, Longman, 1980: 215.

2. At the death of Philip Quacoe in 1816 the SPG had made a total of only 52 converts at Cape Coast.

3. The Roman Catholics re-entered the field in 1880 with Elmina as their base; the AME Zion (1898) and the SPG (1904) operated from their Cape Coast bases.

4. A.F. Walls, 'Missionary vocation and the ministry: The first generation', in Kalu (ed): 22; R. Gray, 'The origins and organization of the ninteenth century missionary movement', in Kalu (ed): 10; Paul Jenkins, *A short history of the Basel Mission*, Texts and Documents, No 10, Basel Mission, Basel, May 1989: 1–4.

5. Jenkins: 3.

6. Jenkins: 3.

7. Jenkins: 3.

8. Jenkins: 3.

9. Jenkins: 11; also Paul Jenkins, 'Villagers as missionaries: Towards a definition of Pietism in Würtemberg as a missionary movement in mid-nineteenth century', Unpublished Seminar Paper, I.A.S. Legon, 1979.

10. M.A. Kwamenah-Poh, 'The Basel Mission and the development of the cocoa industry in Ghana, 1858–1918', Unpublished Seminar Paper, Department of History, March 1994: 14. Zimmermann was head of the Abokobi mission station.

11. R. Addo-Fenning, *Akyem Abuakwa 1700–1943: From Ofori Panin to Sir Ofori Atta*, Legon: Ghana Universities Press, 1995: 88. By the end of 1868 the Christian congregations at Kukurantumi and Kyebi had acquired 18-acre and 20-acre lands respectively, for use as Salem.

12. Addo-Fenning: 264. See also, H.W. Debrunner, *A history of Christianity in Ghana*, Accra: Waterville Publishing House, 1967: 130.

13. See, David Kimble, *A political history of Christianity in Ghana*, Oxford: Clarendon Press, 1963.

14. Jenkins: 11.

15. Jenkins: 11.

16. Debrunner: 130.

17. N.T. Smith, *Presbyterian Church of Ghana 1835–1960: A younger church in a changing world*, Accra: Ghana Universities Press, 1966: 38.

18. Kwamenah-Poh: 16.

19. Addo-Fenning: 313.

20. Kwamenah-Poh:18–19.

21. Kwamenah-Poh: 18–19; Kimble, 1963.

22. Kwamena-Poh: 19.

23. Kwamena-Poh: 20.

24. Addo-Fenning: 316.

25. Addo-Fenning: 315.

26. Addo-Fenning: 316.

27. Kimble: 8.

28. Kimble: 71.

29. Kimble: 62.

30. Kimble: 63.

31. Kimble: 64.

32. Kimble: 64.

33. Kimble: 64.

34. Kimble: 64.

35. Asante's Report for 1877, dd 28 Jan, 1878, No 239. Paul Jenkins, *Abstracts from the Gold Coast correspondence of the Basel Mission*, BV 3625. G5 J41, Balme Library, Legon: 592. Asante travelled 21 days and his Catechists, 169 days.

36. After 15 years of preaching (1853–68) the Basel Mission congregation in Akyem Abuakwa numbered about 80-odd souls: 42 at Kyebi and 20 at Kukurantumi. See Addo-Fenning: 87.

37. Kromer's 3rd and 4th Quarterly Reports for 1859, dd 29 Oct 1859 and 12 Jan 1860. Jenkins, *Abstracts*: 43.

38. Addo-Fenning: 87; Mohr's 2nd Quarter Report for 1877, dd 28 May 1877, Jenkins, *Abstracts*: 73.

39. Addo-Fenning:, 87; Also Christaller's Report for 3rd Quarter 1866, dd 1 Oct 1866 no 22. Jenkins, *Abstracts*:530. Eisenschmid's Report for 1866, dd 8 Jan 1867, No Akim 25, Jenkins, *Abstracts*:525.

40. Addo-Fenning: 87–107.

41. Addo-Fenning: 130 (fn 45).

42. Jenkins, *Abstracts*: 681.

43. Eisenschmid's Report for 1867, dd 7 Jan, 1868, No Akim 8. Jenkins, *Abstracts*: 532.

44. Rossler's Report on the Akim Boarding Schools in 1886, dd 28 Jan, 1887, No II 64, Jenkins, *Abstracts*: 668.

45. Jenkins, *Abstracts*: 516, 528, 552, 617.

46. Report of the Year 1878 by Nath Date, 31 Dec. 1878; Rossler's Report on Akim Middle School during 1885, dd 6 Feb 1886, Jenkins, *Abstracts*: 658.

47. Rossler's Report on the Akim Middle School during 1885 dd 6 Feb 1886, Jenkins, *Abstracts*: 658.

48. Kimble: 71.

49. Nath Date's Report on the Boarding School in 1877, dd 9 Feb 1878, Jenkins, *Abstracts*: 593. Also Nath Date's Report for the year 1878, dd 31 Dec 1878, Jenkins, *Abstracts*.

50. Kramer's Report for the 1st Quarter of 1869, dd 15 April 1869, Jenkins, *Abstracts*: 544. In 1869, 3 or 4 pupils of the Kyebi Primary School who could not, or were unwilling to, enter the Akropong Middle School on account of old age or poor academic attainment, were apprenticed to a carpenter. The fourth was sent to Osu to be apprenticed to a lock-maker.

51. Kimble: 80.

52. J.P. Mackay et al, *A history of world societies* (3rd ed), Boston: Houghton Mifflin Co, 1992: 873.

53. Mackay: 872–73.

54. N.T. Smith: 217. J B Danquah, *The Akim Abuakwa handbook*, London: F.Groom, 1928: 91.

55. Nath Date's Report to the Evangelical Basel Mission Society, 1 July 1882, Jenkins, *Abstracts*.

56. Addo-Fenning: 269. In Akyem Abuakwa taking a wife cost 'something like $18.00 and several pieces of cloth' on the average, besides the extra demand for Tri-sika (literally head-money).

57. Minutes of a Station Conference at Akropong, 28th Aug. 1857, Jenkins, *Abstracts*: 36.

58. Mohr's Jahresbericht for 1879 dd 22 Jan 1880; Asante's Report for 3rd Quarter of 1876, dd 11 Oct 1871, Jenkins, *Abstracts*:III, 390. Also Addo-Fenning: 296 (fn 141).

59. Rossler's Report on the Akim Middle School 1885, dd 6 Feb 1886, Jenkins, *Abstracts*: 657.

60. Huppenbauer's Report for the 2nd Quarter, 1883, dd 19 July. Jenkins, *Abstracts*: 181.

61. Stations Conference Protocol, dd 1 Nov 1878 (No 230), Jenkins, *Abstracts*: 106. With interest rates at 50–100%, a pawn was virtually a permanent slave.

62. Addo-Fenning: 303 (fn270).

63. Deacon Theophilus Opoku to the Committee of the Evangelical Mission Society at Basel, 31 Dec 1882. Jenkins, *Abstracts*.

64. Asante to Basel: A Report on the Kibi Boarding School in the 3rd Quarter of 1876, dd 18 Oct 1876. Jenkins, *Abstracts*: 591.

65. Mohr's Report for the 1st Quarter of 1880, dd 10–26 April 1880. Jenkins, *Abstracts*: 129. One Ntim of Begoro alone held 60 pawns who owed him a total of £450.

66. Mullings Report dd July 1882, Jenkins, *Abstracts*: 630. Sofia Korama of Asiakwa on her death bed told Mullings that she became a Christian out of gratitude to God following the emancipation of herself, her mother and her two children who had all been sold into slavery, her mother and herself for £1 each, her children for £4 each.

67. Buck's Report for the 3rd Quarter 1883, dd 8 Sept 1883, Jenkins, *Abstracts*: 642.

68. Petro Obako, 'a slave from Hausa country' who had lived at Heman (Fankyeneko) for 20 years made the village his domicile. Also John Ayebinim from Salaga who had nobody to support him was adopted by the Basel Mission. See Mohr to Basel, dd 7 Jan, 1880, Munz to the Twi District Inspector of schools dd 20 June, 1882, Asante, Mohr and Werner to the SEC, dd 26 June, 1875, Jenkins, *Abstracts*: 129, 634, 585.

69. Asante, Mohr and Werner to the SEC, dd 26 June 1875, Jenkins, *Abstracts*: 585a.

70. Munz to the Twi District Inspector of schools, dd 20 June 1882, Jenkins, *Abstracts*: 634.

71. The only school outside the control of the two Christian Missions was the Cape Coast Castle School. The Government opened nine more schools in 1856. See, Kimble: 71.

72. Enrolment in Methodist schools was made up of 900 boys and 230 girls. In addition to the Cape Coast Castle School, the Government opened 9 more schools in 1856. Kimble: 71.

73. Kimble:73.

74. Kimble: 86.

75. Mfantsipim began in 1876 as Cape Coast High School. In 1906 it received a new lease of life through the merger of a private High School opened in 1905 and the Wesleyan Collegiate School. Its first headmaster, the Rev W.T. Balmer, raised the enrolment from 8 in 1907 to 91 in 1911. See Kimble: 86.

76. Charles Bannerman was trained in England. G.E. Fergusson, T. Hutton Mills, J.E.

Casely Hayford and his elder brother attended the Wesleyan Boys' High School in Freetown. See Kimble: 84, 89.

77. By 1905 there were only 81 certified teachers in Ghana. From 1902 the Akropong Seminary attracted an annual Government grant-in-aid. Kimble: 76.

78. Rev F. Eggyir Asaam founded Asaam's Grammar School in 1892; John Mensah-Sarbah collaborated with others to set up the Mfantsi National Education Fund for 'the proper education and technical training of Fante youth' in the 1890s. In 1903 he again collaborated with W.E. Sam to promote Secondary School education.

79. Kimble: 86. Accra Grammar School was the first secondary school to receive a Government grant of £100 in 1906.

80. Addo-Fenning: 285. C.E. Okai offered his house in 1935 for the Asafo Secondary School that became Abuakwa State College in 1937.

81. Kimble: 85.

82. Addo-Fenning: 271.

83. Rules given to King Amoako Atta II on the occasion of his reinstatement, 3 Dec, 1900, N.A.G. Adm 11/1/3.

84. In Akyem Abuakwa the list included David Kwaku Asare (1902–05), Joshua Gyamera (1905–07), Kwaku Otupiri (1908–12), Antwi Awua (1912–19) all of Begoro; John Robert Oware (1905–10) of Kwabeng; John Kofi Boobae (1905–18) of Apiramang and Nana Sir Ofori Atta I (1912–1943).

85. John Martin and Theophilus Opoku were the first African ministers to be ordained in the Wesleyan and Basel Missions respectively, the former in the 1850s, the latter in 1872. See Kimble: 64.

86. See C.G. Baeta, 'Missionary and Humanitarian interests 1914 to 1960', in L.H. Gann and P. Duignan (eds.), *Colonialism in Africa 1870–1960, Vol ii*, Cambridge: Cambridge University Press, 1970: 434. Christaller's work was entitled *Dictionary of the Asante and Fante language called Tshi*. By 1671, the whole Bible had been translated into Twi.

87. In Akyem Abuakwa for example, population increased by 50% from 90,306 (1921) to 140,462 (1931). See N A G Adm 11/1/1077. Cuse No.8/1931, chief census officer to SNA, 11 June 1931.

88. Dysentery was cured with Holleinstein pills.

89. Bauer's Report on the Begoro Middle School and the Kyebi (Primary) Boarding School in 1893, dd 1 Feb 1893, Jenkins, *Abstracts*: 67.

90. Addo-Fenning: 316. James Kwaku Donko of Asiakwa began the first of his 12 cocoa farms in the 1880s; the village of Yaw Koko was built on land bought for a cocoa plantation by Teacher Ahwireng and Mr Okanta, a Basel Mission Agent at Akropong; James Okai, the successful cocoa farmer of Asamankese worked previously as a school teacher at Oda and Manso in the 1890s, before taking to cocoa farming in 1898.

91. Addo-Fenning: 316. Polly Hill comments that Akuapem farmers 'many of whom had originally been trained by the Basel Missionaries' minister of religion, catechists, teachers and prominent Christians, generally were among those most sensitive to the possibilities of the new crops'. See, Polly Hill, *Migrant cocoa farmers of Southern Ghana: A study in rural capitalism*, Cambridge: Cambridge University Press, 1963.

92. Addo-Fenning: 344 (fn 78). Also Jenkins, *Abstracts*: 613, 33, 106, 116, 605.
93. Addo-Fenning: 309–10.
94. Jenkins, *A short history of the Basel Mission*: 14. Emphasis added.
95. Addo-Fenning: 281.
96. Debrunner: 174.
97. Baeta: 441. Also R Addo-Fenning, 'Church and State: A historical review of interaction between the Presbyterian Church and traditional authority', *Research Review* 1 (2), 1985; Jarle Simensen. 'Christian Church, "Native State" and African culture: The Presbyterian mission in Akim Abuakwa, Ghana', Unpublished Ms, University of Trondheim.
98. A.A. Boahen, *Ghana: Evolution and change in the nineteenth and twentieth centuries*, London: Longman, 1975: 63.
99. Boahen: 119.
100. N.A.G. Adm 11/1778 Speech by His Excellency the Governor at Kibbi, 11 May 1920. Emphasis added.
101. There were 62 missionary schools in Akyem Abuakwa in 1927, 47 of which belonged to the Presbyterians. See Simensen: 7.
102. Sitzler to Basel 5 May 1888, Jenkins, *Abstracts*, (supplement): 8.
103. N.A.G. Adm 11/1778, H.E.'s Reply to a Petition presented at Kibbi, Jan 25, 1922.
104. Boahen: 88.

Part Four

AFRICAN CHRISTIAN
IDENTITY

Chapter Ten

'Globecalisation' and Religion: The Pentecostal Model in Contemporary Africa.

Ogbu U. Kalu

Introduction: Contours of Contemporary African Scariscape

The contemporary religious landscape or scariscape in Africa is characterised by an enormous numerical growth of all religious forms, but especially of Christianity and, in recent times, by the enlargement and virtual resurgence of religion in the public space. The growth of Christianity is such that there is another shift of the centre of gravity from the Northern hemisphere to the South. In the past the centre has shifted from the Mediterranean origins through the Maghrib to Europe and now back to the South. There are more Christians living now in Latin America, Africa and Asia in that order than in the North. The financial power has disengaged from the cultic power. It is not merely a matter of numbers but what David Martin calls 'geological shift in religious identification', which may be lost to those who still assume that 'political and economic spheres are primary realities' in understanding Christianity.[1]

These shifts have immense implications on how the shape and flow of the Jesus movement is discussed. Moreover, amidst the decimation of civil society under predatory leaders in Africa, the churches, with their vast networks within the communities, remained as the only instruments of restraint in spite of a history of collusion. Church leaders brokered the demise of dictators during the Second Liberation of Africa. In the West, church leaders served as Presidents in Conferences for democratisation in Ghana, Togo, Benin and Cameroon; in the Central region, Central African Republic, Zaire and Rwanda; in the Southern region, South Africa, Zimbabwe, Zambia, Malawi; in the Eastern region, Uganda, Kenya as well as Mozambique and Madagascar. Eyebrows have been raised whether the trend was fortuitous, however undeniable. Indeed, the resurgence in old Marxist enclaves such as Angola and Guinea has led to the speculation that there were no purist Marxist states in Africa.[2]

Commentators acknowledge that much of the growth resulted from the new salience of Pentecostals outside the mainline churches and Charismatic groups operating within the mainline churches.[3] It is as if any church that wants to survive must create some space for charismatic Christianity or risk exodus to where the Spirit is moving. Growth of charismatic movements may have resulted from an encapsulation strategy, indicating the force of 'the wind of God' as the Pentecostal movement has been described.[4] It has challenged all religious forms, alleging that mission churches suffer from power failure, demonizing the earlier African Independent Churches for their use of means which are seen as cultic and calling Islam a religion of the 'bond woman', while the theosophic or new science religions as Rosicrucians, Freemasons and Grail Movement are characterised as the revival of ancient Egyptian mystery religions with many shared similarities with Roman Catholicism. With such a colourful diatribe threatening the pluralistic religious scariscape, rebuttals abound.

The interest here, however, is the conjuncture in time and space with the concept of globalisation and the shift of theory of knowledge from Enlightenment and modernity to post-modernity. Is this fortuitous? There is very little doubt about Pentecostal avid exploitation of modernity. The movement is so locked into the modernity project through shared resources that questions are raised whether Pentecostalism world-wide serves as the enchanted cultural version of globalism. Is African Pentecostalism an aspect of Western religious, global influence, 'an extension of American electronic church'? How has African Pentecostalism responded to the external dimensions of the religious surge, or utilised what Bayart calls 'the resources of externality'? In other words, to what extent has the salience in the African religious landscape been a reproduction of the extravenous factor rather than African indigenous creativity?

An attempt to answer these questions will begin by standing on 'the dry high ground' or theoretical exploration of the concepts of globalisation and its application to local religious contexts, what I have called in this article 'globecalisation.' This is understood as the process of domesticating the global in local contexts. Then, there will be an anatomy of African Pentecostalism focusing on its identity, specificity and character. The 'marshy terrain' charts the African map of the Universe, the worldview which serves as the backdrop and raises the questions which all religious forms must perforce answer, even if differently. The heartbeat of this article is the 'globecalisation' or Pentecostal colouring of the map.

How does globalisation impact local cultures and how do local cultures respond? The appropriation of global forces within local contexts and communities or the relationship of the macrocosm to the microcosm has intrigued scholars, raising the question about how local cultures gestate, absorb, internalize, domesticate or respond to external change agents. It might be useful to turn the question around to explore how African Pentecostalism utilises the resources of an African worldview. Do they merely implant global cultural forms? The argument here is that Pentecostalism is in fact coloured by the texture of the African soil and from its interior derives idiom, nurture and growth. It does not merely adapt but gestates the resources of externality, transforming along the grooves of resonance to serve its needs. This explains why Pentecostal fruits, therefore, answer more adequately the challenges (of power and evil) in the African ecosystem than the fruits of earlier missionary endeavours.

The High Dry Ground:
Defining Globalisation and Globecalisation

Since the literature has burgeoned, suffice it to summarise that globalisation is a relational concept to explain the increasing culture contact which has reduced distances in space and time and brought civilizations and communities into closer degrees of interaction. In the 1960s, when Marshall McLuhan talked about the 'global village', he pointed to the impact of communication on cultures; how, from Gutenberg's invention of the printing press, communication technology had webbed the world in such a manner that whatever happened in one part of the globe was immediately known in another part.[5] Electronic media especially have knotted many cultures, societies and civilizations together into unavoidable contact, depriving them of their isolation and particularity. All are caught in the integration and differentiation of global societies. This not only affects the theory of knowledge but has two other results: the emergence of a new culture and the intensification of culture and value clashes. As cultures are pressed together, the problem of identity looms large. Some argue that the new culture is not from any particular region. Others believe that it is a product and internal requirement of capitalism. Some fear Fukuyama's 'end of history' and American dominance. What is certain is that globalism has acquired many characteristics based on the lenses used to interpret how certain cultural forces and values (economic, social and political) have woven the *oiukumene* into a certain order sharing identical values and bound by economic, cultural, religious forces which are so strong that some inherited values must be surrendered and development trajectories modified or abandoned. This is an emergent culture utilizing technology, commerce and monetary power to weld together disparate peoples and cultures. Sometimes the cord is so strong that a sneeze at one end causes flu at the other end. Sometimes the bind is so ineluctable that even losers cannot extricate themselves. But matters have shifted from the global village concept to a rather bewildering disintegration and flux. One aspect is the pace and direction of change. The other is that, at the core, globalism is a power concept bearing the seeds of asymmetrical power relations. There is no guarantee of equality or benefit for all. Globalism is akin to the New Testament concept of *kosmos, the world order*, controlled by an inexplicable, compulsive power, dazzling with allurements or *kosmetikos*. Some wonder whether friendship with it is not enmity with God's design because it breeds poverty at the periphery. From this perspective, its pursuit of democratic order is designed to create a friendly socio-political environment for a consumer market economy. The embedded concepts of economic interdependence and mutual interest do not diminish the fact that Africa's disadvantage is not addressed. She is the Cinderella in this global dance but she is not the only one fearful of homogenisation and Americanisation. Coca Cola and McDonald hamburgers bear the terrorizing signature tune of the New World Order into many nooks of the globe.

The key concern here is the application of the model in the study of religious systems and Pentecostalism specifically. A few examples will suffice to make the point from the works of Roland Robertson, P. Beyer, Karla Poewe, Mike Featherstone, David Lyon, Rosalind Hackett, Brigit Meyer and Ruth Marshall-Fratani.[6] Much of the early concern, to which Robertson drew attention, was about the world-wide resurgence of religion contrary to the earlier predictions about the death of religion and ethnicity in the insurgence of modernity. Jeff Haynes analysed the contrary trend in the Third World and especially Africa,[7] while Peter Beyer demonstrated the failure of the prophecies on secularism with the insurgence of religious fundamentalism and ecological spirituality in many parts of the globe. It was Karla Poewe who re-interpreted Pentecostalism in South Africa as a form of global Christianity, contradicting those who imaged it as the religion of the disoriented or logged it into the fundamentalist mould or as part of American right-wing insurgence into Africa. Rather, she argued, Pentecostalism reflected the journey of a spiritual flow, with an ancient source, coursing through the Azusa Street impulse into the interior of the globe, including Africa.. 'What is global are traditions that reach across national boundaries, take on local colour, and move on again'.[8] Interest soon shifted to the conjuncture with modernity and post modernity, probing the impact of media and technology as they empower religious crusaders, the cultural discontinuities which must follow and how Pentecostalism becomes an agent in spreading the psychology of modernity: its understanding of the self, the other and perception of the past.[9] Does it attack the communalism in Africa by legitimating individualization and the nuclear family or by liberating its members from the burden of the past? These efforts explored the religious expression of the cultural disjuncture of globalism.

Robertson first applied the concept of glocalisation to deal with the global-local theme, borrowing from the Japanese *dochakuka*, a micro-marketing technique for adapting a global outlook to local conditions. Long before then, *traditionalization* was the favoured term, also using the example of Japanese patterns of industrialisation along the grooves of traditional mores. Factories operated as families, using the deference system and loyalties derived from traditional ethics. David Lyon tested the glocalisation concept on the Toronto Blessing or Laughter, a charismatic flow from America into Canada, in which people would be slain in the spirit and fall down laughing. However, this test case was within a culturally homogenous context and may be unhelpful for Africa, which is a cross-cultural context.

Moreover, the glocalisation discourse webbed Pentecostalism into the post modernity project, which might be useful for the West but less so for Africa where modernity is still acquiring tensile roots. The power relations compel a new discourse which allows Africans and other powerless peoples to participate in the globalism project; the playground is not even and the risk is to do our reflections within circumscribed boundaries. The question should be posed with a new discourse as *globecalisation*, a shift designed to explore the *interior dynamics and process of culture contacts in contexts of asymmetrical power relations.*

It is not globalised religion or increased homogeneity and sameness. Rather 'globecalisation' is a discourse on how global, transnational cultural forms are set on wheels, domesticated or refracted through local cultural lenses. Viewed from several perspectives at once, it is the motor in the process between the encoder and the decoder; the interconnectedness of local distinctiveness and global generality, akin to the biblical understanding of the indigenous and pilgrim principles in Christianity.[10] It emphasizes the initiative and creative responses and character of the local. Africa was not a *tabula rasa* on which foreign culture-bearers wrote their scripts with abandon. By combating the blurring of boundaries and identities in the globalism discourse, it becomes possible to demonstrate how global cultural forms are mediated in everyday lives of ordinary people in local places, which Comarroff calls, 'the epic of the ordinary'.[11] Finally, it emphasizes the sense of fluidity and flux in social analysis by restoring the initiative to the underdog and taking the wind off the triumphalism of the presumed top dog in this dog's life of ours! Globalism has been usually defined with the ideological bias of where one is located in the process. But local conditions and cultural patterns do still filter global flows. As Marshall-Fratani puts it: 'Appropriation of the new occurs in an endless inventive process of cultural bricolage'.[12]

Anatomy of African Pentecostalism

Pentecostalism in Africa has indigenous roots while it has benefited from external interventions and spiritual flows. There was a spiritual revival which hit Africa in the 1970s creating the modern Pentecostal movement, but there had been an avalanche of spiritual flares in the pre-1970 period some of which fed into the new forms. The dynamics of the new forms have been so vibrant that the character of the movement has changed in the decades of the 1980s and 1990s. Thus, a chronological analysis of the movement will distinguish between four periods of the pre 1970s and each of the decades from 1970–1990. For instance, in the first period, many indigenous prophets responded to colonial Christianity by founding charismatic movements and some movements, such as the Balokole, spread across many national boundaries, coursing from Rwanda through Uganda and Kenya into Tanzania in the 1930s. In West Africa, Wade Harris, Garrick Braide and Sam Oppong created enormous Christian resurgence between 1910–22, but did not found churches while the African Independent Churches organised into formal groups from 1925, as did the Zionists who spread from South Africa into Malawi and Zimbabwe through mine workers. In Central Africa, some, like the Kimbaguists, became politically important in primary resistance to authoritarian colonial regimes which colluded with mission churches to frustrate such spiritual revivals. Adrian Hastings has traced the importance of these associations in the rapid vertical growth of Christianity between 1910–60.[13] A proper typology indicates much complexity, just as a cultural-historical analysis would show that the negative missionary culture policy was important in these movements. They sought to bring African indigenous spirituality in appropriating and expressing the gospel. Perhaps, translation of the Bible into the vernacular opened their eyes into the creative possibilities in liturgy, polity and ethics from an African cosmological background.

The spiritual flow of the 1970s can best be understood from a providential model or the finger of God in history. A spiritual revival hit young people in one country after another. From Secondary Schools to Universities, they surged out to preach the gospel and exhibit all manner of charismatic gifts. Examples have been described in Ghana,[14] in Nigeria;[15] in Zambia, Uganda and Cameroon,[16] in Liberia;[17] in Malawi,[18] in Zimbabwe,[19] to mention only a few. This new phenomenon distinguished itself from the Zionist and Aladura groups or African Indigenous Churches described by Sundkler, Oosthuizen, Baeta, Turner, Peel and Daneel between 1961–1981.

In the 1980s this new form grew more intense and widespread in association with the Faith Movement and Prosperity Gospellers to whom tele-evangelism gave high public profile. A functionalist or instrumentalist model has been used to analyse this period which coincided with the collapse of African economies, authoritarian regimes, abuse of human rights and environmental degradation. Paul Gifford perceived this backdrop as essential for understanding the allure of prosperity and faith-claim theology.[20] The pangs of economic Structural Adjustment Programmes and Debt repayments drove many to the warm embrace of hot religion. It is an old model popularised by Vittorio Lanternari's 'Religions of the Oppressed'.[21] While recognising the force of the pressures put on individuals and old networks by the collapse of economies and the ensuing political instability, the limits of this model are also clearly that such movements have occurred under more prosperous economic conditions. In the 1990s, there was a strong voice of sobriety calling the born-again back to the holiness emphasis of old. Equally, the note of pro-active politics of engagement became louder. Intercessors for Africa built a number of National Prayer Houses and grew as the prosperity gospel was publicly under attack. The Third Wave among American Evangelicals allied themselves more with intercessory Third World ministries. At each period, the varieties within the movement increased.

Meanwhile, the typology of the Pentecostal movement, predicated on professional emphases, broadened into at least ten types: inter-denominational fellowships, evangelistic ministries, deliverance, prosperity gospellers, Bible distribution, Children ministries, rural evangelism, intercessors for Africa, classical Pentecostal missions from Europe and charismatic movements in various mission churches. Except in Southern Africa, there was no direct connection between these movements and the Azusa Street Revival of 1907. In most cases, the external intervention was on the invitation of indigenous agents. In the colonial period it was a means of escaping the hostility of the regime. In more recent times, it served to enhance prestige by inducing a sense of belonging to a world-wide movement with funding, training and ministerial formation and a recovery of perceived African contribution to World Christianity. Many feel that the maturity of local Christianity is demonstrated by opportunities to witness in the Western world. Externality may not always mean dependence; evidence abounds that ministries in Africa take pride in funding themselves.

As is typical of such a complex movement, there are many differences in theological emphases and practices and much internal criticism. The core messages include justification by faith, sanctification by the Holy Spirit (a second experience of new birth), manifestation of the charismata, divine healing, prosperity or victorious living and second coming. The temper is ecumenical as Christians are urged to become spirit-filled. These affirmations are propagated through emphases on 'power evangelism' and growth, enormous liturgical vitality and a sense of urgency in the triple task of re-evangelisation, intensification and reconstruction of Christian experience. The media and modern technology are exploited to convey the new experience and millenarian theme and weave together the rural, urban and global contexts. Large quantities of printed materials, newsletters, pamphlets and books, audio and video cassettes, posters and stickers, television and radio programmes, drama and preaching are all pressed into the good cause. 'Dislocation' discourse best describes the mood. Instead of the old type of church-setting, the Pentecostals create new forms of polity and move to cinema houses, stadia, converted warehouses, school buildings and modern expansive buildings conveying newness and size for church services. The entire communal space is turned into religious space: buses, taxis, motor parks, offices, homes become disseminating and preaching points. The community is doused in total immersion into the hot gospel with boldness. They deconstruct the ethnic structures and provide large opportunities for individuals to become agents of change.

Despite criticism that the mission churches diminished the pneumatic dimension of the gospel in their collusion with the Enlightenment project, racism and inane cultural policy, Pentecostals 'set to work' missionary teachings, recovering the lost spirit of Evangelicalism based on biblicism, conversionism, crucicentrism and social activism. It could be imaged as the 'third response' of Africans to the missionary after the responses by the 'Ethiopianism', the cultural nationalists of the nineteenth century and the second and pneumatic response of the Zionists and Aladura at the turn of the century. This third form arose from inside the mission churches urging for the full gospel. From this perspective, it betrayed an African initiative which rejected the hegemonic pattern which missionary vision essayed to install. It challenged missionary theology to incarnate or root the gospel into the culture of the people without diminishing the fact that Christ judges all cultures. They did not reject the tension between the indigenous and pilgrim principles. Pentecostal cultural policy, therefore, becomes intriguing because they have been imaged as hostile to African indigenous cultures. It shall be shown more clearly that their message is a 'fit' into an African worldview, since it seeks to recover the deep structural level in African primal religion. Evans M. Zuesse argued that there are deep structures or existential meanings that tie together a wide variety of folk practices in different cultures of Africa and, working from these, African responses to Christianity have often focussed on the charismatic dimension, which corresponds to what they always wanted their religions to do for them.[22]

The Marshy Terrain: African Map of the Universe

Many of the studies on African Pentecostalism dwell on the impact of modernity on the African scariscape sometimes understood as the effects of Western in-put in funds, manpower, literature, techniques and technology. The numbers of missionaries, resources and expertise translate into power, 'westernisation' and dependence. The cynical argument continues that since Africa is so dependent on the West in other spheres, 'it is natural to ask whether the balance between the local and external within Christianity is different.'[23] Thus, modernity is defined by the resources of Western culture, especially media and technology, which can re-define time, space, human psyche and mental and material cultures. Thus, some commentators go beyond media to highlight shifts in locality, values and imagination as the individual is incited to re-imagine life within membership in the transnational family of born again people. Is Pentecostalism the vehicle for transferring these signifiers of modernity into Africa? This may lead to questions about what is really African about African Pentecostalism; whether the global, the importance of extraversion has not overwhelmed it as Africans mime what they read, hear and watch on television. The approach is to come from the opposite direction and explore how Pentecostals utilize the resources of externality while standing firmly on a certain worldview. This intellectualist approach is often neglected except among the Third Wave American scholars, such as Charles Kraft and C.P. Wagner.[24] Worldviews, or the map of the universe, enable people to mentally organize reality so as to explain why things are the way they are, predict and control space-time events. When exposed to change agents, the impact is quickly filtered through the worldview. Robin Horton, therefore, sought to explain conversion by examining how the negotiation at the level of the map of the universe occurred.[25] The argument here is that an aspect of Pentecostal success could be found in the engagement with the map. They refashion it instead of jettisoning it, as the old missionary cultural policy did, and do not throw away the baby with the bath water.

Worldviews usually start with creation myths and, in many African versions, from a marshy terrain which a blacksmith was delegated by the Creator to blow dry. We shall not mine the structures but rather point to a few salient characteristics, in full awareness that there are varieties of such myths in the complex web of cultures in the huge continent. Perhaps, there is a common structural denominator based on a cyclical perception of time and a three-dimensional perception of space. Paul Hiebert organized the content of worldview into three categories: cognitive, affective and evaluative.[26] These refer to the abstract ideas, inter-personal structures and ethical values. Charles H. Kraft concluded that:

> At the core of culture and, therefore, at the very heart of all human life, lies the structuring of the basic assumptions, values, and allegiances in terms of which people interpret and behave. These assumptions, values and allegiances we call worldview.[27]

Worldview is a picture which points to the deep-level assumptions and values on the basis of which people generate surface-level behaviour; it provides the motivation for behaviour and gives meaning to the environment. Like the rest of culture, it is inherited unconsciously but deliberately transmitted. It could be encrusted in customs, myths, proverbs and folk-lore, music and dances.

Cultural change can often be detected as battering waves chipping away the crusts, initiating a process of separation, reconstruction and re-prioritisation as a new way of viewing the world emerges. Like theory-building, it enables us to search for the underlying simplicity in our complex world and brings into causal relationships wider vistas of reality and every-day life. On the religious front, it helps us to dig deeper than the *structures* into the *allegiances* which constitute the core of religiosity.

Africans conceive time in a cyclical pattern. Life moves from birth to death and back to life by reincarnation. Mircea Eliade has argued that this movement of time is derived from the agricultural cycle among pre-industrial peoples.[28] As their predominant economic activities move from planting to harvest and back to planting, as the sun and moon appear and disappear only to return in an endless cycle, life is conceived to follow a similar pattern. Reality is divided into two: the human world and the spirit world. But each is a replica of the other; thus if an achieved person or a chief dies, he will still live like his former self in the spirit world. This explains why some communities bury slaves to continue serving their master in the spirit world. Tied to this is an anthropology in which a creator deity delegated subalterns to mould human beings from clay while he himself breathed life-giving breath into them. The blood transmits the life into all the body system. At death, the personality-soul or life-breath continues a new life cycle in the spirit world, now as an ancestor who is still a member of his earthly family. This is the concept of the living-dead. Death is not an end but the beginning of a new vista of living. Imbued with vibrant spiritual powers, the ancestor provides a guardian role for the earthly family. Ethical constraints bind either party: a person must have lived a moral life to merit the status of an ancestor. This may be indicated by the fact that the person did not die from certain inexplicable diseases suggesting of a punishment from the gods or by being struck by lightning which will be an overt display of godly anger and punishment for a wicked secret offence. The desire of everyone is to live to old age, with dignity and qualify in death as an ancestor. The human family celebrates the death with appropriate rituals, spaced out into first, second and even third burial ceremonies. If they fail to provide a decent burial or to maintain any of the covenanted obligations with spirits woven by the dead person for the prosperity of the family, he will visit them, making demands and causing troubles for them until they learn to satisfy the conditions. If all obligations are kept, the dead will travel through the spirit world and reincarnate. Thus, when a child is born, diviners will be consulted to indicate who has returned. The umbilical cord would be put in a calabash, sprinkled with certain herbs; an old man of the family would speak incantations on it and bury the calabash under a tree at the back of the family's compound. The child is rooted to the earth, the land of his ancestors. The identification would determine the name which will be given on the eighth day. Various rites of passage would be performed as the individual progresses from adolescence through adult roles to the status of an elder of the community. Different social organizations further root the person into a sense of community: some are achieved, others ascribed; some are open, others are secret.

It should be mentioned that this cyclical perception contrasts with the New Testament conception of time which has informed Western imagination. It is as if the circle is stretched out; time is imaged as linear, a continuum, moving ineluctably from the past to the present and to the future. The Greek, abstract time as *kronos*, measured out chronometrically

is contrasted with African concept of time as *kairos, time as event.* Time
is peopled with events and so reckoned. The past and the present are very
dynamic but the future is attenuated; the notion of eternity or *eschaton* is
foreclosed by the myth of eternal return. However, in the New Testament
conception, the intrusion of the not-yet period into the here-and-now
period brings the two aeons together and creates an organic conception of
the world similar to that prevalent in the symbol of the circle which unites
the spiritual and the earthly realms in the African worldview.

This organic perception is underscored by the conception of space. The
African perceives three dimensions of space: the sky, the earth (consisting
of land and water) and the ancestral or spirit world. It is a living universe,
as each space is populated with some of the four components of spiritual
powers: the *Supreme Being* as the creator and the major subaltern *divinities* inhabit the sky. Manifested as the sun, lightning, thunder, moon and
stars, they serve as oracles, arbiters in human affairs and agents in ritual
dynamics. The major force or divinity on the earth is the *Earth deity,* which
is responsible for fertility and the nurture of life of humans, animals and
plants. Land looms large in this cosmology. In many myths of origin, it is
said that, during creation, the *Supreme Being* sent some deities to perch on
anthills and dry the marshy earth; thus was the world formed. Some stayed
back and inhabited rocks, trees, caves, streams and rivers and thus imbued
physical nature with divine power. Beyond *nature spirits* are *patron spirits* for
certain professions such as farming, hunting, fishing, blacksmithing, trading
and other economic pursuits. Thus, all the realms of life are sacralised; there
is no distinction between the sacred and the profane.

There are *human spirits* on the land because each human being has
a guardian spirit who determines his or her fate in the passage through
life. In some cultures, the individual would make a wooden figure of the
personal daemon and sacrifice to it daily for empowerment in the pursuits
of life. In the gender construct, the marine spirits are imaged as daughters
to the Earth deity. Marine spirits can be munificent and give riches to
devotees. Barren women propitiate marine spirits for children; musicians
consort with them for melodious songs; so do artists seek for inspiration.
The connection between commerce and the arts with marine spirits runs as
deep as the depths of seas. But marine spirits could be wicked, making those
they control to be morally unstable and wayward. Their flashy gifts do not
last; marriages contrived by them do not succeed and children from marine

spirits are often plagued by inexplicable illness. These elements of instability force the afflicted to diviners who will assist to extricate the individual from covenants made by parents or by the person with marine spirits.

Next to the deities and spirits, the third component consists of ancestral spirits which inhabit the earth-beneath. Imbuing the whole of the world of the living are the fourth component, spiritual forces which individuals can acquire through rituals for enhancing life-force. They are non-personal beings such as they call mana in the Oceania: mysterious, ubiquitous power which permeates all areas of life and can be used for good or in an anti-social manner to harm or diminish the capability of another person's life force, fortunes and resources. The negative uses could be operated through words, thoughts, attitudes and behaviour in sorcery or witchcraft practices. Witchcraft is the use of human psychic powers to do evil, unlike sorcery which employs magical incantations, implements, objects, medicine and other paraphernalia. With either method, curses can be put on individuals and families by the envious or wicked people. Evil forces are without bodily forms; so, they embody people, animals and physical objects and manipulate these to harm people. The vision of existence is a precarious one as evil forces, which invest the human world as a siege, endeavour to ruin the capacity of individuals, families and communities from living a prosperous life. Ruth Marshall-Fratani has shown that this scenario holds as equally good for the modern urban setting in Africa:

> With increasing economic hardship and zero-sum struggle for survival, great strain is put on the extended family as the basic domestic unit. Relatively successful family members often resent the pressure put on them by a variety of near and distant relatives ... Young people striving for upward mobility not only desire a relative freedom from such pressures, but also protection from resentment and jealousy in the form of witchcraft, most feared and dangerous in the hands of blood relatives. Apart from the anxiety created by the continued influx of dangerous strangers to urban centres as a result of increased rural-urban migration, the extreme instrumentalisation of social relations, as well as the break-down of many patron-client networks during the past decade have introduced a kind of urban paranoia about evil doers who are out to cheat, deceive, rob and kill. A kind

of Hobbesian sense of all against all prevails; the old forms of community – ethnic, kinship, professional, hometown, neighbourhood – have proved unreliable sources of support.[29]

Rituals of sacrifices, libations, offerings, prayers, taboos and other forms of sacred acts are employed in seeking the interventions of the good spirits in the combat with evil spirits. While some spirits are propitiated, others are driven away through prescribed rituals. J.S. Mbiti in *The Prayers of African Religion* has recorded the liturgy for driving away an intrusive nature spirit among the Banyankore of Uganda:

> Come and go with yours –
> This is your goat –
> This is your road –
> Go and don't return.[30]

Affliction is a pivotal issue in the traditional worldview of Africans. It can be caused by a contravention of moral code. For instance, the Earth deity supervises the moral order on the land. Matters such as stealing, adultery, incest, other forms of wrong-doing and a breakdown in social relations are abomination to her. Failure to propitiate her is visited with afflictions which take different forms, such as illness or misfortune. The manifestation may be individual or communal. Political instability, economic disaster, upsurge in mortality rate, increase in robbery and other unwholesome social facts are regarded as disease, requiring divinatory diagnosis and spiritual cure. Disease could, therefore, be caused by religious, social and natural causes. To re-establish the security of the moral order and reconcile broken social relationships, medicine becomes important. A diviner diagnoses the problem and provides curative and protective spiritual powers – either through herbs or by covenanting the individual or community to protective spirits. Festivals, dances, masquerades and commensality are employed to re-energize ancestral and other covenants and heal the community from untoward conditions. Finally, it has been shown through a survey of six hundred and fifteen spirits which occupy the religious ardour of the Igbo of South-Eastern Nigeria, that different culture theatres in Africa prioritise which deities are central for their needs. The challenges of the eco-system are core determinants for prioritising their choices.

This is a religious worldview. Going through life is like a spiritual warfare and religious ardour may appear very materialistic as people strive to preserve their material sustenance in the midst of the machinations of pervasive evil forces. Behind it is a strong sense of the moral and spiritual moorings of life. It is an organic worldview in which the three dimensions of space are bound together; the visible and the invisible worlds interweave. Nothing happens in the visible world which has not been predetermined in the invisible realm. The challenge for Christianity is how to witness to the gospel in a highly spiritualised environment where the recognition of the powers has not been banished in a Cartesian flight to objectivity and enlightenment. The power question is ultimate and suffuses an African primal worldview, demanding an answer from the new Christian change-agent. It points to the need for continuity in change. Earlier missionary efforts to sidestep this issue with charitable institutions and a Western worldview failed, leaving the field open for re-evangelisation. The born-agains have picked up the gauntlet. To repeat, the argument here is that Pentecostalism in Africa derived her colouring from the texture of the African soil and its idiom, nurture and growth from the interior of an African worldview.

'Globecalisation': Colouring the African Map of the Universe

Pentecostals engage the African worldview and mediate global resources in many ways. A partial list of the way Pentecostals do this would include the following:

1) They engage the interior African worldview from a biblical perspective;
2) They appropriate modernity as a tool of hope and thereby construct a new theology of hope;
3) They provide the transformation of the dark sides of the modern socio-economic and political culture, just as Evangelicals of old responded to the dark consequences of the Industrial Revolution. In this way, they construct a political theology of engagement which empowers them in the midst of a dominant African pathology;[31]
4) They weave a transnational character which contests the asymmetrical power structures through South-South as well as North-South relationships;[32]

5) They contribute to Western religious contexts that is perceptible in a 'reverse flow' of missionary activities from Africa to the West;

6) They impact on the rise of Third Wave theology among American Evangelicals and thus enhance the role of African Churches in the West.[33]

The major contribution of the Pentecostal movement is how they address the continued reality of the forces expressed in African cultural forms. Contrary to the early missionary attitude, which urged rejection of African cultures, Pentecostals take the African map of the universe seriously, acknowledging that culture is both a redemptive gift as well as capable of being hijacked. They perceive a kindred atmosphere and resonance in a biblical contrast between a godly covenant and the snares of other covenants and, therefore, the need for testing of spirits. They appreciate the tensile strength of the spiritual ecology in Africa and the clash of covenants in the effort to displace the spirits at the gates of individuals and communities with a legitimate spiritual authority. Salvation is posed in a conflict scenario. As the Garrick Braide people used to sing: 'Jesus has come and Satan has run away!' Pentecostals, therefore, explore the lines of congruence which go beyond deconstruction to a new construction of reality.

First, at the structural level, there is an identical myth of creation and the perception of a three-dimensional space shared by both biblical and African world views in spite of a cyclical concept of time. This is clear in the declaration that at the name of Jesus, 'every knee shall bow', whether it exists in the heavenlies, earth (land and water) or in the earth-beneath (ancestral world). Second, at the dynamic interior both affirm that the connection between manifest and unseen realities, 'things which are seen are made of things which are not seen' (Heb. 11:3b), the supernatural and inexplicable are valid aspects of reality, and that conflicts in the manifest world are first decided in the spirit world. Therefore, 'the weapons of our warfare are not carnal'. Third, both are spiritualised cosmologies; therefore, the strict dichotomy between the secular and the profane diminishes. Fourth, the biblical worldview is that life is just as precarious as the traditional African imagines; the enemy is ranged in a military formation as principalities, powers, rulers of darkness and wickedness in high places. R.J. Gehman has shown the wide vista of resonance between an African understanding of demons and the biblical perspective, and also areas of divergence.[34] The

Pentecostal goes through life as keenly aware of the presence of evil forces as the African does. Fifth, there are human beings who are given false powers by evil forces to exercise control over individuals, families and communities. Satan even promised Jesus some of these if he complied. Thus, Pentecostals perceive dictatorial and corrupt rulers as being 'possessed'. Sixth, the Pentecostal's anthropology enables a keen awareness and reality of witchcraft and sorcery as soul-to-soul attack. Seventh, both accept the power of the Word. Situations and circumstances can be spoken into being or out of being. *Onoma* is metonym where the part represents the whole and the name of Jesus can be used to achieve effects in the physical realm. Eighth, both approach the human-divine relationship as covenantal, and, therefore, Christian evangelism is a power encounter in which two covenant traditions are opposed. Salvation is imaged as the liberation from the obligations of one covenant with freedom to be re-covenanted to Jesus.

The Pentecostal adopts the New Testament worldview in such a manner as to exploit the areas of resonance before creative transformation. They do not ignore the fact that the word, *kosmos*, can refer to the material universe and the inhabitants of the world, but fasten on the third usage referring to worldly affairs: the worldly goods, endowments, riches, pleasures and allurements (*kosmetikos*) which seduce people away from God. Thus, behind the classical idea of kosmos as orderly arrangement is a mind behind the system, a world system established after the Fall by a *kosmokrator*, a world ruler, the prince of this world, in rebellion. Friendship with him is enmity with God. It is a short step from here to perceive territorial spirits allocated to various spaces for un-Godly activities. This idea was, after all, very prominent in Judaism and in the early church. There is a confluence of the spiritual and material worlds denying the myth of materialism.

Walter Wink has explored the language of power in the New Testament and concluded that

> Every power has a visible and invisible pole, an outer and inner spirit or driving force that animates, legitimates and regulates its physical manifestation in the world. Principalities and powers are the inner and outer aspects of any given manifestation of power. As the inner aspects, they are the spirituality of institutions, the within of corporate structures and systems, the inner essence of outer organizations of power.[35]

Analysing further, he argues that the language of power pervades the whole New Testament and while it could be liquid, imprecise, interchangeable and unsystematic, a clear pattern of usage emerges. Powers could be used to refer to heavenly, divine, spiritual, invisible forces as well as earthly, human, political and structural manifestations as long as we realize that 'the world of the ancients was not a physical planet spinning in empty space in a rotation around a nuclear reactor, the sun; it was a single continuum of heaven and earth, in which spiritual beings were as much at home as humans'.[36] Paul used *dunamis* to focus on the spiritual dimension of power in its capacity to determine terrestrial existence for weal or for woe. Later, it assumed more the designation for God's enemies, engaged in a cosmic struggle to assert lordship over the earth.

Some have assumed that African Christians have manufactured demons and enlarged their space in theology. They abound, however, in Jewish literature as defecting angels, sired giants who were drowned in the flood, but whose spirits live on as demons, evil spirits or 'powers of Mastema'. Their leaders were variously called Azazel, Mastema, Satan and Belial. Early Christians devised elaborate instructions on how to discern them. The ministry of Jesus was very much a cosmic battle in which Jesus rescued humanity from evil powers. African Pentecostals have appropriated the resonance of this factor in the two traditions to domesticate the new and construct tools of hope with symbols of transcendence. The first step is to equate principalities, powers and demons with the various categories of spirits in the worldview and as enemies of man and God. They reinforce the causality pattern in the African worldview before providing a solution beyond the purviews of indigenous cosmology.

By turning the Bible into a canon of tribal history and by interweaving the African and biblical worldviews, Pentecostals directly address the problems of evil forces. They mine the interior of the worldviews to establish that the same covenantal structure exists in both. Therefore, the solution to the problem of affliction and defeat in life is to exchange the covenant with the wicked spirits for the covenant with Christ. They produce large quantities of literature as discourses which expose these forces and show individuals and communities how to overcome their dangerous and destructive influences. They enable individuals and groups to constitute historical agents, empowered to do battle with these principalities and powers and they incite public testimonies about the works and victory over the wicked forces.

Former agents of the spirits describe in gory details their years of bondage serving the false spirits. Testimonies in public worship become ceremonies of degradation and bridge-burning as well as narratives of biographical reconstruction. The subtlety in Brigit Meyer's discussion of the use of the past could be lost[37] and, as Ruth Marshall-Fratani argued, they do not reject the past wholesale but engage with it, refashioning the history and domesticating it; they combine a wide range of self-help discourses with exposures of spiritual machinations at ground-level, occultic and territorial spirit levels.[38]

With spiritual diagnosis of social malaise goes the raising of an army to recapture the land. Contrary to Hackett's assertion, the Pentecostal does not stress individualization and the nuclear family but in fact emphasises the African value of community.[39] To be born again might require re-packaging an individual identity but one is supposed to ensure that one's family members can attain the rapture and that the village will be delivered from evil forces. The 'brethren' constitute a community for personal support and ministry. From the vantage of community, people foray into the public space. This explains the emphasis in biographies of great leaders, such as Benson Idahosa or E.A. Adeboye of the Redeemed Christian Church of God, which describe how they evangelised their parents, families and villages. It is believed that if a soldier of Christ has not dealt with family and clan roots, the old covenants will make demands on the person and hinder the growth of the ministry. One can neither rest content with the conversion of the nuclear family nor escape from the obligations to support one's extended family. Rather, it is the force of secularisation and urbanization which raised the problem.

Pentecostals are not apolitical but run commentaries on public affairs. One is urged to be well informed so as to know the strategies or 'wiles' of the enemy. For instance, corruption is attributed to the operation of the hunter or Nimrod spirit among African rulers, descendants of Ham. The shedding of blood through fratricide (civil wars) brings curses reminiscent of the Cain/Abel saga in which the land withheld her increase. Africa's economic woes are caused by polluting the land with blood. Emigration follows ineluctably as the earth spews out her people.

All of life is subjected to the authority of Christ and, while not denying personal responsibility, it recognizes that individuals and circumstances could be driven by forces beyond their control. The Pentecostal explanation for witchcraft and sorcery by appeal to a biblical anthropology is fascinating. Arguing that God formed man and breathed Himself into the body and man became *nephesh*, a living soul, the fall is imaged as a house which collapsed, burying the spiritual resources. The soul (*psuche*), consisting of the intellect, will power and emotions, constitutes the strongest part of the human being, seeking to dominate both the spirit person (*pneuma*) and the body (*soma*). Salvation comes by the spirit of God, taking over the *pneuma* and exuding the power into the *psuche,* redeeming the constituent parts and the recovering the *soma* which is driven by lusts of the flesh, lust of the eyes and pride of life. In this anthropology, witchcraft operates in the quest to tap the latent powers of the soul and using these to perform false miracles or hurt other people by a soul-to-soul attack. Sorcery worsens matters by using things which provide contact with the victim. It could be the hair, clothes, food and such-like. Since incantations are used and curses pronounced, Christians are admonished to speak the reversal, using the name of Jesus, the blood and the resources of the Holy Spirit. The text often cited is 1 John 5:8 and many others recounting the powers of Jesus and his position in the God-head. They avoid the use of instruments, limiting these to olive oil and anointed handkerchiefs and laying on of hands.

The language of God in Pentecostal liturgy buttresses this fact. They explore the language which communities use in addressing their sustaining divinities, ancestors and the Supreme Being and use these to describe God and Christ, showing that they are superior to all the powers available in the people's map of their universe. The reconstructed world is brought home to individual lives and circumstances by applying what I have termed, 'bumper sticker' hermeneutics.[40] Karla Poewe calls it 'experiential literalism'.[41] Cheryl B. Johns said that Pentecostal hermeneutics is praxis-oriented, with experience and Scripture being maintained in a dialectical relationship. The Holy Spirit maintains the ongoing relationship. The truth must be fulfilled in life experiences. Lived faith is the result of a knowledge of the Scriptures.[42] The emphases are on the experiential, relational, emotional, oral faith, immediacy of the text and a freedom to interpret and appropriate the multiple meanings of the biblical texts. By a pneumatic illumination, it recognizes a spiritual kinship between the authors and readers and ongoing continuity with the New Testament church. Personal and corporate experience weave into the hermeneutical task. The literature on this matter has burgeoned; suffice it to point to the emphasis on the power of the Word in spiritual formation, resisting forces which could lead one to backslide, reversing curses, deliverance and commanding the things which the Lord's hands have made. The 'brethren' arrive for bible studies and Sunday worship with notebooks to take down the message or 'revelations' so as to apply these during the week for victory. Everyone is urged to be an overcomer and 'demon destroyer'. This is hermeneutics for conscientization choreographed with a vigorous homiletic which mines the people's experiences, dramatized these, props them with 'real-life' testimonies and brings the promises in the bible to bear on personal problems, so that no one should leave bearing the burdens of yesterday.

An illustration commonly used in Pentecostal sermons has the pastor telling the story of a woman who is carrying a heavy load on her head. A car stops and offers to assist the woman. She accepts the offer, gets into the car but continues to carry the load on her head instead of setting it down. The congregation typically responds by shouting that this was a foolish thing to do. The sermon would be interrupted with choruses to bring home the message. Pentecostal homiletic is language crafted in a transformative manner and choreographed as a ritual of validation and commitment. As Rambo argues, the songs, dances and yells elicit audience participation and aid believers to perform religiously before rationalizing the process.[43] Such rituals offer knowledge in a distinct form which enables the believer to understand, experience and embody the new way of life.

To craft a tool of hope in the midst of the dark side to the politics of modernization, Pentecostals utilize the concept of the land. The approach is derived from the African map of the universe and employed in response to the legitimacy crises and economic collapse of the 1980–90s. For instance, when there is drought, famine or social distress, Africans look to the land, to their relationship with the earth deity. Economic and moral order are within her purview. The Pentecostals bring to the problem the importance of the land among Israel. As Brueggemann said, for the people of Israel, land referred to actual earthly turf and also symbolically expressed the wholeness of joy and well-being characterized by social coherence and personal ease in prosperity, security and freedom.[44] Land as promise and as a symbol of the covenant relationship with God has tremendous resonance in the attitude to land in African primal societies. The 'brethren' plumb these resonances and move to the impact of pollution caused by the actions of rulers and the ruled. Shrines, festivals to Baal and Ashteroths, witchcraft and corruption are all listed as sources of the woes. The International Monetary Fund and the World Bank are portrayed as the evangelists of the Beast, a force equally behind the European Union and the divinity of the market economy which is 'sapping' African countries with debt repayment. sap is Structural Adjustment Program and comes with 'conditionalities'. Certain literature on the End Time Prophecies from the West provide the armoury for this application of the Bible to both contemporary events and the African primal map of the universe. Both the internal and external forces are brought under the anvil of the gospel in a manner which the unlettered could understand and to show that behind the macro- economics of the global market is a divine will. Pentecostals urge members to avoid judging by sight but by revelation as to which spirits are operating behind manifest events. Land deliverance is only one of the strategies employed. It is subtle and avoids overt iconoclasm: believers can 'walk' around hostile ground or polluted ground and command the spirits to leave; sometimes, at emotional crusades, those with authority over the land and affairs of the community will be asked to confess the iniquities of the fathers which are being visited upon their progenies and to hand over the land to the authority of Jesus. This will ensure prosperity for all the people. In these ways, the born again brethren in Africa bring a spiritual solution to the great issues of the day, taking the context, the worldview and the ecology seriously but within the gospel mandate. Beyond the cultural dimensions and charitable works (eg Nigerian Pentecostals engaged in relief work in Liberia), they engage in direct political actions in the belief that when the righteous are in authority the people will rejoice. So, many run for elective offices and seek leadership positions in the secular world.

Conclusion

I have tried to demonstrate in this article that African Pentecostalism is essentially a form of African Christianity, which is rooted in primal religiosity. It can best be understood within the strand in African Church historiography that has urged attention to the interweaving between religious ecology and the forms of Christian allegiance. It is a response to the deep-level challenges of the eco-theatre, applying the pneumatic resources of biblical theology which missionary theology and practice had muted. Working within African maps of the universe, African Pentecostals have shown how a creative use of biblical promises can transform the lives of many with tools of hope in the midst of the darkness which has hit Africa at noontide. They, therefore, utilize modern technology to re-interpret reality and craft a new theology of hope.

This strategy exploits the elasticity in the African worldview, and makes use of its adaptive capacity to create room within its inherited body of traditions for new realities or resources, which though seemingly coming from outside, fulfil aspirations within the tradition and, thereby, contribute quite significantly to African Pentecostal self-understanding and identity. Kwame Bediako says this is precisely what Paul did with Jewish traditions in the letter to the Hebrews.[45] In Africa today, Pentecostals have fleshed out the faith in the context of contending religious and social movements. This process of gestation, mediation and transformation of global forces in local contexts, riddled as it with vulnerability, defines exactly what I have meant in this article by the term 'globecalisation'.

Notes

1. D.A. Martin, *Tongues of fire: the explosion of Protestantism in Latin America*, Oxford: Blackwell, 1990.

2. See, P. Gifford, 'Some recent developments in African Christianity', *African Affairs* 93, October 1994: 513–534; K. Bediako, *Christianity in Africa: The renewal of a non-Western religion*, Edinburgh: Edinburgh University Press, 1995; J.C. McKenna, *Finding a social voice: The Church and Marxism in Africa*, New York: Fordham University Press, 1997.

3. D.B. Barrett, 'The twentieth century Pentecostal/Charismatic renewal in the Holy Spirit, with its goal of world evangelization', *International Bulletin of Missionary Research*, July 1988: 119–129.

4. O.U. Kalu, 'The wind of God: Pentecostalism in Igboland, 1970–1991', lecture presented at the Centre for the Study of Christianity in the Non-Western World, University of Edinburgh, 1992.

5. M. McLuhan and B. Powers, *The global village: Transformation in world, life and media in the 21st century*, Oxford: Oxford University Press, 1989.

6. R. Robertson, 'Humanity, globalisation and worldwide religious resurgence', *Sociological Analysis* 46 (3), 1985: 219–242; R. Robertson, 'Glocalization: Time-space and homogeneity-heterogeneity', in M. Featherstone, *Global modernities*, London: Sage, 1995; P. Beyer, *Religion and globalisation*, London: Sage, 1994: K. Poewe, *Charismatic Christianity as a global culture*, Columbia, South Carolina: University of South Carolina Press, 1994; M. Featherstone (ed.), *Global modernities*, London: Sage: 1993; D. Lyon, 'Glocalization and contemporary religion' in M. Hutchinson and O.A. Kalu (eds.), *A global faith: Essays on evangelicalism and globalisation*, Sydney: Centre for

the Study of Australian Christianity, 1998: 47–68; R.I.J. Hackett, 'New diretions and connections for African and Asian charismatics', *Pneuma* 18 (1), 1996:69–77; R.I.J. Hackett, 'Pentecostal appropriation of media technologies in Nigeria and Ghana', *Journal of Religion in Africa* 28 (3): 258–277; B. Meyer, 'Make a complete break with the past: Memory and post-colonial modernity in Ghanian Pentecostalist discourse', *Journal of Religion in Africa* 28 (3), 1998: 316–349; A. Corten and R. Marshall-Fratani, *Between Babel and Pentecost: Transnational Pentecostalism in Africa and Latin America*, Bloomingon, Indiana: Indiana University Press, 2000.

7. J. Haynes, *Religion and politics in Africa*, London: Zed Press, 1996.

8. Poewe: 17.

9. A. Appadurai, *Modernity at large: Cultural dimensions of globalisation*, Minneapolis: University of Minnesota Press, 1996.

10. A.F. Walls, 'African Christianity in the history of religions', in C. Fyfe and A.F. Walls (eds.), *Christianity in Africa in the 1990s*, Edinburgh: University of Edinburgh Centre of African Studies, 1996.

11. J.L. Comaroff, *Of revelation and revolution: Christianity, colonialism and consciousness in South Africa*, Chicago: University of Chicago Press, 1991.

12. R. Marshall-Fratani, 'Mediating the global and the local in Nigerian Pentecostalism', *Journal of Religion in Afirca* 28 (3), 1998: 280.

13. A. Hastings, *The Church in Africa: 1450–1950*, Oxford: Clarendon Press, 1994: chapter 12.

14. C. Omenyo, 'Charismatic renewal movements in Ghana', *Pneuma* 16 (2), 1994: 169–185; E.K. Larbi, 'The development of Ghanaian Pentecostalism', Unpublished Ph.D. thesis, University of Edinburgh, 1995; A.J. Gyadu, 'The Pentecostal/Charismatic experience in Ghana', *Journal of African Christian Thought* 1 (2), 1998: 51–57.

15. M. Ojo, 'Deeper Life Christian ministry', *Journal of Religion in Africa* 18 (2), 1988: 141–162; M. Ojo, 'Charismatic movements in Africa', in C. Fyfe and A.F. Walls, 1996; M. Ojo, 'Charismatic movement in Nigeria' in P. Gifford (ed.), *New dimensions in African Christianity*, Nairobi: AACC, 1992; R. Marshall-Fratani: 278–315; O.U. Kalu, *Embattled gods: Christianisation of Igboland, 1841–1991*, London/Lagos: Minaj Publishers, 1996; O.U. Kalu, 'The third response: Pentecostalism and the reconstruction of Christian experience in Africa, 1970–1996', *Journal of African Christian Thought* 1 (2), 1998: 1–21; O.U. Kalu, 'The practice of victorious life: Pentecostal political theology and practice in Nigeria, 1970–1996, *Journal of Mission Studies* 5, 1998: 229–255.

16. P. Gifford, *African Christianity: Its public role*, Bloomington, Indiana: Indiana University Press, 1998.

17. P. Gifford, *Christianity in Doe's Liberia*, Cambridge: Cambridge University Press; P. Gifford, 'Some recent developments in African Christianity', *African Affairs* 93, 1994: 513–534.

18. K. Fiedler, 'The Charismatic and Pentecostal movements in Malawi in cultural perspective', unpublished manuscript, Chancellor College, Theology Conference, 1998.

19. D. Maxwell, 'Delivered from the spirit of poverty? Pentecostalism, prosperity and modernity in Zimbabwe,' *Journal of Religion in Africa* 28 (3), 1998: 350–373.

20. Gifford, 'Some recent developments in African Christianity'.
21. V. Lanternari, *The religions of the oppressed: A study of modern messianic cults*, London: MacGibbon and Kee, 1963.
22. E.M. Zeusse, 'Perseverance and transmutation in African Traditional Religions', in J. Olupona (ed.), *African Traditional Religions in contemporary society*, St Paul: Paragon House, 1991: 167 ff.
23. Gifford, *African Christianity: Its public role*: 47.
24. C. Kraft, *Behind enemy lines*, Ann Arbor: Servant Books, 1994; C.P. Wagner, *Warfare prayer*, Tunbridge Wells: Monarch, 1992.
25. R. Horton, 'African conversion' *Africa* 41 (2), 1971: 85–105.
26. P.G. Hiebert, *Anthropological insights for missionaries*, Grand Rapids: Baker Books, 1985.
27. C. Kraft, *Anthropology for Christian missions*, Maryknoll, New York: Orbis Books, 1996: 10
28. M. Eliade, *The sacred and the profane: The nature of religion*, New York: Harcourt, Brace, 1959.
29. Marshall-Fratani: 283.
30. J.S. Mbiti, *The prayers of African religion*, London: SPCK, 1975: 106.
31. Kalu, '*The practice of victorious life*': 229:255.
32. Hackett, 'New directions and connections': 69–77.
33. M. Burgess and G.B. McGee, *Dictionary of Pentecostal and Charismatic Movements*, Grand Rapids: Zondervan Publishing House, 1988: 843–844; W. Ma, 'A first waver looks at the third wave,' *Pneuma* 19 (2), 1994: 189–206.
34. R.J. Gehman, *African Traditional Religion in biblical perspective*, Kijabe, Kenya: Kesho Publications, 1989: 172–173.
35. W. Wink, *Naming the powers: The language of power in the New Testament*, Philadelphia: Fortress Press, 1984: 5.
36. Wink: 15.
37. Meyer: 316–349.
38. Marshall-Fratani: 278–315.
39. R.I.J. Hackett, 'Pentecostal appropriation of media technologies in Nigeria and Ghana', *Journal of Religion in Africa* 28 (3): 258–277.
40. Kalu, 'The third response': 22.
41. K. Poewe, 1994.
42. C.B. Johns, *Pentecostal formation*, Sheffield: Sheffield Academic Press, 1993: 86.
43. R. Rambo, *Understanding conversion*, New Haven: Yale University Press, 1993: 113–116.
44. W. Brueggemann, *The land: Place as gift, promise and challenge in biblical faith*, Philadelphia: Fortress Press, 1977: 2.
45. Bediako: 84.

Chapter Eleven

Old Wine in New Wine Bottles: Prophetic Experiences in the Celestial Church of Christ[1]

Afe Adogame

Introduction

The Celestial Church of Christ[2] (CCC) represents one of the most popular and pervasive prophetic movements in West Africa. It emerged out of the visionary experience and charismatic initiative of Samuel Bilehou Oschoffa, a Nigerian carpenter/timber merchant who turned a prophet following a spiritual 'trauma' in 1947. He was born and nurtured in Porto Novo-Dahomey (now Benin Republic) as the only surviving child of his parents who had migrated and sojourned there following incessant inter-ethnic wars in Yorubaland (Nigeria). He claimed that part of the message he received from this vision was to found a church which will be charged with 'cleansing the entire world'. What started as an obscure 'ethnic' religious movement has grown and transcended geo-ethnic boundaries with at least 3,000 branches scattered world-wide and a membership strength estimated at several millions today. This study concentrates on the status, role and activities of prophets/prophetesses within the CCC. It examines the meaning and functions of prophecy, visions and dreams in the life of the church, and in what ways they are employed to explain, predict and control events around the life of members. It further investigates into how these 'charismatic' ingredients have helped to shape the CCC worldview as well as provide members with a sense of identity and belonging.

The Status of *Wolidah/Wolijah* in CCC hierarchical structure

CCC organization is structured around the centralized authority of the Pastor. As both the spiritual and administrative head, the Pastor has the unchallengeable authority on all matters affecting the church. He exercises this authority through his personal charisma. Papa Oschoffa as the *Oludasile* (the founder) was greatly respected; all spiritual, social, economic and political issues within CCC were referred to him. He was referred to as Reverend, Pastor, Prophet and Founder. Following his demise in 1985, the mantle of leadership fell on A.A. Bada who was able to evince before his members such charismatic potentialities noticed in his predecessor.

The internal organization of CCC under the Pastor provides a complex hierarchical structure which could be classified into the lower and top cadres. The lower category provides a vertical progression along three separate but corresponding axes, namely line of Leader, *Wolidah/Wolijah* (prophet/ prophetess), and Elder. Though, not necessarily equal in rank, the three lines correspond with one another at the terminal posts of Superior Senior Leader, Superior Senior *Wolidah/Wolijah* and Superior Senior Elder. These represent the highest rank to which members may normally be elevated by promotion in the hierarchy. The upward mobility of these ranks to the top hierarchy rests solely on the discretion of the Pastor, or through the Pastor's ratification of nominations made by the Pastor-in-Council and other special committees. It is based essentially on the 'spiritual achievements' and the duration of service of the member. The top and lower hierarchies can be further categorized into the administrative and the prophetic offices. It is only the Pastor, by virtue of his status and role, who ostensibly combines the two structures simultaneously. Both lines are expected to be balanced in the leadership of every CCC parish, such that where the Shepherd emerges from the administrative line, his assistant must necessarily be chosen from the prophetic line and vice versa.

The status and role of *Wolidah* (prophets) and *Wolijah* (prophetesses) is vital to the total well-being of the church. New entrants, usually referred to as brother/sister, have to spend a minimum of two years before they can participate in a rite of passage which facilitates their upward mobility into any of the three but corresponding lines in the leadership ladder. The anointment ritual or unction is a very central feature of CCC. It is a rite which bridges movement from one rank to another. If a new entrant is observed during the liminal phase of transition 'to deliver spiritual messages that are true and tested', then on his first anointment, he or she may on the authority of the Pastor or his representative (Shepherd), be referred to as *Woli* (prophet/prophetess). From this level, the unction is reiterated at least every two years for promotion to the next higher rank as Assistant *Wolider/Wolijah*, *Wolider/Wolijah*, Senior *Wolider/Wolijah* and Superior Senior *Wolider/Wolijah* respectively. Through the enactment of the ritual of anointment, members enter into the phase of incorporation.

Prophets/Prophetesses as Receptors and Transmitters of CCC Hymns

CCC is governed by tenets, rules and regulations which are believed to have been revealed and channelled through the Pastor-Founder, prophets and prophetesses under the influence of the Holy Spirit. While most of them are now contained in the CCC Constitution, Pastoral Council Order, 'spiritual' hymns and other church literature, some of them were also made known through sermons during the lifetime of the Pastor-Founder. These represent the basic well-spring from which CCC hymn repertoire developed. Such songs emerge especially when the prophets and prophetesses experience a state of vision or trance. The first 'revealed' song/hymn to the church came during the first week in October 1947, five days after Oschoffa's traumatic experience in which he claimed to have received the 'divine commission'. It was believed to have been revealed to Oschoffa during a prayer service with the nucleus group, he fell into ecstasy and began to sing a song in Yoruba language as:

Enyin ara 'nu Krist	Fellow faithfuls in Christ
E gbe orin soke	Raise up songs
K'e si gbo ohun ti	And lift it up with a strong voice
Jehovah nso	Jehovah demands to know
Ere di re t'e fi wa	The purpose of your gathering
Ninu Ijo Mimo yi?	In this Celestial Church?
Ere di re t'e fi wa	The purpose of your gathering
Ninu egbe nla yi?	In this large congregation?
Ki Maria Iya wa	So that Mary our mother

243

Le e wa a sin wa lo   May accompany us
K'Eni Mimo rere yi   May this holy one
Wa ma sin wa lo   Accompany us[3]

The song was memorized and sung collectively by all present. It is believed that from this period onward stems the practice of singing only hymns revealed in visions during devotional worship.

Yah rih gorimah
Yah rih goriyeh
Ngo yeh
Yah rih yah[4]

The above hymn was claimed to have been revealed through Mawunyon[5], Oschoffa's relative, who was directed 'by the Holy Spirit' from his father's house a mile away. He arrived Oschoffa's house singing the above song (in an unknown language), and translating it at the same time into Egun, Yoruba and English languages as follows:

Egun	Yoruba	English
'Mi pa oku na	*'E yin Oluwa*	O praise ye the Lord
Won di pa emi	*Enyin omo ogun*	All ye Heavenly hosts
O ji re lo	*Asiko*	The great hour
Ko soso	*Na ti de*	Is at hand

He was said to have rendered the song in a kneeling position when he arrived at the house. In other cases, the hymns, when revealed, are quickly noted and put into writing or later taught to members by prophets and prophetesses who were mainly illiterates or semi-illiterates. The prophet or prophetess sometimes kept repeating the 'revealed' hymn while the congregation sang continually until they understood the wordings and could render them fluently. All hymns used for devotional services are expected to be only those that are given to the church through the mouth of prophets/prophetesses while possessed by the Holy Spirit, and they are usually songs which no one or any church is believed to have ever offered or known.[6]

It is forbidden to copy for use the hymns of other Christian denominations during the devotional services. 'Many more songs' according to the Pastor-Founder 'will the Holy Spirit give unto the church if we (members) adhere strictly to this injunction. If we use our songs alone, the Holy Spirit will manifest itself'[7]. Even minute details like the next song to sing in worship – its syntax and form – are believed to be dictated by the Holy Spirit. A tape-recorder is often part of the gadgets of worship in some parishes to record new songs that may be dictated and sponsored by the Holy Spirit. The hymns are therefore important not only for their euphonic value; they also constitute the 'spiritual' doctrines of ccc. The hymns have been employed to reveal the worldview and *raison d être* of the church.

The detailed procedure for the acceptance of ccc hymns according to them helps to put in check spurious and alien hymns. New hymns delivered through prophets/prophetesses are accepted for general use in devotional services only after vetting by the Pastor. Such hymns requiring acceptance are sent to the Pastor either in writing (with the tonic sofa) or on tape, accompanied by the name and details of the bearer through whom the hymn was delivered as well as the date and time of delivery. Once such a hymn is accepted by the Pastor, it shall then be the subject of a Pastoral Council Order proclaiming it for general use. On the whole, the 'spiritual' songs in the Yoruba hymn book number 925, though 712 were reflected originally. The difference in these figures explains the reservation already made for songs yet to be revealed. They believe that the revelation of new 'spiritual' songs is an unending, continuous process. Members believe that more new hymns/songs will be descended in the present and future times so long as the Holy Spirit continues to inspire prophets and prophetesses within ccc. Each hymn/song is believed to have its own motive, use and efficacy. The English Versions are essentially translations of the Yoruba hymns/songs.

An indigenous feature found in ccc hymnal repertory is the use and presentation of words/phrases in esoteric 'spiritual' languages. Such words and phrases include, for example, *Jerih mo ya mah; Yah rah Sarah Yah rah Samahtah; Yah rah man Hi Yah rah man; Yagol lolah Mariyanga rih yeh; Yah-Kirah-hihi-jah; Zevah Riyah, Zava Raye e.*[8] These are usually well-structured phonetically at the first stanza, or the first few lines of each stanza. In other cases, they are symmetrically transposed within the text or arranged interchangeably with their Yoruba or English interpretations. They were usually interpreted by the individual who receives them in a vision, trance or dream. Even though the meanings of some were also revealed in Egun, Yoruba and English languages, they were preserved in their original forms irrespective of the translated language. Such esoteric words used in their hymnal are not necessarily intelligible to non-members or even the indigenous Yoruba speakers. This represents perhaps an apparent form of glossolalia. Members believe that the charismatic gift of glossolalia was granted to only a few chosen ones, especially the prophets and prophetesses. The speaking in such esoteric language during trance or vision is seen as glossolalic.[9] CCC does not encourage speaking in tongues in the congregation, unless the speaker interprets.[10]

Purification Ritual for the Re-invigoration of *Agbara Emi*

The ritual services held every Friday of the week in CCC are referred to as *Esin Ojo Agbara* (Power Day Services). The underlying feature in all the three types of services is the quest for *agbara emi* (spiritual power), material and spiritual help to cope with the existential problems of life. The observance of Friday as a sacred day is linked with the day on which Jesus Christ died on the cross of Calvary for humankind. *Esin Ojise, Alala, Ariran* (Service for prophets, prophetesses, dreamers, visioners and seekers of spiritual power) is held between 12 noon and 1.00 P.M. at the Mercy land. This ritual must be conducted by the Shepherd-in-Charge and all those involved must be present with a bottle of water and a stick of candle each. Ritual purification of the Mercy land through the fumigation of incense and the sprinkling of holy water usually takes place prior to the commencement of the service. This is done either to put any existing malevolent forces on their heels or to create spiritual barricades within the sacred space.

One feature of such ritual worship is that petitions are made and prayers are enacted for forgiveness of sins, acquisition and reinforcement of spiritual power, sanctification, victory and protection of members. The prayer ritual is led at different stages by the highest ranking prophet, prophetess, the service conductor. There is also provision for the three-member prayer on various themes and the individual silent prayer where each member entreats God for spiritual power, peace, rebirth and accurate prophecy. Songs of mercy and power are sung:

Jesu Olugbowo mi	Jesus my great assistant
Tani mo ni laiye yi	Who else have I in this world

Bi ko se Re Baba Mimo	If not thou the Father Divine
Sunmo mi pe'lu Emimo	Draw near with thy spirit
Mo teriba 'waju Re	In humility I bow
Ma je ki nlo lowo ofo	Let me not go empty-handed
Maikeli Mimo Ode Orun	Holy Michael Defender
Wa so eru mi ka le	Give rest to my wearied soul
Gba mi Ajagun-segun	Save rest our warrior and con-
	queror

(Y.H.N. 158 / E.V. 22)

All the hymns and Bible lessons selected for the service are based on the essence of the Holy Spirit and the acquisition and retention of *agbara emi*. Sermon, announcements and sometimes admonition are based on the conduct and behaviour of prophets and prophetesses, and their punctuality to ritual services. Towards the apogee of the ritual, all members synchronously chant 'seven Halleluyahs to the four corners of the world' facing one direction at a time and lifting their hands heavenwards. At the last recitation, all members kneel down, bowing and touching the earth with their foreheads. The gesticulation is completed with making the 'sign of the cross' on the forehead or on the chest region.

The leader conducts the ritual cleansing of their bodies with the altar cloth, while participants are kneeling with their bottles of water and their candle lit in front of them. Afterwards, the leader sprinkles some of the holy water on them. At this stage of the ritual, many of the participants fall into 'spiritual sleep' through which they are believed to commune with the benevolent powers in visions, trance and dreams. They remain in this state for a while, always an indefinite period of time. Upon recovering from this semi-conscious state, they will drink out of the now sacralized water and take the remaining home also for drinking or other ritual purposes. Water is also obtained from the sacred well in the Mercy land. Such 'holy' water is believed to be potent, and thus used for prophylactic and therapeutic functions.

Visions, Prophecy, Trances and Dreams as Channels of Communication

There is a characteristic difference between the role ascribed to visions, prophecy, trances and dreams by the mainline churches and in CCC. While the CCC generally resent the belittling of visions, dream-life in the mission churches, in contrast, they attach great value to visions, prophecy, trances and dreams. The charismatic gift of vision is constitutive of CCC. The CCC seem to assimilate visions and prophecy, in fact, it is almost uniquely seen as visions. Prophecy through dreams and visions is regarded as the supreme manifestation of spiritual power. The priority which the church accords to these agents of revelation is evidence of the spiritual orientation of the church. The Pastor-Founder represents the head of the visioners and prophets in CCC. The vision, as visible manifestation of the power of the Holy Spirit acting in the church, is in the centre of their religious experience, even though not every member can acquire the gift.

Visions serve as a sort of 'watchdog' for the church. They inform constantly about the life of the church and of its members, revealing the causes of and solutions to their existential problems. Every existing CCC parish is expected to have a number of visionaries. The absence of revelation would be considered as a loss of spiritual power or force. Visions are also believed to be capable of revealing the 'spiritual' tensions underlying the situation in the church or of an individual member as well as to indicate in a premonitory way how the spiritual forces move towards and around them. The diagnosis given by the vision is most often completed by the indication of 'spiritual' action or works that are to be undertaken in order to remain, or to return 'under the power of God'.

CCC makes a comparison between 'visionaries' who may have revelations through dreams and visions (clairvoyance) and the hearing of voices (clairaudience), but unless they actually prophesy, they do not attain the status of a 'prophet'. A prophet or prophetess may be said to prophesy when they pass on to others revelations or 'messages' based on what has been seen or heard through the special work of the Holy Spirit. The visioner describes what he/she is seeing (Cf. Ezekiel 1:3–2:14); the prophet says the word of God, and his discourse is often recognizable through the phrase 'word of God' (Cf. Isaiah 43:1–13). CCC do not make a clear-cut distinction between the status and functions of visioners and prophets/prophetesses. They are seen to function complementarily. Strictly speaking, a CCC 'prophet' is more of a 'visionary' or 'diviner' in that he has the faculty of 'seeing' and 'finding remedies', than the Old Testament-type prophet as the spokesman of God and foreteller of doom. This relationship is further explained by the fact that the same purificatory ritual is enacted for prophets, prophetesses, visioners, dreamers and seekers of spiritual power.[11] Prophets/Prophetesses form a fundamental nerve-centre in the life of CCC. They are referred in CCC as *Ojise Oluwa* (messengers of God) or *Woli* (prophet). The duty of a prophet/prophetess is to edify the church and the individuals (1 Cor. 14:3).

Ala (dreams) are also received with a premonitory value in CCC. Both *Woliders* and *Wolijahs* have a similar leadership status, but the *Wolider* has the additional gift of being able to interpret dreams. *Ala* plays a role parallel to visions. However, it is less important, less spectacular too. It justifies an unction only if accompanied by the gift of vision. Those who seek 'spiritual' diagnosis to their problems may be advised to sleep on the floor of the nave of *Ile Esin/Ile Adura* or remain within the church precincts indefinitely or for a specified period in anticipation for the dream-sent revelations they desire. Such dreams, if and when they occur, are then interpreted by the dreamers or by other leaders such as the *Wolider*, gifted with the interpretation of dreams. The *Wolider* may also be asked to seek dreams or visions concerning a member's problems. Every existing parish is expected to have at least a leader from the prophetic hierarchy. The number of prophets/prophetesses, visioners and dreamers in any one parish vary depending on its size and numerical strength.

Visions, dreams and prophecy are common phenomena, especially during devotional services, prayer and revival services, power, thanksgiving and mercy services, night vigil and so forth. They could also become manifest anywhere, but their occurrence is more profound at the *Ile Esin* (house of worship/prayer), their 'heavenly' space on earth which serves as a centre for the dramatization of the 'heavenly' spiritual forces. During the prayer ritual, visionaries, prophets and prophetesses are often seen making frenzied and staggering movements, some falling, kneeling or prostrating on the floor and uttering both coherent and unintelligible sounds. When in this state, a visionary is said to be 'in spirit', 'falls in spirit', or falls into a long half-conscious state known as trance. At this time, the person experiencing the vision is no longer aware of what is happening in the immediate surroundings, nor is the visionary conscious of having sensations. The person is believed to be 'agitated by the Holy Spirit'. While some have very calm visions, others are shaken by trembling, sometimes very heavily. Most of the visionaries do not remember what they have seen, heard or said during the vision. The duration of the trance state varies from a few minutes to hours, days, or even weeks, without food or water.

After a prolonged rhapsodic state, the visionary 'returns in flesh', 'is brought back into flesh' or leaves a state of being 'in spirit' in order to come back 'in flesh'. While the visionary 'emits', that is, pronounces words telling what is seen and heard during the vision, a literate member of the church is immediately assigned to note the emission either in writing or by recording it in a tape recorder. Sometimes, the emission is incomprehensible or not very clear; words are difficult to be understood due to the spontaneity the utterances assume. The emission may simply be grunting sounds like *hon, hon, han, han, hun, hun* .... At other times, the visionary can be 'in spirit' without any signs of emission and exudation. The vision is conceived by CCC as what builds the church and what reminds it that it does not exist for itself, but for God that is manifest in the power of the Holy Spirit. Owing to the fact that the visionaries are particularly sensible to 'the Spirit', members believe that they could also be exposed to being tempted, troubled or deceived by the evil spirit. Therefore, precaution is taken and the vision itself is submitted to a spiritual discernment by a CCC authority. Shepherds or senior members such as the Superior Senior *Wolider* try to discern the spirit that inspires the visionaries. Depending on the content and object of the message received, the Pastor or his representative (Shepherd) are immediately intimated with the message. Complex 'spiritual messages', which concern the entire church or a parish as a whole, are often handled with caution. They go through and subject the contents to 'spiritual' scrutiny. They are believed to possess the power with which to discern the source of the message. It is only after ratification has been obtained that such a message can be disclosed to the individual or the church community as a whole. This, members claim, is a strategy against the infiltration of fake visionaries or spurious messages.

A prophet/prophetess' message after a vision or trance state may announce forthcoming blessings, danger or disaster. In such cases, a special prayer is embarked upon after the worship service or sometimes during the main devotional service. At the end of each service, members are often found in small groups, engaging in *eto adura* (prayer ritual) with the Shepherd, prophet or prophetess, or an elder presiding. Children also receive special prayer at the end of each service, for protection from accidents, sickness, death and the attack of evil spirits. Members may also go for special prayers during the week depending on the 'spiritual work', a certain course of action prescribed by the prophet/prophetess. Spiritual messages could also be revealed on certain occasions such as during 'special prayers' for an individual. On all days of the week, some members are found sleeping in the church premises with a number of candles lit around them. The duration varies from the details of the 'spiritual work' to the nature of the problem or need.

Abe abo (spiritual incubation or confinement) is a common feature in CCC. Members are believed to receive 'spiritual' protection by staying in the 'heavenly' space on earth for a number of days, weeks or months. While here, they are made to undergo *ise emi* (spiritual work) which includes fervent prayer ritual either to avert an impending danger or obstacle, or to pave the way for expected blessings or favour from the benevolent powers. Special prayers may also be offered when a member offers thanksgiving for blessings received, or when the church authority directs that such prayers be said at a particular time for specific issues. CCC believe that the benevolent powers can also be invoked and consulted through visionary means. A member who feels threatened by the malevolent, evil spirits, such as the *ajogun, aje and oso*, can request for prayers from a visionary. If the visioner falls 'in spirit', he then will be able to reveal the underlying spiritual forces, and indicate the type of prayer ritual corresponding to the described situation. The visioner can also reveal facts about absent persons or even persons unknown to him/her. Sometimes, the one who follows the vision or took down the messages will then make efforts to obtain details in order to identify the concerned person.

The different types of visions in CCC can be classified as: premonitory, explanatory and approval. The premonitory type announces a blessing, a disease, an impending doom, catastrophe or other forthcoming events, while the explanatory vision reveals the underlying spiritual forces or powers in a given situation, as for example, a disease, sickness, family or professional problems. The visions of approval are those which accept prayers and offertories. We can here cite examples from two vision accounts:

Oluwa ire ni apata mi
Eru kan ki yio ba mi ...
E fi ogun ole ara ole
Emi bu gidi gidi
Ranti lati san majemu
Ti o ba Oluwa da

Mo ti di olori ire
Se ni Ayo mi sese bere ...
Kiyesi ara
Ko ara ti re ni ijanu
Mase fi asiri re han ore
Mase beru
Iwo to duro lo sora
Ma sun gbagbe Olorun
Ni ojo oni ya ohun irin
se yi si mimo AQ 706 LSD
Imole tan
Edun okan re Agba
Se ore ofe si tan pepe

The above vision text was handed over to me on a letter-headed paper (titled 'CCC Ijeshatedo Parish I 'Oluwaseyi' – Notes of Spiritual Revelations) signed by a Prophetess simply identified as Adewumi, and the scribe Bisi. On October 6, 1996, during a routine visit to the above mentioned parish in Lagos, I was waiting to meet my appointment with the Shepherd-in-Charge of the parish when my attention was drawn to a prophetess dressed in *aso emi* (white sutana) standing beside the motor car which I drove to the church premises. On reaching the scene I observed the woman already 'in spirit', shaking and jerking involuntarily with her eyes firmly closed. She was heard uttering some unintelligible and incoherent sounds which were simultaneously recorded by the female scribe standing beside her. She immediately beckoned on me to kneel down in front of the Prophetess who had claimed to have been 'directed in the spirit to me'.

At the end of a prolonged 'vision state', she was 'brought back into the flesh'. When she finally opened her eyes, she directed the scribe to explain details to me. Due to the language barrier (she spoke in Yoruba), I requested that the message be explained in English, which she immediately translated as follows:

God of blessing is your rock, you should not fear. Pray and wage spiritual war against loss of life and loss of property. Do not forget to fulfil the covenant you had with the Lord. You have been blessed with the good things in life. Your blessings (joy) have just begun. Be careful of people (friends, family members, enemies etc.) and be watchful (with your tongue, what you eat, drink etc.). Do not give away your secrets to your friends. Do not be afraid. He that stands, be careful. Do not sleep and forget God. Today, you have to sanctify this means of transport with Reg. No. AQ 706 LSD. Light one candle, your heart must accept and be in agreement. An elder will supervise the benediction/grace at the altar.

The 'message' required that I subject the car to a sanctification ritual within the church premises by lighting a candle stick before the altar and reciting the 'benediction' under the supervision of an elder. For obvious reasons, I reluctantly accepted the earlier prescription but not the latter. Consequently, 'holy water' was obtained and sprinkled on both the interior and exterior parts of the car while the prophetess rendered some prayers. However, as I discovered afterwards, a candle stick had been used to write or draw a cross symbol on all the doors and windscreen of the car prior to my arrival. This was done without my consent and approval. The second example represents a vision which occurred during a naming ritual in a CCC parish:

> Hon! Hon!
> The angels, the angels still
> come down, come down
> from everywhere, everywhere
> in the choir, in front of the altar
> I see, I see
> that great, that great light
> coming down, coming down from heaven
> coming to fill the altar, the choir
> Hon! Hon! Hon!
> They come, they come
> to this holy, holy, holy place
> Hon! Hon!
> The angels, many
> are in the middle of us
> and take, they take our offertory
> in the hand, in the hand

Oh! they go up, go up to heaven
Hon! Hon! Hon!

This vision took place during a child naming ceremony. The prophet, who was carrying the child, 'fell in spirit' during the reading of psalms. As we can see from these two examples, besides the announcement and the explication, the vision can also indicate the type of prayer ritual corresponding to the described situation. So there can be all possible combinations of types and objects of prayer. Visions can also announce an accident, describe a celestial worship, indicate the state of relationship between a member and the spiritual forces, manifest hidden spiritual forces underpinned to a situation such as disease, envy or hatred. It can also announce the manifestation of a spiritual force and indicate what has to be done to prepare its reception.

CCC and Religio-Cultural Identity

The concepts 'culture' and 'ethnicity' in contemporary socio-scientific discourse have become highly problematic in terms of the specificity of use and the somewhat nuanced connotations they are seen to imply. However, in our discussion here, we suggest that the notion and understanding of identity in the CCC may be seen within the contours of both religion and ethnicity (with emphasis on the cultural element). Hans Mol's tripartite schema of personal, group and social identity is quintessential in relation to the experience of ethnicity as well as religion.[12] Knott aptly remarks that 'religion and religious choices are clearly influenced by the modes of self-perception of the individual, the group and the society'. At the individual level, the degree of religious participation may well be determined by a desire to be identified as part of an ethnic enclave. The same is true for groups'. She adds, 'the formation of an identity of ethnic groups and their members is thus not without influence on their religion and religiousness'.[13] For instance, the increasing proliferation of African Christian churches in Europe and elsewhere lends credence to the way in which the migration experience has affected religion at this group level.[14]

Knott demonstrates how religion makes its own impact on identity at the personal, group as well as social levels. She identifies the enormous impact that life cycle rites, and the beliefs and practices which are related to them, have on the nature of personal identity; and shows that traditions of religious authority and organization play significant roles in the shaping of a group's ethnic experience. At the level of social identity, Knott uses the example of ecumenism to show the influence of religion.[15] Religion reinforces ethnic identity, although the nature of this process varies and depends on the particular ethnic group and its situation.[16] Religion is seen as functioning in a certain way for ethnic identity. In another sense, the relationship may be reciprocal in terms of viewing the effect of religion on ethnicity and the corresponding impact of ethnicity on religion.

Ter Haar's use of public identity implicates on Christian identity on the one hand, and African identity on the other. Although, her view that 'African Christians in the Netherlands identify themselves first and foremost as Christians and only secondly as Africans or African Christians' may be somewhat problematic and contested in terms of the prioritisation, yet her identification of Africans (African Christians) and their adherence to Christianity as integral constituents of their public identity is germane to our discussion here.[17] This leads us further to another vital argument echoed in Ter Haar's concise paper, that is, the insistence on religious self-definition by 'insiders' as opposed to ascription and imposition of (ethnic or religious) identity by 'outsiders'. She corroborates Taylor's view which maintains that the definition of identity should result from a process of negotiation in which the people concerned participate.[18] What then is ccc's own sense of identity (self-definition) or and how do they define their identity? To what extent does the ccc serve as a bastion for religious and cultural identity? What constitutes the identity of a religion or what makes the identity of a religious system? Is a religious system the same as a religion?

Appiah sees identity as 'a coalescence of mutually responsive (if sometimes conflicting) modes of conduct, habits of thought, and patterns of evaluation; in short a coherent kind of human social psychology'.[19] According to Seiwert, it is certainly not the substance of the norms which defines the identity of a religious system. The reasons he adduced are that norms are not static, but may be susceptible to change.[20] It is thus problematic to define the identity of a religion, as the contents of a religion may change almost beyond recognition in both time and space. It is not the content or the substance of the norms, that is what is actually believed and practiced, that is decisive for the identity of a religion, but the authority referred to. Evidently within the different religious systems could be found substantially the same norms, especially in the realm of ethics. Seiwert argues that 'the identity and unity of a religious system are defined by the recognition of the source or the sources of authority on which the system is founded'.[21] The validity of a system of norms depends on the recognition of the authority which is defined by the system itself. It is exactly this source of authority which marks the boundaries of a given authority. Seiwert aptly identifies the well-spring of authority as pivotal in the delineation of identity and unity of a religious system. However, the beliefs and practices, in some respects, may also be momentous in determining the identity of a religion as well. Each religion has its own style, inner dynamic, special meanings and uniqueness.

I have shown elsewhere that the CCC exhibit cultural identity by taking on certain elements from Yoruba tradition, although features which are not necessarily diametrically opposed to biblical belief, and giving them a new meaning in their ritual context.[22] The use of concrete objects such as *omi agbara* (green water), *omi iyasimimo* (sanctified water), *mariwo ope / ida* (palm fronds) are elements which have affinity with Yoruba tradition but which have been legitimised and given biblical basis by the Pastor-Founder. Other examples are traditional rituals such as *Isomoloruko* (rite of naming) and *Esin Ipari Osu* (new moon ritual). In the same vein, biblical belief and Christian liturgical tradition have been made more intelligible and expressive in their own religio-cultural milieux. Christian ritual symbols such as in the Eucharist have been localized. The *Esin gbigba Ara ati Eje Oluwa* (Holy Communion) in the church has been located through 'inculturation' to give new meaning. Biblical belief was localized by replacing the ritual symbols of 'bread' (the Body of Jesus) and 'wine' (the Blood of Jesus) with the elements of 'fruits' and 'fruit juice' respectively. The consequence is the redefinition of Christian rites in Yoruba experience, while also explaining traditional rites in Christian paradigms.

On the level of religious system, the CCC maintains and insists on a self-identity as a Christian church. In this way it portends discontinuity with Yoruba tradition. The CCC beliefs are of immense significance to its members as they lie behind the praxis, rituals, worship, membership and decisions of the church. CCC is governed by tenets, rules and regulations which are believed to have been revealed and channelled through the Pastor-Founder, prophets and prophetesses under the influence of the Holy Spirit.[23] Members see the Bible as the source and foundation of all their knowledge and beliefs, and vehemently refuse any connecting nexus with the traditional religion. Several CCC hymns reveal the ingredient for the establishment of the CCC as 'the power of the blood of Jesus' in order to show her potency. The fervency of the belief in this commitment is such that all members of the CCC always insist on their identity being made perfectly clear and simple. The self-image of the CCC as *Oko igbala ikehin* (the last ship for salvation) best exemplifies the *raison d'être* of the church as they claim that the church 'is a branch of the heavenly church which was descended directly through the Pastor-Founder and charged with the task of cleansing the world'.[24] As elements of a religious system, many have been embodied, transformed and given biblical interpretation (new meaning), and vice versa.[25] The CCC insist on a self-identity that is essentially Christian, but the striking affinity with Yoruba cultural matrix is the elements that are given new meanings or interpretations. While we do recognize a great deal of affinity in both cosmological and ritual traditions, yet the inner meaning of the member's faith, the deeper conceptual and ritual procedures intrinsic to traditional Yoruba cosmology is left in our view largely untouched in the CCC. Herein lies the politics of cultural or religious identity in the church. It is pertinent as in the assessment of the nature and extent of this synthesis, that a distinction be made between elements and meanings which form the basic units in the entire process.

Conclusion

I have demonstrated in this article that CCC cosmology is weaved through and through with biblical belief, Christian ritual patterns and Yoruba thought and praxis. The prescription of rules, codes of behaviour, and procedures by the CCC derive largely from both religious (Christian) and cultural (indigenous Yoruba praxis). Many of these practices are also new indigenous inventions or innovations. In this way, CCC belief system and ritual tradition provide members with a sense of identity and belonging. The emphasis on visions, dreams, prophecy and spirit possession in CCC is in a sense evidence of the continuity with Yoruba religious *Weltanschauung*. The idea that the paranormal world is directly accessible by ritual specialists such as the *babalawo* (traditional diviner/medicineman) is also integral to Yoruba cosmology. We can possibly see a certain parallel between the attitude of members and the role visions play in CCC and the conception of and attitude towards the traditional Yoruba divination system (*Ifa* for example), even though the church itself points to scriptural support and evidence of the same phenomena. The anxieties and existential problems brought to a CCC prophet/prophetess are akin to those brought before the *babalawo*.

In the traditional setting, most situations of failure, diseases, sickness, other misfortunes and in fact whatever goes beyond human imagination is believed to be extra-ordinary or an influence of the malevolent spirits. People resort to the *babalawo* either to find out the causes or to know the wish of the *orisa* (divinities). CCC members still recognize that this desire for 'explanation' still exists and that problems never change or cease to exist, only the means or sources of 'prediction and control', and the power invoked has varied. Traditional Yoruba divination system contains in fact the three types of revelation that we have seen above. However, the traditional divinatory system 'acts' in most if not all cases when consulted, not spontaneously. The sources of revelation have also changed in the case of CCC from what they would refer to as evil spirits to benevolent spirits. That is why members insist on the fact that it is useless and disastrous to turn to *Ifa* or other systems of divination, exhibiting dubious or evil forces, while God Himself can be consulted[26]. It can therefore be said that what has changed in the CCC worldview is more of the sources, channels and nature of revelation or divination rather than in the attitude towards it.

A cursory look at the contents of prophetic messages in the CCC does not reveal prophecies of collective doom or of a revolutionary nature, a characteristic of Old Testament prophets or the early itinerant African prophets such as William Wade Harris, Kimbangu and Garrick Braide. In the present day, itinerant prophets still exist in the Church of the Lord – Aladura and the Cherubim and Seraphim. They are often seen with a bell and a Bible preaching during the wee-hours of the day or at other times. This phenomenon is completely alien to CCC as prophets are always warned never to engage in this evangelistic strategy[27]. In this sense, therefore, the role of the CCC prophet/prophetess is not so much as a catalyst or as an agent of social change, but rather as an oracular source of hidden knowledge concerning the past, present and future of an individual and the measures to be adopted to remedy certain existential problems and situations. Thus, the heaven sent revelations (visions, dreams, prophecy) are diagnostic as well as therapeutic, similar to the divination *Odu Ifa* (Ifa poems) chanted by the *babalawo*. The panacea assumes the form of 'spiritual work or activity' (i.e *Eto Adura* and *Iyasimimo*) as opposed to the *ebo* (offerings or sacrifices) to the *orisa*.

Notes

1. The original version of this paper was read at the British Association for the Study of Religions (BASR) Annual Conference on 'Religious Experience', Harris-Manchester College, Oxford University, UK. 11–13 September 1997.

2. For an extensive history of the CCC, see A. Adogame, *Celestial Church of Christ: The politics of cultural identity in a West African Prophetic-Charismatic Movement*, Frankfurt am Main: Peter Lang, 1999. Excerpts from this book have been reproduced here in this paper.

3. Celestial Church of Christ, *Constitution*, Nigeria Diocese, Board of Trustees for the Pastor-in Council, 1980; Cf. Yoruba Hymn Number 762. English translation by author.

4. Celestial Church of Christ, *Constitution*: 24. Cf. Yoruba Hymn Number, 331.

5. Mawunyon played a major role as one of the earliest prophets in the formative years of CCC. For instance, it was through him that some of the injunctions about Holy Communion, Candleholder, Pajaspa-Collection Pouch were revealed. See for instance Celestial Church of Christ: *Constitution*, 1980: 24–25.

6. See, Celestial Church of Christ, *Pastoral Order number 6*.

7. See *Alaye Lori Esin Ijo Mimo ti Kristi lati Orun wa-Lati enu Oludasile Ijo*, Celestial Church of Christ, CC Ijeshatedo 1-Oluwaseyi Parish, August 6, 1974: 8.

8. See *Orin Isipaya Mimo lati enu awon Woli Oluwa*, Yoruba and English (Combined Edition), Celestial Church of Christ International Headquarters, Ketu-Lagos. n.d. Yoruba Hymn Numbers 1, 2, 3, 56, 462 and 712 respectively. There are several other hymns which reflect these holy words/phrases.

9. Personal Interview with Olatunji Akande at CCC International Headquarters, Ketu-Lagos on September 23, 1996.

10. S.O. Odeyemi, *The spiritual heritage of Celestial Church of Christ*, Lagos: Femyet Outreach Publishing Company, 1993: 132.

11. See, Celestial Church of Christ, *Order of service (revised edition)*, Ketu-Lagos: Celestial Church of Christ International Headquarters, 1995: 63–64.

12. H. Mol, (ed.), *Identity and religion: International cross-cultural approaches*, Beverly Hills: Sage, 1978.

13. K. Knott, 'Religion and identity, and the study of ethnic minority religions in Britain,' in V. Hayes (ed.), *Identity issues and world religions*. Selected Proceedings of the Fifteenth Congress of the International Association for the History of Religions, Australia: Australian Association for the Study of Religions, 1986: 170.

14. See also, G. ter Haar, *Halfway to paradise. African Christians in Europe*, Cardiff: Cardiff Academic Press, 1998; A.U. Adogame, 'A home away from home: The proliferation of the Celestial Church of Christ (CCC) in Diaspora-Europe' *Exchange* 27 (2), 1998: 141–160.

15. Knott: 170.

16. See, F. Lewins, 'Religion and ethnic identity', in H. Mol (ed.), 1978.

17. G. ter Haar, 'Imposing identity: The case of African Christians in the Netherlands', *Diskus* (Web Edition) 5, 1999.

18. C. Taylor, *Multiculturalsim: Examining the politics of recognition*, Princeton: Princeton University Press, 1994.
19. K.A. Appiah, *In my father's House: Africa in the philosophy of culture*, Oxford: Oxford University Press, 1992.
20. H. Seiwert, 'What constitutes identity of a religion?', in V.C. Hayes (ed.): 5.
21. Seiwert: 5.
22. Adogame, *Celestial Church of Christ*: 212.
23. Celestial Church of Christ, *Constitution*: 29.
24. Adogame, *Celestial Church of Christ*: 147.
25. Adogame, *Celestial Church of Christ*.
26. Personal Interview with S.O. Odeyemi (Coordinator of ccc Bible Fellowship and Youth Programme) at the University of Lagos Senior Staff Quarters on August 27, 1996.
27. Personal Interview with Olatunji Akande at ccc International Headquarters, Ketu-Lagos on October 4, 1996.

Chapter Twelve

Who Defines African Identity?
A Concluding Analysis

Gerrie ter Haar

IN DIFFERENT WAYS the various articles in this volume reflect African perceptions of selfhood, with a specific focus on national, cultural and educational identities. As James L. Cox suggests in his introductory chapter, they are perhaps best understood as reflections about identity through discussions of what Western scholars have come to refer to in recent years as 'alterity', or the study of Otherness. Seen in this way, the African views put forward in this volume are as much statements about the West as they are about Africa itself. The intellectual point proposed by such a reading of the texts concerns the way in which the common divide between the Self and the Other may be bridged.

This has become a more than normally important matter in recent years due to the mass migration of sub-Saharan Africans to the West, notably to Europe, which has taken place during the last two decades. International migration has become a hallmark of our times, and Africans are in the forefront, largely due to the social and political condition of many African countries. Although reliable figures on the presence of sub-Saharan Africans in Europe are lacking, for various reasons including the large number of undocumented migrants, in the mid-1990s the total number of documented Africans within the countries of the European Union was officially estimated at about one million.[1] The large number of black Africans in Europe, including in places without any significant history of African presence, poses questions about African identity and its supposed unique character with particular urgency.[2] It also implies a need to bridge the perceived divide between, in this case, the European self and the African other.

The present chapter suggests that Europeans at present, far from eliminating the divide between identity and alterity, seem to be busy widening the gulf between the two. That is, the concept of African identity appears to be employed mainly as a way of emphasising the perceived existence of alterity, in this case in the form of an ascribed 'unique' ethnic identity. One of the most striking features of European politics today is the attempt to justify the erection of a wall – at times even literally![3] – between Europe and Africa, and between Europeans and Africans, with the objective of preventing the latter from settling in the West. Even more striking is the emergence of a Europe-wide official policy based on a consensus that the proper place for Africans is in Africa, and not in Europe. To legitimise such a view, it is essential to have a theory which justifies the fundamental difference between the Self and the Other. This is precisely what has happened with regard to Africans in Europe, as I will argue below on the basis of extensive research carried out among African migrant communities in Europe.

In the early and mid-1990s I did research among newly-established African Christian communities, particularly in the Netherlands, but to some extent also elsewhere in Europe. This resulted in the book *Halfway to Paradise: African Christians in Europe,* published in 1998.[4] One of the preoccupations of the book is with the concept of identity, which often appears a problem in the relations between African Christians in Europe and their counterparts in various European countries, as well as – in a more general sense – with people adapted to a Western-Christian culture, although the precise nature of the relationship seems to depend much on the circumstances and conditions of individual countries in Europe. In any case, my research has led me to conclude that identity and ethnicity are among the most misused concepts in the study of religious minority groups today. Exemplified by the case of African Christians in the Netherlands, I argue in the book that it is of vital importance to determine who fixes ethnic categories and who is subsequently allocated to these.

The Rise of African Congregations

In recent years many Africans have migrated to Europe in search of work. Many of them are Christians, who have founded new and independent churches in all the countries where they have settled, thus adding a new (and unexpected) dimension to Europe's multicultural society. The rise of African congregations may be a new phenomenon for the Netherlands and for most of the European continent, but this is not the case for one of its outlying regions, the United Kingdom. As one of the former colonial powers in Africa, the United Kingdom has been home to African Christian congregations for several decades. Unlike elsewhere in Europe, the majority of these were originally founded by Nigerians. On the continent, the founding of new congregations has largely been at the initiative of Christian believers from Ghana. Former Zaire, recently renamed as the Democratic Republic of Congo, also has a strong Christian tradition which is today perpetuated in Europe.

Few would have foreseen the religious changes which are taking place all over Europe as a result of worldwide immigration. In the Netherlands, which together with Germany is in the forefront of these developments, a large number of African-initiated churches now exists, most of which were founded only in the 1990s. As in other countries they are located in or near the big cities where African immigrants have settled to find work. Thus, Amsterdam, Rotterdam and The Hague have become main locations for African Christian worship. The most important of these is Amsterdam, where today some seventy to eighty African-initiated churches exist, of different size, mostly founded by Ghanaians and mostly situated in one particular district of Amsterdam, the Bijlmermeer. The latter is no surprise considering that the majority of African migrants in the Netherlands have taken up residence there. Most of these churches are of an evangelical and charismatic character and international in their orientation, which is often expressed by including or adding the word 'international' to the name of the church. In addition to these institutionalised congregations, there are many other organised groups of worshippers, such as prayer-groups, whose existence is hard to detect because they usually meet in private. In fact, nearly all the African church communities started their life as small house congregations where people gather for Bible study and prayer.

Taking the situation in the Netherlands as an example, we may for analytical purposes divide the African Christian communities into four different categories. First, there are fully independent churches which were founded in the Netherlands and have no immediate counterpart elsewhere, either in Africa or outside. The best example of this is the True Teachings of Christ's Temple, the oldest church of this sort in the country, which has now also established branches in Hamburg and London. This church owes its existence entirely to the diaspora situation of its members in the Netherlands. A second category consists of churches which maintain links with a church in the home country. In most cases, the initial contact has been made by the congregation in the Netherlands which felt an acute need to be assisted in its work by a long-established, experienced church. Often, the initiators belonged to such a church in their home country. In Ghana this may either be an influential mother-church such as the Church of Pentecost or the Resurrection Power and Living Bread Ministries or, as is increasingly the case, one of the more recently established independent churches, such as the Praise Valley Temple or the Damascus Christian Church. Depending on the organisational structure and type of affiliation the relationship may also imply some link with the United States, such as in the case of the Assemblies of God or the Rhema Bible Church.

Third, there are African religious communities which are part of a world-wide organisation, such as the Roman Catholic Church. Due to its hierarchical structure the Roman Catholic Church has developed its own ways to accommodate newcomers. In Amsterdam, for example, special services are held in English and French to assemble Catholics from abroad where African Christians worship together with English- and French-speakers from other parts of the world. Yet, the African spirit of independence can also be seen here. Within the Catholic Church, English-speaking Africans, mainly from Ghana, have formed their own congregation, known as the All Saints Church, which was officially inaugurated by the Bishop of Haarlem under whose jurisdiction it falls. Finally, there are some previously existing churches in the Netherlands which are frequented in numbers by Africans, such as the Seventh Day Adventists or the Dutch *Pinkstergemeente* or Pentecostal Church. Such churches do not belong to the mainstream Christian tradition in the Netherlands, which consists essentially of the Reformed Protestant Churches and the Roman Catholic Church. Another example of a 'non-mainstream' church that also attracts African believers is the Dutch Catholic Church, an episcopal church which, despite its name, is not related to the Roman Catholic Church but is an independent organisation which adheres to the laws and principles of the early Christian Church and follows the ancient rites. In Amsterdam, for example, there are quite a few Nigerians among the congregation.

'African Churches'?

It is in these circumstances that the question has emerged how important or how relevant the issue of African identity is to African Christians in Europe. In the Netherlands, the label 'African churches' is commonly used by the Dutch to refer to the African Christian congregations in their midst. It is a type of ethnic labelling which bears a relation to the way in which Dutch society has traditionally been organised at all levels, and whose hallmark is 'pillarisation' (*verzuiling*). This designates a system of social organisation which is itself traditionally marked by a form of exclusive group affiliation based on religious persuasion and thus easily leads to the relative isolation of those who are not part of one of the pillars. It is in fact a system which encourages the development of groups along separate lines – a system which has worked well in the past for the emancipation of different social groups in the Netherlands but which, because of its imposition on others, has also led to excesses such as the South African system of apartheid. Although the system of pillarisation has eroded over time with the increasing secularisation of society, the mental structure remains deeply embedded in Dutch society.

In my book *Halfway to Paradise* I have argued that African Christians in the Netherlands look at themselves in a different way and, without denying their African background, first and foremost define their own identity in terms of being Christian. This is also expressed in the fact that, unlike their Dutch counterparts, they do not refer to their own churches as 'African' churches but as 'international' churches'. This self-chosen label is a clear indication of the fact that they do not wish to operate in a form of splendid isolation imposed on them by the Dutch but, as a matter of principle, want to be open to all believers irrespective of their individual and collective backgrounds. Thus, in effect, African Christians in the Netherlands try to locate their identity not in what separates them from Dutch Christians, but rather in what binds them together with them.

Thus, African Christians in the Netherlands identify themselves first of all as *Christians* and only secondly as Africans or *African* Christians.

In their own view, their adherence to Christianity constitutes the most important element of their public identity. Yet, there is a general tendency on the part of their Dutch counterparts to insist on their perceived African identity, while ignoring their common Christian identity. In effect, this tendency leads to the segregation of Africans in Dutch society and as such is in striking contrast to the general outcry for the integration of foreigners. It takes us back to the vital question of whether an identity is self-imposed or ascribed by others, and whose interests are served in respective cases. With specific reference to the situation in the Netherlands, I would like to argue that the discussion regarding the need for African Christians in Europe to develop their 'own' identity as African Christians is being led by their European counterparts and serves European rather than African interests. It would be interesting to compare the Dutch attitude with the situation in other countries of Europe, where different social mechanisms exist for the integration of foreigners.[5]

Rather than labelling them as 'African' churches it would be more appropriate, I argue in my book, to refer to the African-initiated churches in Europe today as African international churches, an appellation which would do justice to the historical significance of these churches in a globalised world, while at the same time showing their continuity with the past by providing the well-known abbreviation of AIC with new meaning. Originally known as African independent churches or, in short AIC's, the content of the 'I'-initial has been subject to change ever since these churches emerged on the African continent in the late nineteenth and early twentieth centuries. Apart from African 'independent' churches, these churches have been labelled over time as African 'indigenous', African 'instituted', and African 'initiated' churches. The change of appellation is a telling illustration of the change of perspective it implies on a historic phenomenon at different points of time. The rise of African congregations in the Netherlands and other parts of the European continent reflects yet another change of perspective which can best be expressed with the term African 'international' churches, a term which does justice to both the subjective perspective of the insider who has chosen this term, and the objective view of the outsider who cannot ignore the international distribution of these churches today. The latter, however, requires a change of outlook on the part of Western observers who are often inclined to neglect or underestimate the global character of these churches.

African Identity

In his book on multiculturalism and the politics of recognition, Charles Taylor argues that identity is often shaped by the *mis*recognition of others.[6] My research findings concerning African Christians in the Netherlands seem to support Taylor's thesis. The difference between the ascribed ethnic identity of African Christians and their religious self-definition is too important to ignore and leads one to suspect underlying motives, of either a religious or a political nature. The insistence by many non-Africans on the existence of a specific African identity may be inspired by a concern for religious orthodoxy, or otherwise respond to a need of white Christian communities to distinguish themselves from black Christian communities in their midst, whom they believe to be different. Demarcation is also furthered by the tendency of intellectuals of various sorts to ascribe a special identity to African Christians in Europe derived from their ethnic background, due to an intellectual attachment to the notion of multiculturalism. Hence, academic specialists tend to emphasise migrants' African roots, in preference to seeking the meaning of their lives in Europe, where they now live. This contributes to the segregation of Africans and non-Africans in this part of the world, and also ignores the religious element in their current identity. In a different way, the same process is furthered by the public insistence that Africans in Europe should develop their own – meaning 'African' – identity. This is not to deny that Africans in Europe have such a right; my argument is simply that the necessity to promote this should not be imposed on them.

One of the problems recurring throughout my book has been to decide how to refer to people who have moved their place of residence from Africa to Europe. Are they Africans who happen to live in Europe? Are they black Europeans? How long must a foreigner live in Europe to qualify as a European? The laws of various European states provide answers to these questions, since there are specific circumstances under which an immigrant may become a naturalised citizen of a new country, and children born in Europe of immigrant parents may be defined as nationals of the places where they live. But although the law is generally precise on these matters, at present the laws governing immigrants from Africa are subject to frequent change, usually in the sense of making it harder to regularise a stay in Europe. In any case, the perceptions of various groups of people often do not coincide exactly with the text of whatever legislation is currently in force. A person born in Ghana, and naturalised as a citizen of one or another European country, or at least having official permission to live there, may still be regarded by native Europeans as an African, and therefore an alien, particularly recognisable by his or her skin colour. On the other hand, a black Briton, for example, whose parents emigrated from a Caribbean island which had itself known a long period of British government and cultural influence, may nevertheless insist on being regarded as having some sort of African origin, an 'Afro-Saxon'.

These considerations apply not only to people but also to their ideas and their institutions. If we refer to a church established in Amsterdam by a person born in Ghana, and attended overwhelmingly by others from Africa, as an 'African' church, it is to imply strongly that it is not for Europeans. If we refer to the faith which African immigrants profess when they are in Europe as African Christianity, it may equally imply that this is of a special ethnic brand, not for European use. But to achieve any degree of clarity at all in analysing this subject, it is almost inevitable that an author will refer to 'African Christians', even when these live in Europe. It is thus understandable that many commentators refer to their places of worship as 'African churches', even when these regard themselves as fully international and open to people of all races and nationalities.

In *Halfway to Paradise* I have striven to avoid such a usage, referring rather to African-initiated churches, a term quite widely used in the literature to refer to a catagory of churches in Africa which have been founded and are led by (black) Africans. I have coined the term 'African international churches' to refer to a similar type of churches which have been initiated by Africans in Europe, and at the same time owe much to their African origin. Since these churches may maintain links all over the world, notably with Africa as well as within Europe and with Asia and America, their scope is clearly international. In fact, so cosmopolitan has church life become in Africa that there are today churches on the African continent which can also usefully be described as African international churches. This is particularly true of the new generation of evangelical or pentecostal churches in Ghana, many of which are preoccupied with spreading the gospel and some of which have established efficient bureaucracies intent on evangelising overseas, notably in Europe. Hence, the African international churches represent the latest stage of development in the life of churches initiated and led by Africans.

Nevertheless, all this is still to make use of an ethnic adjective in describing these institutions and the religious and cultural ideas with which they are associated. What is of crucial importance, therefore, is the precise significance which is attached to these labels. In this respect the connotations attached in Europe to any label which has 'African' written on it are powerful ones, summarising all the respects in which Africans are generally believed to be different from Europeans. The insistence – which I noted before – of many non-Africans on the existence of a specific African identity, whether inspired by religious orthodoxy or by intellectual liberalism, is in effect a continuation of the old colonial and early missionary discourse and praxis regarding the perceived 'otherness' of Africans.[7] Concepts of otherness, like all ideas, have a history, and in the case of Europe it is one which includes the experiences of colonialism and nineteenth-century missionary enterprise as well as ideas generated by media reports of more recent events, including famines and wars. All of this provides part of the ideological baggage which many Europeans carry with them and which they may unpack when they read a description of somebody or something as 'African'. This baggage is a legacy of the past, which cannot be wished away. But in applying labels and descriptions today it seems important to be aware of the great speed with which Africa itself is changing and with which its links with other parts of the world are being reforged, sometimes in surprising ways.

Personally, I would like to argue not only that the definition of identity should result from a process of negotiation in which the people concerned participate (as Taylor also argues), but also that the formation of an ethnic identity is closely associated with the personal security of the individuals concerned. Obviously, the mechanisms for that are influenced by the size of a particular minority group vis-à-vis the majority population. Africans in Europe are a relatively small minority and have little or no power as a group. For many of them, their (Christian) religion helps them to achieve a degree of security and inner strength which may well encourage them in future to reconsider their self-identity specifically in terms of being African Christians. Or, alternatively, the experience of exclusion, inspired by racism or other excluding mechanisms, may have a similar effect. This is the case, for example, in the United Kingdom where, due to the circumstances of an entirely different context, African and Afro-Caribbean church leaders tend to insist on their African identity in the experience of their faith.[8]

It is useful, at this stage, to have a quick look at North America. Compared to Europe, debates on multiculturalism in America often risk being caught between two ideological positions, on the one hand a demand for the recognition of a homogeneous equality, and on the other hand the promulgation of ethnocentric rights and rules.[9] This applies to society at large and to its various institutions, including the churches. It is said that ethnic minorities in America tend to feel excluded from the liberal democracy in which they are living. They often do not regard the political decisions which are taken, even when this is by a majority vote, as reflecting their views. When such a situation arises, excluded communities have a broad choice between either conforming or protesting.[10] If we apply this insight to Europe, it has certain implications for the relationship between African Christian communities and their European counterparts, of the sort I have discussed at length in various chapters of my book. It may also imply the development of a process in which African communities, having been defined in ethnic terms, come to regard themselves as excluded from political society, and be faced with a similar choice between conformity and protest.

To take a specific example of such a process in operation it is appropriate to turn once more to the Bijlmer district of Amsterdam, the focus of attention throughout my book. Black members of the district council, claiming that they are excluded from the centre of political power, have formed what they call a *Zwart Beraad*, a Black Consultation Group. It is significant that they have chosen to organise themselves under this label, which emphasises their blackness as their common characteristic. In fact most of the group are Surinamers, but it could be said that, by describing themselves as black politicians, they are claiming to represent a constituency of black people as a whole, which includes Africans. In theory, a similar process could take place among the churches in the Bijlmer if, in the course of time, they too were to perceive themselves as excluded from the mainstream of society. A sign of that happening would be if they were to advertise themselves as black or African churches, rather than simply as Christian ones, as they now do.

Religion and Ethnicity

In studying African communities, whether in or outside Africa, the scholarly focus is often on ethnicity and ethnic adherence, and often at the expense of the religious factor. The question is: why is this so? Or, in the particular case under discussion: why is it that Western scholars prefer to single out ethnicity in their efforts to understand the development of the African diaspora in Europe? The focus on ethnicity rather than on religion is no doubt partly due to the fact that analysts who themselves view the world in secular terms tend to regard religion either as a form of false consciousness or at best as a symbol of some other force, such as an expression of ethnicity. In a broader sense, it may also be a consequence of the fact that African communities, wherever they manifest themselves, are often seen as the almost exclusive domain of anthropology. So prevalent is the study of ethnicity in modern anthropology that a leading American anthropologist, Sally Falk Moore, has wondered if, in terms of anthropological theory, ethnicity has become the *avatar* of tribe.[11] Anthropologists, like other Western observers, were until quite recent times accustomed to think of Africans as forming political and social groups called 'tribes', and to consider that such groups were a phenomenon characteristic of Africa and other parts of what would later be called the developing world. The idea, prevalent until the mid-twentieth century, that Africans lived in 'tribes' which were the vehicle of their ethnic identity, was also a racial one, combined with notions of hierarchy and evolution. While the concept of race is no longer scientifically respectable, and that of 'tribe' is also avoided by many social scientists, the concept of ethnicity has come to enjoy wide currency.

The concept of ethnicity, in other words, has tended to replace the concept of race in the study of African communities in modern times, while the content has remained substantially the same. Ethnicity, like race, is an elusive concept. Both are essentially modern notions generated by the global expansion of European societies since the late fifteenth century when the gradual shrinking of the world brought Europeans into contact with human societies whose main characteristic seemed to be a physical one, most noticeable in the colour of their skin.[12] In its modern form, the concept of race developed in the seventeenth and eighteenth centuries as one of the products of the Enlightenment and further developed into a science of race during the nineteenth century when scientific theories came to replace religious beliefs in some respects.

Given the scientific discrediting of the concept of race, the concept of ethnicity provides in principle an alternative way of thinking about human diversity as it introduces other categories for defining differences between human populations. There appears to be no consensus as to how to define ethnicity, but most commentators tend to stress the cultural element. In other words, they tend to refer to some sort of cultural distinctiveness as the mark of an ethnic group. As always, there are different schools of thought in this matter, but an important one seems to adhere to the idea that ethnicity is most of all a matter of the processes by which boundaries are created and maintained between different groups.[13] That makes it an interesting and relevant question by whom and how these boundaries are delineated. In modern Europe, when the identity of certain social groups thought to be ethnically distinct is brought into debate, such as in the case of African Christians, the delineation is usually ascribed to the wish of that particular minority to preserve or define its specific identity. This is usually considered in terms of a specific cultural identity, of which religion forms a part. The argument I have advanced in the case of African Christian communities notably in the Netherlands has been the opposite, namely that the drawing of boundaries is a conscious or unconscious act on the part of the host society and as such the social and intellectual concomitant of the current political process of segregating human societies.[14]

The term 'ethnic' is often used as synonymous with people who are thought of as culturally different, almost as if 'naturally' culturally different. This is conceived in the absence of clear standards, and either ignores or underestimates the importance of non-biological elements or mechanisms which are central to defining humans' ability to create culture.[15] Its main attraction lies in its usefulness in distinguishing between 'us' and 'them', thus furthering the process of 'othering'. In practice, as the British sociologist David Mason has pointed out, the essential characteristic for membership of a so-called ethnic minority often appears to be the possession of a skin which is not 'white'. In this way, the equation of cultural difference and ethnicity may become an instrument of social and political power, as with the designation of race. Or, in sociological terms, the attribution of ethnicity to others can thus become part of a process of denying the legitimacy of claims on resources by those concerned.[16] This, it seems to me, is eminently the case in present-day Europe where a main occupation today is the exclusion of those who try to come and share in its wealth.

Notes

1. This figure refers exclusively to African countries south of the Sahara and therefore does not include North African migrants. The figure has been compiled on the basis of statistics provided by Eurostat, the statistical office for the European Union. Note that this is a general figure which needs to be seen more as a guideline than an accurate assessment. This is due to the differing ways of data collection in individual countries and the fact that European migration statistics are always several years behind. It is often suggested that the official figures should be doubled or even tripled if we take into account the estimated number of undocumented migrants in Europe.

2. Whereas in the past African presence was largely limited to former colonial powers in Africa, notably including the Ununted Kingdom and France, today we find a large African presence in countries such as Germany and the Netherlands and others without recent colonial connections with Africa.

3. This notably concerns the Spanish enclaves on the North African coast, Ceuta and Melilla, which are both considered weak spots in the defence of Fortress Europe. In Ceuta a barbed wire wall has been erected around the enclave financed by the European Union. See, M. Carr, 'Policing the frontier: Ceuta and Melilla', in L. Fekete (ed.), *Europe: The wages of racism*, 1997: 61–66.

4. Gerrie ter Haar, *Halfway to paradise: African Christians in Europe*, Cardiff: Cardiff Academic Press, 1998. In 2001 the book was republished in a special edition for Africa by Acton Press in Nairobi under the title *African Christians in Europe*.

5. One may refer here, for example, to the study carried out in London by Gerd Baumann, *Contesting culture: Discourses of identity in multi-ethnic London*. Cambridge: Cambridge University Press, 1996.

6. Charles Taylor, *Multiculturalism: Examining the politics of recognition*. Princeton: Princeton University Press, 1994.

7. See e.g. the critical comments made by Teresia Hinga in her short essay entitled 'Inculturation and the otherness of Africans: some reflections' , in: Peter Turkson and Frans Wijsen (eds), *Inculturation: Abide by the otherness of Africa and the Africans*, Kampen: Kok, 1994: 10–18.

8. See Patrick Kalilombe, 'Black Christianity in Britain', in: Gerrie ter Haar (ed.), *Strangers and sojourners: Religious communities in the diaspora*, Leuven: Peeters, 1998: 173–193. In 2001 this volume of essays was republished in a special edition for Africa by Acton Press in Nairobi under the title *Religious communities in the diaspora*.

9. Taylor, 1994.

10. Taylor, 1994.

11. Sally Falk Moore, *Anthropology and Africa: Changing perspectives on a changing scene*, Charlottesville and London: University Press of Virginia, 1994: 129.

12. See David Mason, *Race and ethnicity in modern Britain*, Oxford: Oxford University Press, 1995: 5. The whole argument of this author concerning race and ethnicity is based on the assumption that these are *relational* concepts.

13. Mason: 12–13.

14. See Gerrie ter Haar, *Chosen people: The concept of diaspora in the modern world*, Leeds:

British Association for the Study of Religions (BASR) Occasional Paper No. 16, 1996.

15. Note that 'culture' is also a much-debated concept and that there is no overall consensus as to its precise meaning. Today it is often taken among anthropologists to refer to 'a class of phenomena, conceptualised for the purpose of serving their methodological and scientific needs'. On the basis of that, culture is seen as 'composed of patterned and interrelated traditions, which are transmitted over time and space by non-biological mechanisms based on man's uniquely developed linguistic and non-linguistic symbolising capacity' (Charlotte Seymour-Smith, *Macmillan's Dictionary of Anthropology*, London: Macmillan, 1986: 65).

16. Mason, 1995: 14.

General Bibliography

Abia State Government White Paper. 1996. 'The Ogo/Church conflict in Afikpo', *Afikpo Today*, 1 (7).

Achebe, Chinua. 1978. *Things fall apart*, London: Heinemann, 1978.

Adamolekun, Ladipo. 1976. *Sékou Touré's Guinea*, London: Methuen.

Addo-Fenning, R. 1985. 'Church and State: A historical review of interaction between the Presbyterian Church and traditional authority', *Research Review* 1 (2).

Addo-Fenning, R. 1995. *Akyem Abuakwa 1700–1943: From Ofori Panin to Sir Ofori Atta*, Legon: Ghana Universities Press.

Ade Ajayi, J.F. 1965. *Christian missions in Nigeria, 1841–1891: The making of a new elite*, London: Longmans.

Adeleye, R.A. 1971. *Power and diplomacy in northern Nigeria 1804–1906: The Sokoto Caliphate and its enemies*, Harlow: Longman.

Adiele, S.N. 1996. *The Niger mission: Origin, growth and impact 1857 –1995*, Aba: Isaeco Press.

Adogame, A. 1998. 'A home away from home: The proliferation of the Celestial Church of Christ (CCC) in Diaspora-Europe' *Exchange* 27 (2): 141–160.

Adogame, A. 1999. *Celestial Church of Christ: The politics of cultural identity in a West African Prophetic-Charismatic Movement*, Frankfurt am Main: Peter Lang.

Ainger, Geoffrey. 1995. 'Profile: Geoffrey Parrinder', *Epworth Review* (January): 29–38.

Aja, R.O. 1996. 'Religion and culture in Afikpo society', *Afikpo Today* 1 (7): 34–35.

Akintoye, S.A. 1971. *Revolution and power politics in Yorubaland 1840–93: Ibadan expansion and the rise of Ekitiparapo*, New York: Humanities Press, 1971.

Alphen, E. van. 1991. 'The Other Within', in R. Corbey and J.Th. Leerssen (eds.), *Alterity, identity, image: Selves and others in society and scholarship*, Amsterdam and Atlanta: Rodopi, 1–16.

Anagbogu, Ifeanyi. 1995. *History of Awka*, Awka: Chiston.

Anderson, G.H. and T.F. Stransky,(eds.) 1981. *Christ's Lordship and religious pluralism*, Maryknoll, NY: Orbis Books.

Anyanwu, U.D. 1997. *Local government democracy in Nigeria*, Okigwe: Whytem Publishers, 8–21.

Appadurai, A. 1996. *Modernity at large: Cultural dimensions of globalisation*, Minneapolis: University of Minnesota Press.

Appiah, K.A. 1992. *In my father's house: Africa in the philosophy of culture*, Oxford: Oxford University Press.

Assimeng, Max. 1989. 'Historical legacy, political realities and tensions in Africa,' in Lutheran World Federation, *Encounters of religions in African cultures*, Geneva: Lutheran World Federation.

Austin, D. 1964. *Politics in Ghana*, London: Oxford University Press.

Austin, J.L. 1963. 'Performative-constative', in C.E. Caton (ed.), *Philosophy and ordinary language*, Urbana, Chicago, London: University of Illinois Press, 22–54.

Awolalu, J.O. 1991. 'African Traditional Religion as an academic discipline'. in: Uka, E.M. (ed.), *Readings in African Traditional Religion: Structure, meaning, relevance, future*, Bern: Peter Lang, 123–138.

Ayandele, E.A. 1996. *The missionary impact on modern Nigeria 1842–1914: A political and social analysis*, London: Longmans.

Baeta, C.G. 1971. *The relationships of Christians with men of other living faiths*, Accra: Ghana University Press.

Baeta, C.G. 1970. 'Missionary and humanitarian interests 1914 to 1960', in L.H. Gann and P. Duignan (eds.), *Colonialism in Africa 1870–1960*, Volume 2, Cambridge: Cambridge University Press.

Balagangadhara, S.N. 1994. 'The Heathen in his blindness…': Asia, the West and the dynamic of religion*, Leiden: E.J. Brill.

Banda, Jande. 1995. 'Aspects of current constitutional change debate in Malawi, Paper presented at Social Change in Malawi Conference, Chancellor College, 1 July 1995: 12–13.

Barrett, D.B., 1968. *Schism and renewal in Africa: An analysis of six thousand contemporary religious Movements*, London: Oxford University Press.

Barrett, D.B. 1982. *World Christian Encyclopedia: A comparative survey of churches and religions in the modern world*, Oxford: Oxford University Press.

Barrett, D.B. 1988. 'The twentieth century Pentecostal/Charismatic renewal in the Holy Spirit, with its goal of world evangelization', *International Bulletin of Missionary Research* (July): 119–129.

Barth, K. 1957. *The Word of God and the word of man*, New York: Harper.

Batchelor, S. 1998. 'The other Enlightenment project: Buddhism, agnosticism and postmodernity', in U. King (ed.), *Faith and praxis in a postmodern age*, London: Cassell, 113–27.

Baumann, G. 1996. *Contesting culture: Discourses of identity in multi-ethnic London*, Cambridge: Cambridge University Press.

Bayart, J-F. 1989. L'etat en Afrique: la politique du ventre, Paris: Fayard

Beach, D.N., 1973, 'The Initial Impact of Christianity on the Shona: the Protestants and the Southern Shona', in J.A. Dachs (ed.), *Christianity south of the Zambezi, volume 1*, Gweru: Mambo Press, 25–40.

Bediako, K. 1992. *Theology and identity: The impact of culture upon Christian thought in the second century and modern Africa*, Oxford: Regnum Books.

Bediako, K. 1995. *Christianity in Africa: The renewal of a non-Western religion*, Edinburgh: Edinburgh University Press, 1995.

Bediako, K., 1996, 'Understanding African theology in the twentieth century', *Bulletin for Contextual Theology in Southern Africa and Africa* 3 (2): 1–11.

Beek, W.E.A. van and T.D. Blakely, 1994. 'Introduction', in T.D. Blakely, W.E.A. van Beek,, and D.L. Thomson, (eds.), *Religion in Africa*, London: James Currey and Portsmouth, New Hampshire: Heinemann, 3–20.

Beyer, P. 1994. *Religion and globalisation*, London: Sage.

Bhebe, N.M.B. 1979. *Christianity and Traditional Religion in Western Zimbabwe, 1853–1923*. London: Longman.

Blake, J.W. 1937. *European beginnings in West Africa 1454–1578*, London: Longmans.

Boahen, A.A. 1975. *Ghana: Evolution and change in the nineteenth and twentieth centuries*, London: Longman.

Bolink, P. 1967. *Towards church union in Zambia: A study of missionary cooperation and church-union efforts in central-Africa*, Franeker: T. Wever.

Bourdillon, M.F.C. 1996. 'Anthropological approaches to the study of African religion', in J. Platvoet, J. Cox, and J. Olupona (eds.), *The study of religions in Africa: past, present and prospects*, Cambridge: Roots and Branches, 139–154.

Bourdillon, M.F.C. (ed.). 1977. *Christianity south of the Zambezi, volume 2*, Gweru: Mambo Press.

Bovill, E.W. 1958. *The golden trade of the Moors*, London: Oxford University Press.

Bowdich, T.E. 1873. *Mission from Cape Coast Castle to Ashantee*, London: Griffith and Farran.

Brueggemann, W. 1977. *The land: Place as gift, promise and challenge in biblical faith*, Philadelphia: Fortress Press.

Brunschwig, H. 1966. *French colonialism: 1871–1914: Myths and realities*, London: Pall Mall Press.

Bujo, B. 1992. *African theology in its social context*, Maryknoll, New York: Orbis Books.

Burgess, M. and G.B. McGee, 1988. *Dictionary of Pentecostal and Charismatic Movements*, Grand Rapids: Zondervan Publishing House.

Burns, E. 1974. *World civilizations*, New York: W.W. Norton.

Carr, M. 1997. 'Policing the frontier: Ceuta and Melilla', in L. Fekete (ed.), *Europe: The wages of racism*, London: Institute of Race Relations, 61–66.

Cartwright, J.R. 1978. *Political leadership in Sierra Leone*, London: Croom Helm.

Celestial Church of Christ. 1980. *Constitution*, Nigeria Diocese, Board of Trustees for the Pastor-in Council, 1980.

Celestial Church of Christ. 1995. *Order of service (revised edition)*, Ketu-Lagos: Celestial Church of Christ International Headquarters.

Chavhunduka, G. 1978. *Traditional healers and the Shona patient*, Gweru: Mambo Press.

Chinweizu, A.J. and I. Madubuike, 1980, *Toward the decolonisation of African literature*, Enugu: Fourth Dimension Publishing.

Chirwa, C.W. 1994. 'The politics of ethnicity and regionalism in contemporary Malawi', *African Rural and Urban Studies*, 1 (2).

Clifford, J. 1988. *The predicament of culture, twentieth-century ethnography, literature, and art*, Cambridge: Harvard University Press.

Comaroff, J.L. 1991. *Revelation and revolution: Christianity, colonialism and consciousness in South Africa*, Chicago: University of Chicago Press.

Corbey R. and J. Leerssen, 1991. 'Studying alterity: backgrounds and perspectives', in R. Corbey and J.Th. Leerssen (eds.), *Alterity, identity, image: Selves and others in society and scholarship*, Amsterdam and Atlanta: Rodopi: vi–xviii.

Corten, A. and R. Marshall-Fratani, 2000. *Between Babel and Pentecost: Transnational Pentecostalism in Africa and Latin America*, Bloomingon, Indiana: Indiana University Press.

Coupland, R. 1964. *The British anti-slavery movement*, London: F. Cass.

Cox, J.L. 1995. 'Ancestors, the sacred and God: Reflections on the meaning of the sacred in Zimbabwean death rituals', *Religion* 25 (4): 339–355.

Cox, J.L. 1996. 'Methodological considerations relevant to understanding African Indigenous Religions', in J. Platvoet, J. Cox and J. Olupona (eds.), *The study of religions in Africa: past, present and prospects*, Cambridge: Roots and Branches, 155–171.

Cox, J.L. 1998. *Rational ancestors: Scientific rationality and African Indigenous Religions*, Cardiff: Cardiff Academic Press.

Cox, J.L. (ed.). 1998. *Rites of passage in contemporary Africa*, Cardiff: Cardiff Academic Press.

Crowder, M. 1968. *West Africa under colonial rule*, London: Hutchinson.

Cruise O'Brien, D.L. 1971. *The Mourides of Senegal: The political and economic organization of an Islamic brotherhood*, Oxford: Clarendon Press.

Cullen, T. 1994. *Malawi: A turning point*, Edinburgh: The Pentland Press, 1994.

Dachs, J.A. (ed.). 1973. *Christianity south of the Zambezi, volume 1*, Gweru: Mambo Press.

Daneel, M.L. 1971. *The background and rise of southern Shona Independent Churches*, The Hague: Mouton.

Daneel, M.L., 1976, 'Independent Church leadership South of the Zambezi', *African Perspectives* 2: 81–99.

Daneel, M.L. 1987. *Quest for belonging: Introduction to a study of African Independent Churches*, Gweru and Harare: Mambo Press.

Daneel, M.L. 1991. 'The liberation of Creation: African Traditional Religions and Independent Church perspectives', *Missionalia* 19 (2): 99–121.

Daneel, M.L. 1991. 'Towards a sacramental theology of the environment in African Independent Churches', *Theological Evangelica* 24 (1): 2–26.

Danquah, J.B. 1928. *The Akim Abuakwa handbook*, London: F. Groom.

Davis, D.B. 1966, *The problem of slavery in Western culture*, Ithaca, New York: Cornell University Press.

Dawe, D.G. 1981, 'Introduction', in Anderson and Stransky 1981: 1–6.

Debrunner, H.W. 1967. *A history of Christianity in Ghana*, Accra: Waterville Publishing House.

Delavignette, R.L. 1964. *Christianity and colonialism*, London: Burns and Oates.

Denton, J. 1917. 'History of Fourah Bay College', in *Jubilee Volume of the Sierra Leone Church*, London.

Deveneaux, G. 1973. 'The political and social impact of the colony in northern Sierra Leone 1821–1896', unpublished Ph.D. dissertation, Boston University.

Deveneaux, G. 1976. 'Public opinion and colonial policies in the nineteenth century Sierra Leone' *The International Journal of African Historical Studies* 2: 45–67.

Deveneaux, G. 1978. 'The frontier in recent African history', *International Journal of African Historical Studies* 11 (1): 63–85.

Dickson, K.A. 1984. *Theology in Africa*, Maryknoll, NY: Orbis Books.

Dike, K.O. (Chairman). 1962. *Report on the review of the educational system in eastern Nigeria No 19*.

Donge, J.K. van. 1995. 'Kamuzu's legacy: The democratisation of Malawi. or searching for the rules of the game in African politics', *African Affairs* 94: 227–257.

Dovlo, Elom. 1991. 'Religious pluralism and Christian attitudes', *Trinity Journal of Church and Theology* 1 (2): 40–52.

Dovlo, Elom. 1993. 'Religion and politics in Ghana's presidential election', *Uhuru Magazine* 5 (1): 42–47.

Dovlo, Elom. 1994. 'Religious pluralism and nation-building in West Africa', *Trinity Journal of Church and Theology* 4 (1).

Dzimbiri, L.B. 1993. 'The Malawi referendum of June 1993', *Electoral Studies* 13 (3): 229–334.

Ekechi, F.K. 1971. Missionary enterprise and rivalry in Igboland 1857–1914, London, Frank Cass.

Ekejiuba, Felicia I. 1995. 'Down to fundamentals: Women-centered hearth-holds in rural West Africa', in Deborah Fahy Bryceson (ed.), *Women wielding the hoe: Lessons from rural Africa for feminist theory and development practice*, Oxford: Berghahn.

Ela, Jean-Marc. 1986. *African cry*, Maryknoll, NY: Orbis Books.

Eliade, M. 1959. *The sacred and the profane: The nature of religion*, New York: Harcourt, Brace, 1959.

Etherington, N. 1983 'Missionaries and the intellectual history of Africa: A historical survey', *Itinerario* 7: 116–143.

Evans-Pritchard, E.E. 1956. *Nuer religion*, New York and Oxford: Oxford University Press.

Evans-Pritchard. E.E. 1965. *Theories of primitive religion*, Oxford: Oxford University Press.

Ezeala, J.O.L. 1991. *Can the Igboman be a Christian in view of the Osu caste system?* Orlu: Nnaji and Sons Press.

Featherstone M. (ed.). 1993. *Global modernities*, London: Sage: 1993.

Fiedler, K. 1996. 'Joseph Booth and the writing of Malawian history', *Religion in Malawi 6*.

Fiedler, K. 1998. 'The Charismatic and Pentecostal movements in Malawi in cultural perspective', unpublished manuscript, Chancellor College, Theology Conference, 1998.

Fitzgerald, T. 1990. 'Hinduism and the "World Religion" Fallacy', *Religion* 20 (2): 101–118.

Forster, P.G. 1994. 'Culture, nationalism, and the invention of tradition in Malawi', *The Journal of Modern African Studies*, 32 (3): 477–497.

Forstner, A.K. 1969. *The conquest of the Western Sudan: A study in French military imperialism*, London: Cambridge University Press.

Freud, S. 1949. *An outline of psycho-analysis*, Trans. by James Strachey, London: The Hogarth Press.

Fyfe, C. 1962. *A history of Sierra Leone*, London: Oxford University Press.

Fyfe, C. (ed.). 1964. *Sierra Leone inheritance*, London: Oxford University Press.

Fyfe, C. 1972. *Africanus Horton, 1835–83: West African scientist and patriot*, New York: Oxford University Press.

Gaba, C.R. 1975. 'The African traditional way of nation-building', ORITA: *Ibadan Journal of Religious Studies* 9: 3–22.

Gehman, R..J. 1989. *African Traditional Religion in biblical perspective*, Kijabe, Kenya: Kesho Publications.

George, S. 1988. *A fate worse than debt*, New York: Grove Press.

Gibb, H.A.R. 1961. *Mohamedanism*, London: Oxford University Press.

Gifford, P. 1993. *Christianity in Doe's Liberia*, Cambridge: Cambridge University Press.

Gifford, P. 1994. 'Some recent developments in African Christianity', *African Affairs* 93: 513–534.

Gifford, P. 1994. 'Ghana's charismatic churches', *Journal of Religion in Africa* 24 (3): 241–265.

Gifford, P. (ed). 1995. *The Christian churches and the democratisation of Africa*, Leiden: Brill.

Gifford, P. 1998. *African Christianity: Its public role*, Bloomington: Indiana University Press.

Goldthorpe, J.E. 1986. *The sociology of the Third World: Disparity and development*, Cambridge: Cambridge University Press.

Grant, D. 1968. *The fortunate slave: An illustration of African slavery in the early eighteenth century*, London: Oxford University Press.

Gray, R. 1980. 'The origins and organization of the nineteenth century missionary movement', in O.U. Kalu, (ed.), *The history of Christianity in West Africa*, London: Longman.

Greene, Sandra E. 1996. 'Religion, history and the Supreme Gods of Africa: A contribution to the debate', *Journal of Religion in Africa* 26 (2): 122–138.

Gruchy, J.W. de. 1994. *Christianity and democracy*, Cambridge: Cambridge University Press and Cape Town: David Philip.

Gundani, P. 1994. 'The Roman Catholic Church and the *Kurova Guva* ritual in Zimbabwe', *Zambezia* 21 (2): 123–146.

Gyadu, A.J. 1998. 'The Pentecostal/Charismatic Experience in Ghana', *Journal of African Christian Thought*, 1 (2): 51–57.

Haar, Gerrie ter. 1996. *Chosen people: The concept of diaspora in the modern world*, Leeds: British Association for the Study of Religions (BASR) Occasional Paper No. 16.

Haar, Gerrie ter. 1998. *Halfway to paradise: African Christians in Europe*, Cardiff: Cardiff Academic Press.

Haar, Gerrie ter. 1999. 'Imposing identity: The case of African Christians in the Netherlands', *Diskus* (Web Edition) 5.

Hackett, R.I.J. 1998. 'Pentecostal appropriation of media technologies in Nigeria and Ghana', *Journal of Religion in Africa* 28 (3): 258–277.

Hackett, R.I.J. 1996. 'New directions and connections for African and Asian charismatics', *Pneuma,* 18 (1): 69–77.

Hackett, R.I.J. 1990. 'African religions: Images and I-glasses', *Religion,* 20: 303–309.

Hallencreutz, C. and A. Moyo (eds.). 1988. *The Church and State in Zimbabwe*, Gweru: Mambo Press.

Hargreaves, J.D. 1974. *West Africa partitioned, volume 1: The loaded pause, 1885–1889*, London: Macmillan.

Hargreaves, J.D. 1985. *West Africa partitioned, volume 2: The elephants and the grass*, Basingstoke: Macmillan.

Hargreaves, J.D. 1996 (2nd ed.). *Decolonization in Africa*, London: Longman.

Hastings, A. 1976. *African Christianity: An essay in interpretation*, London: Geoffrey Chapman.

Hastings, A. 1979. *A history of African Christianity: 1950–1975*, Cambridge: Cambridge University Press.

Hastings, A. 1990 'Christianity in Africa', in: U. King (ed.), *Turning points in Religious Studies: Essays in honour of Geoffrey Parrinder*, Edinburgh: T. and T. Clark, 201–210.

Hastings, A. 1994. *The Church in Africa: 1450–1950*, Oxford: Clarendon Press.

Haynes, J. 1996. *Religion and politics in Africa*, London: Zed Press.

Hellig, J. 1996. 'The study of Judaism in Africa: The case of the South African Jewry', in J. Platvoet, J. Cox and J. Olupona (eds.) *The study of religion in Africa: Past, present, prospects*, Cambridge: Roots and Branches, 343–357.

Hick, J. 1989. *An interpretation of religion. Human responses to the transcendent*, London: Macmillan.

Hiebert, P.G. 1985. *Anthropological insights for missionaries*, Grand Rapids: Baker Books.

Hill, C. 1974. *Irreligion in the Puritan revolution*, London: Queen Mary College.

Hill, Polly. 1963. *Migrant cocoa farmers of Southern Ghana: A study in rural capitalism*, Cambridge: Cambridge University Press.

Hinga, Teresia. 1994. 'Inculturation and the otherness of Africans: Some reflections', in Peter Turkson and Frans Wijsen (eds.), *Inculturation: Abide by the otherness of Africa and the Africans*, Kampen: Kok, 10–18.

Hiskett, M. 1973. *The sword of the truth: The life and times of Shehu Usuman dan Fodio*, New York: Oxford University Press.

Hobsbawm, Eric and Terence Ranger (eds.). 1995. *The invention of tradition*, Cambridge: University Press.

Hobson, J.A. 1938. *Imperialism: A study*, London: Allen and Unwin.

Hodgkin, T. 1956. *Nationalism in colonial Africa*, London: Frederick Muller.

Horton, R. 1971. 'African Conversion,' *Africa* 41(2): 85–105.

Horton, R. 1993. 'Judaeo-Christian spectacles: Boon or bane to the study of African Religions?', in R. Horton, *Patterns of thought in Africa and the West*, Cambridge: Cambridge University Press, 161–193.

Huber, Hugo. 1951. 'Review of Smith, Edwin W. (ed.) *African Ideas of God: A Symposium*, 1950,' *Anthropos* 46: 656–657.

Hunwick, J. 1996. 'Sub-Saharan Africa and the wider world of Islam: Historical and contemporary perspectives', *Journal of Religion in Africa* 26 (3): 230–257.

Idowu, E.B. 1962. *Olodumare: God in Yoruba belief,* London: Longman.

Idowu, E.B. 1973. *African Traditional Religion: A definition*, London: SCM Press.

Idowu, E.B. 1965. *Towards an indigenous church*, London: Oxford University Press.

Idowu, E.B. 1974. 'An introduction: Nation-building', ORITA: *Ibadan Journal of Religious Studies* 8 (2): 87–96.

Igwe, S.O. 1987. *Education in eastern Nigeria 1847–1975: Development and management: Church, state and community*, London: Evans Brothers Ltd.

Imo State Nigeria, *Government White Paper on the Judicial Commission of Inquiry into the Disturbances of 24–25 September 1996 in Owerri, 1997.*

Isichei, E. 1976. *A history of the Igbo people*, London: Macmillan.

Isichei, E. *A history of Christianity in Africa: From antiquity to the present*, Grand Rapids: William B. Eerdmans.

Jenkins, Paul. 1979. 'Villagers as missionaries: Towards a definition of Pietism in Würtemberg as a missionary movement in mid-nineteenth century', Unpublished Seminar Paper, Institute of African Studies, Legon, Ghana.

Jenkins, Paul. 1989. *A short history of the Basel Mission*, Texts and Documents, No 10, Basel Mission, Basel.

Johns, C.B. 1993. *Pentecostal formation*, Sheffield: Sheffield Academic Press.

Johnson, S. 1921. *The history of the Yorubas from the earliest times to the beginning of the British Protectorate*, London: Routledge.

Jordan, J.P. 1949. *Bishop Shanahan of southern Nigeria*, Dublin: Clonmore and Reynolds.

Jules-Rosette, Benetta W. 1991. 'Tradition and continuity in African Religions: The case of New Religious Movements, in: Jacob K. Olupona (ed.), *African Traditional Religions in contemporary times*, New York: Paragon House, 149–166.

Kaba, L. 1981. 'Archers, murketeers and mosquoitos: The Moroccan invasion of the Sudan and the Songhai resistance 1591–1612', *Journal of African History* 22 (4): 457–476.

Kaberry, Phyllis M. 1951. 'Review of *African Ideas of God: A Symposium*', *Africa* 21: 76.

Kalilombe, Patrick. 1988. 'Black Christianity in Britain', in: Gerrie ter Haar (ed.), *Strangers and sojourners: Religious communities in the diaspora*, Leuven: Peeters, 173–193.

Kalu, O.U. (ed.). 1980. *The history of Christianity in West Africa*, London: Longman.

Kalu, O.U. 1992. 'The wind of God: Pentecostalism in Igboland, 1970–1991', lecture presented at the Centre for the Study of Christianity in the Non-Western World, University of Edinburgh, 1992.

Kalu, O.U. 1996. *Embattled gods: Christianisation of Igboland, 1841–1991*, London/Lagos: Minaj Publishers.

Kalu, O.U. 1998. 'The third response: Pentecostalism and the reconstruction of Christian experience in Africa, 1970–1996, *Journal of African Christian Thought* 1 (2): 1–21.

Kalu, O.U. 1998. 'The practice of victorious life: Pentecostal political theology and practice in Nigeria, 1970–1996'; *Journal of Mission Studies* 5:229–255.

Kalu, O.U. 1993. 'Images and lenses: The image of Igboland in early missionary writings 1841–1945', *Journal of Religion and Theology* 1 (1).

Kanyongolo, F.F. 1996. 'State and Constitutionalism in Malawi', Paper presented at Conference on Social Change in Malawi, Chancellor College, Zomba, 28 June.

Kanyoro, M. and Nyambura Njoroge (eds.). 1996. *Groaning in faith: Women in the household of God*, Nairobi: Acton Press.

Kaspin, D. 1995. 'The politics of ethnicity in Malawi's democratic transition', *The Journal of Modern African Studies* 33 (4): 595–620.

Kennedy, Paul. 1988. *The rise and fall of great powers: Economic change and military conflict from 1500 to 2000*, London: Unwin Hyman.

Kiernan, J.P., 1995, 'The African Independent Churches', in M. Prozesky and J. de Gruchy, *Living faiths in South Africa*, Cape Town: David Phillip, 72–82.

Kimble, David. 1963. *A political history of Christianity in Ghana*, Oxford: Clarendon Press.

King, Ursula (ed.). 1990. *Turning points in Religious Studies: Essays in honour of Geoffrey Parrinder*, Edinburgh: T. and T. Clark.

Kirche und Gesellschaft in Malawi: Die Krise von 1992 in historischer Perspektive, 1993. Hamburg: EMW Informationen No. 98.

Klein, M. 1968. *Islam and imperialism in Senegal: Sine-Saloum, 1847–1914*, Edinburgh: Edinburgh University Press.

Knott, K. 1986. 'Religion and identity, and the study of ethnic minority religions in Britain,' in V. Hayes (ed.), *Identity issues and world religions*. Selected Proceedings of the Fifteenth Congress of the International Association for the History of Religions, Australia: Australian Association for the Study of Religions.

Kraft, C. 1994. *Behind enemy lines*, Ann Arbor: Servant Books.

Kraft, C. 1996. *Anthropology for Christian missions*, Maryknoll, New York: Orbis Books.

Kraft, M. 1995. *Worldview and the communication of the Gospel*, Pasadena: William Carey.

Krieger, D. 1991. *The new universalism. Foundations for a global theology*, Maryknoll: Orbis Books.

Kumbirai, J. 1977. '*Kurova Guva* and Christianity', in Bourdillon 1977: 123–130.

Kwamenah-Poh, M.A. 1994. 'The Basel Mission and the development of the cocoa industry in Ghana, 1858–1918', unpublished Seminar Paper, Department of History, University of Ghana, Legon, March.

Lamola, J.M. 1988. 'Towards a Black Church: A historical investigation of African Independent Churches as a model', *Journal of Black Theology in South Africa* 2 (1): 5–14.

Lanternari, V. 1963. *The religions of the oppressed: A study of modern messianic cults*, London: MacGibbon and Kee.

Larbi, E.K. 1995. 'The Development of Ghanaian Pentecostalism', unpublished, Ph.D. dissertation, University of Edinburgh.

Latourette, K.S. 1964. *A short history of the Far East*, New York: Macmillan.

Levtzion, N. 1968. *Muslims and chiefs in West Africa: A study of Islam in the Middle Volta Basin in the pre-colonial period*, Oxford: Clarendon Press.

Lewins, F. 1978. 'Religion and ethnic identity', in H. Mol (ed.), *Identity and religion: International cross-cultural approaches*, London and Beverly Hills: Sage.

Lienhardt, R.G. 1950. 'Review of *African Ideas of God: A Symposium*', *Man* (December): 164–165.

Linden, I., 1980, *The Catholic Church and the struggle for Zimbabwe*, London: Longman.

Living our Faith, 1992. Pastoral Letter from the Catholic Bishops of Malawi, 8 March 1992; also published as *The Truth Will Set You Free* (Church in the World No. 28), London: CIIR, 1992.

Lochman, J.M. 1985. *The faith we confess: An ecumenical dogmatics*, Edinburgh: T. and T. Clark.

Lwanda, J.L.C. 1996. *Promises, power, politics and poverty: Democratic transition in Malawi (1961–1999)*, Glasgow: Dudu Nsomba.

Lynch, H. 1964. 'The native pastorate controversy and cultural ethnocentrism in Sierra Leone 1871–74', *Journal of African History* 31: 395–413.

Lyon, D. 1998. 'Glocalization and contemporary religion' in M. Hutchinson and O.A. Kalu (eds.), *A global faith: Essays on evangelicalism and globalisation*, Sydney: Centre for the Study of Australian Christianity, 47–68.

Ma, W. 1997. 'A first waver looks at the third wave,' *Pneuma* 19 (2): 189–206.

Mackay, J.P., D.H. Bennett, and J. Buckler. 1992 (3rd ed.). *A history of world societies*, Boston: Houghton Mifflin.

MacQuarrie, J. 1965. *An existentialist theology: A comparison of Heidegger and Bultmann*, New York: Harper and Row.

Mandivenga, E. 1983. *Islam in Zimbabwe*, Gweru and Harare: Mambo Press.

Mandivenga, E. 1989. 'The history and "reconversion" of the Varemba of Zimbabwe', *Journal of Religion in Africa* 19 (2): 98–124.

Marcus, George E. and Michael M.J. Fisher. 1986. *Anthropology as cultural critique: An experimental moment in the human sciences*, Chicago: The University of Chicago Press.

Marett, R.R. 1909. *The threshold of religion*, London: Methuen and Company.

Marshall-Fratani, R. 1998. 'Mediating the global and the local in Nigerian Pentecostalism' *Journal of Religion in Africa*, 28 (3): 278–315.

Martin, D.A. 1990. *Tongues of fire: The explosion of Protestantism in Latin America*, Oxford: Blackwell.

Martins Ugonna Okafor, 1997. 'The Nanka and Owerri uprisings: The church connection', *Wisdom Satellite* 4 (4): 17–18.

Marty, Emmanuel. 1993. *African theology: Inculturation and liberation*, Maryknoll: Orbis Books.

Masolo, A. 1994. *African philosophy in search of identity*, Edinburgh: Edinburgh University Press.

Mason, David. 1995. *Race and ethnicity in modern Britain*, Oxford: Oxford University Press.

Mason, P. 1970. *Patterns of dominance*, London: Oxford University Press.

Maxwell, D. 1998. 'Delivered from the spirit of poverty? Pentecostalism, prosperity and modernity in Zimbabwe,' *Journal of Religion in Africa* 28 (3): 350–373.

Mazrui, A. 1973. 'The sacred and the secular in east African politics', *Cahiers D'Etudes Africaines* 52: 667.

Mbayo, L.N. 1988. *The reshaping of African traditions*, Enugu, Nigeria: Spiritan.

Mbefo, L. 1993. 'Nanka martyrs: The shadow side of inculturation', *The Leader*, Owerri, Assumpta Press, 1993.

Mbefo, L. 1994. 'The Church Bishop Shanahan Left Behind', *The Nigerian Journal of Theology* 8 (1), 1994.

Mbiti, J.S. 1969. *African religions and philosophy*, London, Heinemann.

Mbiti, J.S. 1971. *New Testament eschatology in an African background: A study of the encounter between New Testament theology and African traditional concepts*, London: Oxford University Press.

Mbiti, J.S. 1975. *The prayers of African religion*, London: SPCK.

Mbiti, J.S. 1975. *An introduction to African religion*, London: Heinemann.

Mbiti, J.S. 1986. *Bible and theology in African Christianity*, Oxford: Oxford University Press.

McKenna, J.C. 1997. *Finding a social voice: The Church and Marxism in Africa*, New York: Fordham University Press.

McLuhan, M. and B. Powers. *The global village: Transformation in world, life and media in the 21st century*, Oxford: Oxford University Press, 1989.

McVeigh, M.J. 1974. *God in Africa: Conceptions of God in African Traditional Religion and Christianity*, Cape Cod, Massachusetts: Claude Stark.

Mellor, P.A. and C. Shilling. 1994. 'Reflexive modernity and the religious body', *Religion* 24 (1): 23–42.

Memmi A. 1967. *The colonizer and the colonized*, Boston: Beacon Press.

Merwe, van der, W.J. 1981. *From mission field to autonomous church in Zimbabwe*, Transvaal: N.G. Kerkboekhandel.

Meyer, B. 1998. 'Make a complete break with the past: Memory and post-colonial modernity in Ghanian Pentecostalist discourse', *Journal of Religion in Africa*, 28 (3): 316–349.

Milingo, E. 1984. *The world in between: Christian healing and the struggle for spiritual survival*, London: C. Hurst and Company.

Minnis, J.R. 1995. 'Can civil society be a force for political change in Malawi?' Paper presented at Conference on Social Change in Malawi, Chancellor College, 30 June.

Mol, H. (ed.). 1978. *Identity and religion: International cross-cultural approaches*, London and Beverly Hills: Sage.

Moore, Sally Falk. 1994. *Anthropology and Africa: Changing perspectives on a changing scene*, Charlottesville and London: University Press of Virginia.

Moraes Farias, P.F. 1973. 'Great states revisited, Review article of *Ancient Ghana and Mali* by N. Levtzion', *Journal of African History* 15 (3): 470–488.

Mphaisha, C.J.J. 1996. 'Retreat from democracy in post one-party state Zambia', *The Journal of Commonwealth and Comparative Politics* 34 (2): 65–84.

Mudimbe, V.Y. 1988. *The invention of Africa: Gnosis, philosophy, and the order of knowledge*, London: James Curry.

Musopole, A.C. 1996. 'A vision for theology in Malawi', *Religion in Malawi*. 6.

Neill, S. 1950. *Survey of the training of the ministry in Africa, Part 1*, London: International Missionary Council.

Newbigin, L. 1985. *Unfinished agenda: An autobiography*, Grand Rapids Michigan: William B. Eerdmans.

Newell, J. 1995. '"A Moment of Truth?" The Church and political change in Malawi, 1992', *The Journal of Modern African Studies*. 33 (2): 243–262;

Ng'ong'ola, C. 1996. 'Managing the transition to political pluralism in Malawi – Legal and constitutional arrangements', *The Journal of Commonwealth and Comparative Politics* 34 (2) 1996: 85–110.

Njoku, M. O. 1996. 'Conflict between religious groups and Ogo adherents' *Afikpo Today* 1 (7): 32.

Nwabara, S.N. 1967. *Igboland: A century of contact with Britain, 1860–1960*, London: Hodder and and Stoughton.

Nzunda and K.R. Ross (eds.). 1995. *Church, law and political transition in Malawi 1992–94*, Gweru: Mambo Press.

Odeyemi, S.O. 1993. *The spiritual heritage of Celestial Church of Christ*, Lagos: Femyet Outreach Publishing Company.

Oduyoye, M.A. 1986. *Hearing and knowing*, Maryknoll: Orbis Books.

Oduyoye, M.A. 1995. 'Christianity and culture', *International Review of Mission* 84 (332/333).

Oduyoye, Mercy Amba and Musimbi R. Kanyoro (eds.). 1992, *The will to arise: Women, tradition and church in Africa*, Maryknoll: Orbis Books..

Ojo, M. 1992. 'Charismatic Movement in Nigeria', in P. Gifford (ed.), *New dimensions in African Christianity*, Nairobi: All African Conference of Churches.

Ojo, M. 1996. 'Charismatic movements in Africa', in C. Fyfe and A.F. Walls (eds.), *Christianity in Africa in the 1990s*, Centre of African Studies, University of Edinburgh.

Ojo, M. 1996. 'Deeper Life Christian ministry', *Journal of Religion in Africa* 18 (2): 141–162.

Oliver, Roland and J.D. Fage. 1962. *A short history of Africa*, New York: New York University Press.

Oloruntimehin, B.O. 1972. *The Segu Tukulor Empire*, London: Longman.

Olupona, J.K. (ed.). 1991. *African Traditional Religions in contemporary society*, New York: Paragon House.

Olupona, J.K. and Sulayman S. Nyang (eds.). 1993. *Religious plurality in Africa: Essays in honour of John S. Mbiti*, Berlin and New York: Mouton de Gruyter.

Omenka, N.I. 1991. 'The impact of religion on the educational and social development of Nigeria', paper delivered at Nguru Students Day, Nguru, Nigeria.

Omenyo, C. 1994. 'Charismatic renewal movements in Ghana', *Pneuma* 16 (2): 169–185.

Omu, F.J.A. 1978. *Press and politics in Nigeria 1888–1937*, London: Longmans.

Onwubiko, O.A. 1993. *Facing the Osu issue in the African Synod*, Engui, Nigeria: Snaap Press.

Oosthuizen, G.C. 1968. *Post-Christianity in Africa: A theological and anthropological study*, Grand Rapids: William B. Eerdmans.

Otto, Rudolf. 1917. *Das Heilige. Über das Irrationale in der Idee des Göttlichen und sein Verhältnis zum Rationalen*, Breslau: Trewendt and Granier.

Palmer, R.R. 2002 (9th ed.). *A history of the modern world*, New York: A.A. Knopf.

Panikkar, R. 1979. *Myth, faith and hermeneutics*, New York: Paulist Press.

Parrinder, E.G. 1949. *West African religion: A study of the beliefs and practices of Akan, Ewe, Yoruba, Ibo, and kindred peoples*, London: Epworth Press.

Parrinder, E.G. 1954. *African Traditional Religion*, London: Hutchinson.

Parrinder, E.G. 1970. 'Monotheism and pantheism in Africa', *Journal of Religion in Africa* 3: 81–88.

Parrinder, E.G. 1976. *Africa's three religions*, London: Sheldon Press.

Parry, J.H. 1964. *The age of reconnaissance: Europe and the Wider World 1415–1715*, London: Weidenfeld and Nicholson.

Pauw, C.M. 1980. 'Mission and Church in Malawi: The history of the Nkhoma Synod of the Church of Central Africa Presbyterian 1889–1962', D.Th., University of Stellenbosch.

Phiri, I.A., K.R. Ross and J.L. Cox (eds.). 1996. *The role of Christianity in development, peace and reconstruction: Southern African perspectives*, Nairobi: All Africa Conference of Churches.

Platvoet, J.G. 1985. 'Review of Westerlund, D., *African Religion in African Scholarship*', *Journal of Religion in Africa* 15 (3): 244–248.

Platvoet, J.G. 1989. 'The institutional environment of the study of religions in Africa south of the Sahara', in: M. Pye (ed.), *Marburg revisited: Institutions and strategies in the study of religion*, Marburg: diagonal-Verlag, 107–126.

Platvoet, J.G. 1990. *Akan Traditional Religion: A reader*, Harare: University of Zimbabwe, Department of Religious Studies, Classics and Philosophy.

Platvoet, J.G. 1990. 'The definers defined: Traditions in the definition of religion', *Method and Theory in the Study of Religion* 2 (2): 180–212.

Platvoet, J.G. 1996. 'From object to subject: A history of the study of the religions of Africa',. in: J. Platvoet, J. Cox and J. Olupona (eds.), *The study of religions in Africa: Past, present and prospects*, Cambridge: Roots and Branches.

Platvoet,J, J. Cox, J. Olupona (eds.), 1996. *The study of religions in Africa: Past, present and prospects*, Cambridge: Roots and Branches.

Poewe, K. 1994. *Charismatic Christianity as a global culture*, Columbia: University of South Carolina Press

Prozesky, M. and J. de Gruchy (eds.). 1995. *Living faiths in South Africa*, Cape Town: David Phillip.

Rambo, R. 1993. *Understanding conversion*, New Haven: Yale University Press.

Ranger, T.O. 1996. 'Postscript. Colonial and postcolonial identities', in R. Werbner and T. Ranger (eds.), *Postcolonial identities in Africa*, London: Zed Books.

Ranger, T.O. 1995. 'Conference summary and conclusion', in P. Gifford (ed.), *The Christian churches and the democratisation of Africa*, Leiden: E.J. Brill.

Rinsum, H.J. van. 1999. 'Edwin W. Smith and his "raw material": Texts of a missionary and ethnographer in context,' *Anthropos* 94: 351–367.

Robertson, R. 1985. 'Humanity, globalisation and worldwide religious resurgence', *Sociological Analysis* 46 (3): 219–242;

Robertson, R. 1995. 'Glocalization: time-space and homogeneity-heterogeneity', in M. Featherstone, *Global modernities*, London, Sage

Rocchietti, A de. 1989. 'Women and the people of God', in, E. Tamez (ed.), *Through her eyes: Women's theology from Latin America*, Maryknoll: Orbis Books, 96–117.

Ross, K.R. 1994. 'Theology and Religious Studies at the University of Malawi 1988–1993', *Religion in Malawi* 4: 4–5.

Ross, K.R. 1995. 'Not catalyst but ferment: The distinctive contribution of the churches to political reform in Malawi 1992–93', in P. Gifford (ed.), *The Christian churches and Africa's democratisation*, Leiden: E.J. Brill, 98–107;

Ross, K.R. 1995. 'The renewal of the State by the Church: The case of the Public Affairs Committee in Malawi', *Religion in Malawi* 5: 29–37.

Ross, K.R. 1995. 'The truth shall set you free: Christian social witness in Malawi 1992–93', *Journal of Theology for Southern Africa* 90 (March): 17–30.

Ross, K.R. and F.L. Moyo, 1995. *Udindo Wonse*, Zomba: University of Malawi Department of Theology and Religious Studies.

Ross, K.R. 1996. 'The transformation of power in Malawi 1992–95: The role of the Christian churches', *The Ecumenical Review* 48 (1): 38–52.

Ross, K.R. 1997. 'Current Christological trends in northern Malawi', *Journal of Religion in Africa* 27 (2): 160–176.

Said, E. 1978. *Orientalism*, New York: Pantheon.

Said, E. 1989 'Representing the colonized: Anthropology's interlocutors', *Critical Inquiry* 15: 205–225.

Sandbrook, R. 1985. *The politics of Africa's economic stagnation*, Cambridge: Cambridge University Press.

Sanneh, Lamin, 1979. 'Muslims in non-Muslim societies in Africa' in *Christian and Islamic contributions towards the establishment of independent states in Africa,* K.W. Bechold and E.J. Tetsch (eds), Tübingen: Laupp and Göbel.

Sanneh, Lamin. 1989. *Translating the message: The missionary impact upon culture,* Maryknoll: Orbis Books.

Sawyerr, H. 1976. 'Tradition in transit', in J.S. Pobee (ed.), *Religion in a pluralistic society,* Leiden: Brill, 85–96.

Schoffeleers, J.M. 1988. 'Black and African theology in southern Africa: A controversy re-examined', *Journal of Religion in Africa* 18 (2): 99–124.

Schoffeleers, J.M. 1990. 'The theological invention of Africa and the problem of witchcraft', paper read at the XII World Congress of Sociology, Madrid 9–13 July.

Seiwert, H. 'What constitutes identity of a religion?', in V.C. Hayes (ed.), *Identity issues and world religions,* Selected Proceedings of the Fifteenth Congress of the International Association for the History of Religions, Australia: Australian Association for the Study of Religions.

Sharpe, Eric J. 1986 (2nd ed.). *Comparative religion: A history,* London: Duckworth.

Shaw, R. 1990 '"African" Traditional Religion', in: King, Ursula (ed.) *Turning points in Religious Studies: Essays in Honour of Geoffrey Parrinder,* 181–191, Edinburgh: T. and T. Clark.

Shaw, R. 1990. 'The Invention of "African Traditional Religion"', *Religion* 20: 339–353.

Shepperson, G. and T. Price. 1958. *Independent African,* Edinburgh: Edinburgh University Press.

Shorter, Aylward. 1985. *Jesus and the witchdoctor,* London: Geoffrey Chapman.

Smart, N. 1973. *The science of religion and the sociology of knowledge,* Princeton: Princeton University Press.

Smith, Edwin W. 1907. 'The Religion of the Bantu', *Primitive Methodist Quarterly Review,* January.

Smith, Edwin W. 1923. *The religion of lower races, as Illustrated by the African Bantu,* New York: The Macmillan Company.

Smith, Edwin W. 1929. *The secret of the African,* London: Student Christian Movement.

Smith, Edwin W. 1935. 'Africa: What do we know of it?', *Journal of the Royal Anthropological Institute*, 65: 1–81.

Smith, Edwin W. 1936. *African beliefs and Christian faith*, London: Lutterworth Press.

Smith, Edwin W. 1946. *Knowing the African*, London: Lutterworth Press.

Smith, Edwin W. (ed.). 1950. *African ideas of God: A symposium*, London: Edinburgh House Press.

Smith, Edwin W. 1950. 'The whole subject in perspective: An introductory survey', in: E.W. Smith (ed.), *African ideas of God: A symposium*, London: Edinburgh House Press, 1–35.

Smith, Edwin W. 1950. 'The idea of God among South African tribes', in: E.W. Smith (ed.), *African ideas of God: A symposium*, London: Edinburgh House Press, 78–134.

Smith, Edwin W. 1952. 'African symbolism', *Journal of the Royal Anthropological Institute of Great Britain and Ireland*, 82 (January–June): 13–37.

Smith, Edwin W. and Dale, Andrew M. 1920. *The Ila-speaking peoples of Northern Rhodesia*. (2 vols.), London: MacMillan and Company.

Smith, N.T. 1966. *Presbyterian Church of Ghana 1835–1960: A younger church in a changing world*, Accra: Ghana Universities Press.

Smith,W.C. 1978. *The meaning and end of religion*, San Francisco: Harper and Row.

Strenski, I. 1993. *Religion in relation: Method, application and moral location*, London: Macmillan.

Summer, D.L. 1963. *Education in Sierra Leone*, Freetown,: Government of Sierra Leone.

Sundkler, B. 1948. *Bantu prophets in South Africa*, London: Lutterworth Press.

Suret-Canale, J. 1971. *French colonialism in tropical Africa, 1900–1945*, London: C. Hurst.

Tasie, G.O.M. 1976. 'Africans and the religious dimension: An appraisal', *Africana Marburgensia* 9 (1): 34–70.

Tawney, R.H. 1998 [1926]. *Religion and the rise of capitalism*, with a new introduction by Adam B. Seligman. New Brunswick, New Jersey: Transaction Publishers.

Taylor, C. 1994. *Multiculturalism: Examining the politics of recognition*, Princeton: Princeton University Press.

Tempels, Placide. 1959. *Bantu philosophy*, Paris: Présence Africaine.

Therborn, Göran. 1980. *The ideology of power and the power of ideology*, London: Verso.

Thomas, N. 1991. 'Anthropology and *Orientalism*', *Anthropology Today*, 7(2): 4–7.

Thompson, L A. 1975. 'Some classical thoughts on nation-building' *ORITA: Ibadan Journal of Religious Studies* 8 (2): 114–123.

Thompson, T.J. 1930. *The jubilee and centenary volume of Fourah Bay College*, Freetown: Sierra Leone, Freetown: Elsiemary Printing Works.

Thornton, Richard. 1983. 'Narrative ethnography in Africa, 1850–1920: The creation and capture of an appropriate domain for anthropology', *Man* 18: 502- 520.

Thrower, J. 1999. *Religion: The classical theories*, Edinburgh: Edinburgh University Press.

Tillich, P. 1978. *Systematic theology volume 3. Life and spirit. History and the Kingdom of God*, London: SCM.

Townsend, M.E. 1921. *The origins of modern German colonialism: 1871–1885*, New York: Columbia University.

Trimingham, J. Spencer. 1962. *A history of Islam in West Africa*, Oxford: Oxford University Press.

Trimingham, J. Spencer. 1968. *The influence of Islam upon Africa*, London: Longman.

Uchendu, V.C. 1965. *The Igbo of southeast Nigeria*, New York: Holt, Rinehart and Winston.

Uka, E.M. (ed.). 1991. *Readings in African Traditional Religion: Structure, meaning, relevance, future*, Bern: Peter Lang.

Vail, L. and L. White, 1989. 'Tribalism in the political history of Malawi,' in L. Vail (ed.), *The creation of tribalism in southern Africa*, London: James Curry and Los Angeles: University of California Press, 151–192.

Wagner, C.P. 1992. *Warfare prayer*, Tunbridge Wells: Monarch.

Walls, A.F. 1980. 'Missionary vocation and the ministry: The first generation', in O.U. Kalu, (ed.), *The history of Christianity in West Africa*, London: Longman.

Walls, A.F. 1996. 'African Christianity in the history of religions, C. Fyfe and A.F.Walls, *Christianity in Africa in the 1990s*, University of Edinburgh: Centre of African Studies.

Walls, A.F. 1980. 'A bag of needments for the road: Geoffrey Parrinder and the study of religion in Britain', *Religion* 10 (2): 141–150.

Walshe, P. 1995. *Prophetic Christianity and the liberation movement in South Africa*, Pietermaritzburg: Cluster Publications.

Wamue, Grace and Mary Getui. 1996. *Violence against women: Reflections by Kenyan women theologians*, Nairobi: Acton Press.

Warren, M.A. 1967. *Social history and Christian mission*, London: SCM.

Weber, Max. 2001. *The Protestant ethic and the spirit of capitalism.* translated by T. Parsons, with an introduction by A. Giddens, (Routledge classics series), London: Routledge.

Westerlund, D. 1985. *African religion in African Scholarship: A preliminary study of the religious and political background*, Studies published by the Institute of Comparative Religion at the University of Stockholm 7, Stockholm: Almquist and Wiksell International.

Williams, E. 1944. *Capitalism and slavery*, Chapel Hill: University of North Carolina Press.

Wink, W. 1984. *Naming the powers: The language of power in the New Testament*, Philadelphia: Fortress Press.

Wiredu, K. 1980. *Philosophy and an African culture*, Cambridge: Cambridge University Press.

Young, W. John. 1993. 'Edwin Smith: Pioneer explorer in African Christian theology': *Epworth Review* (May): 80–88.

Young, W. John. 2002. *The quiet wise spirit: Edwin W. Smith (1867–1957) and Africa*, Petersborough: Epworth Press.

Zeusse, E.M. 1991. 'Perseverance and transmutation in African Traditional Religions', in J. Olupona (ed.), *African Traditional Religions in contemporary society*, St Paul: Paragon House.

Zvobgo, C.J.M. 1996. *A history of Christian missions in Zimbabwe*, Gweru: Mambo Press.

List of Contributors

Robert Addo-Fenning recently retired from his post as Professor of History in the University of Ghana, Legon.

Afe Adogame lectures in the Department of the Science of Religion in the University of Bayreuth, Germany.

U.D. Anyanwu is Director of the Centre of Igbo Studies, Abia State University, Uturu, Nigeria.

Ezra Chitando is Senior Lecturer in the Phenomenology of Religion in the Department of Religious Studies, Classics and Philosophy in the University of Zimbabwe, Harare.

James L. Cox is Reader in Religious Studies and Convener of the Religious Studies Subject Group in the University of Edinburgh, Scotland.

Gustav H.K. Deveneaux, who died in 1997 and to whom this book is dedicated, headed the Department of History in Fourah Bay College, University of Sierra Leone, Freetown.

Elom Dovlo is Professor in the Department for the Study of Religion in the University of Ghana, Legon.

Gerrie ter Haar is Professor of Human Rights in the Institute of Social Studies, The Hague, Netherlands.

Ogbu Kalu is the Henry Winters Luce Professor of World Christianity and Mission at McCormick Theological Seminary, Chicago, Illinois. Prior to taking up this appointment in 2001, he was Professor of Church History in the University of Nigeria, Nsukka.

Mercy Amba Oduyoye, is Adjunct Faculty and Director of the Institute of African Women in Religion and Culture, Trinity Theological Seminary, Legon, Ghana. She has held numerous academic posts in

West Africa and the United States, including Princeton Theological Seminary, and has served as Deputy General Secretary of the World Council of Churches.

Henk J. van Rinsum is a Senior Administrator in the Faculty of Social Sciences in the University of Utrecht, The Netherlands. He is also a researcher in the same university and until 2001 headed the University of Utrecht's international project (UNITWIN) which linked Utrecht University with universities in Africa and Asia.

Kenneth R. Ross is the General Secretary of the Board of World Mission for the Church of Scotland, prior to which he was Professor in the Department of Theology and Religious Studies in the University of Malawi.

Subject Index

Names Index